No. 1

THE DAILY JOURNAL,

FOR

1859

PUBLISHED ANNUALLY, BY

FRANCIS & LOUTREL,

MANUFACTURING STATIONERS,

45 MAIDEN LANE,

NEW YORK.

MANUFACTURERS OF
Account Books, Manifold Writers,
Croton Inks, &c. &c.

AUGUSTA'S JOURNAL

VOL. III

Augusta Seeks Her Fortune
In Gold Mines of two New Territories:
Colorado; Montana
1860 - 1870

A BIOGRAPHY

BY

MARJORIE LUND CRUMP

&

RALPH EUGENE CRUMP

AuthorHouse™
1663 Liberty Drive
Bloomington, IN 47403
www.authorhouse.com
Phone: 1-800-839-8640

© 2009 Ralph & Marjorie Crump. All rights reserved.

No part of this book may be reproduced, stored in a retrieval system, or transmitted by any means without the written permission of the author.

First published by AuthorHouse 10/21/2009

ISBN: 978-1-4490-2699-8 (e)
ISBN: 978-1-4490-2698-1 (sc)
ISBN: 978-1-4490-2697-4 (hc)

Library of Congress Control Number: 2008902972

Printed in the United States of America
Bloomington, Indiana

This book is printed on acid-free paper.

Contents

ACKNOWLEDGEMENTS. V

INTRODUCTION - AUGUSTA'S JOURNAL. VII

33. *Mr. Diggle January 10, 1859* 1

34. *The Martins' Supper Party, January 12 to January 19 1859* 11

35. *Eldorado - Blissful Days, January 1859*. 21

36. *Eldorado's First Wedding, January 23 to March 2nd, 1859*. 27

37. *Eldorado's First Accidental Death, Spring 1859* 37

38. *Eldorado - An Intriguing Offer from Texas, Late Spring 1859*. . . .57

39. *Eldorado - Abandoned to Indians, Summer 1859*. 71

40. *Chelsea - The Glennis Bemis Story, August 1859*. 83

41. *Eldorado - Adda Returns to Lawrence, August
and September 1859*. 99

42. *Eldorado - Jacob Eastman Chase, September 11
to late September, 1859*. 111

43. *Lawrence - A Visit with Adda, October and November 1859* . . .127

44. *We Settle a Score, November, 1859* 151

45. *News of John Brown's Raid at Harpers Ferry, November, 1859* . .163

46. *Paul, the Disciple, Has a Disturbing Message,
November and December 1859*. 171

47. *Eldorado's First School "Marm", December to
Christmas Eve, 1859* 187

48. *My Strange Social Status, December 1859 to July 1860* 207

49. *Meditations On The Road to Lawrence, March
12 to March 15, 1860* 229

50. *Lawrence D. H. Montague to the Rescue, March 16 to June 1860* *241*

51. *Conversation With A Proslavery Lawyer, June and July. 1860* *257*

52. *Adda and I Sell Our Eldorado Claims, July 8 to July 19, 1860* *279*

Illustrations

Sam Stewart 9
Augusta…the author of. 36
Adda 109
Chase. 125
Augusta 150
Augusta - 20 Years Old 159
John Brown 160

ACKNOWLEDGEMENTS
Volume III

Donnali Fifield of San Francisco who has edited for Forbes Publications and recently translated "March of the Penguins" and other books from French to English, painstakingly edited all fifty-two chapters (and more) …(a task of one and a half years)

My brother, James L. Lund, Esq., inherited Augusta's three original journals from our mother, Hazel. Sometime in the 1980s he passed them on to me.

Dr. Ramon Powers, Executive Director of the Kansas State Historical Society in Topeka in the early 1990s invited us to use their library and gave us access to twelve volumes of the transactions of the Kansas State Historical Society, where several references of the territorial period verified or corresponded to many of Augusta's journal entries, in volumes I through III. Augusta has provided some of the best accounts of the first few years of Eldorado and its founding by her father and a few like-minded abolitionists in the summer of 1857.

Mrs. Kim Stagliano, a professional editor and author, edited this volume for punctuations, typos, etc.

The Kansas State Historical Society, Topeka, KS, graciously gave us permission to use the two pictures of John Brown and one of Sara Robinson.

Augusta's Journal
Introduction: Volume III

With all the well written history, the best of it by witnesses alive at the time, during the Pre Civil War struggle over whether Kansas Territory would be admitted as a state Free of Slavery or with slaves, which was certainly the intent of Presidents Pierce and Buchanan, the Congress and indirectly the Supreme Court (via the Dred Scott decision), you'd think there was nothing more to say on the subject. But, comes now a journal written by one of my ancestors that was seldom, if ever, "cracked open" by any of my relatives, which describes, often in daily detail how ordinary folk, all of them settlers, faired during that unique and turbulent time. The period was unique, if for no other reason than the tremendous national zeal that existed North and South over whether 3.5 million slaves would remain in bondage or would somehow be freed from its aristocracy, different from Louis the XVI's France sixty years earlier only by the suffering of its agricultural workers, little industry and no middle class. Whereas the North had raised and invested $400 million for 20,000 miles of railroads and $60 million for canals, all that and over 100,000 factories had created a very large and prosperous middle class.

The Japanese audacious and militarily very successful raid on Pearl Harbor was followed in four days by a declaration of war by Germany on us. Of course the Germans had been sinking our ships long before that. Those two acts, I'm sure escalated our national zeal between 1941 and 1945 to levels equal to those historians ascribe to Americans, North and South during the fifty year pre Civil War period.

Then all that zeal was replaced by the sobering effects of the war, followed by Lincoln's Proclamation that technically freed the slave.

Augusta's journal…actually three bound journals, written with exquisite penmanship describes how his own zeal caused her father in responding to the enthusiasm of the fire-brand speaker, Jim Lane, to sell his successful sawmill on Lake Erie, a little south of Detroit, buy a wagon suitable for the rigors of the long trek west and in the summer of 1856 took his two daughters to the Kansas Territory…to help outvote the pro slavery population already there as well as to pursue economic opportunity, particularly cheap land.

But pursuit is always more complicated. When Sam, the girls and several thousand more abolitionists arrived in the territory that summer, they discovered that most of the problem there was being caused by semi-organized gangs from Missouri (east of and adjacent to the Kansas Territory) regularly coming over, voting illegally, harassing the few "free soil" settlements, burning their homes, stealing or killing their live stock and trying to make it difficult for those in the minority, but, opposed to slavery, to want to stay in the territory.

Missouri had unlawfully blocked the use of riverboats carrying Northern settlers. The U. S. Army turned a blind eye to this. The U. S. Army was ordered to interdict incoming overland trains, detain them, search the wagons for arms and confiscate what they considered excess beyond what the settlers needed to shoot game or defend themselves against the Indians. The local sheriff and his people were pro slavery, so the Free Soilers got no comfort from him or the courts for that matter, when complaints were filed about the Missouri raiders.

Well, old John Brown, who had brought part of his large family to settle in the territory, responded to this aggravation with such terrible and bloody vengeance that authorities placed a bounty on his head; a bounty never collected.

The Free Soilers had elected their own governor, but he and his well-educated Yankee wife and a hand full of like-minded abolitionists were already in a P.O.W. camp charged with treason when Sam and his two daughters arrived.

Now that Jim Lane and his Committee representing the Northern States had primed the pump and thousands of immigrants were pouring in, the most able-bodied of them were organized into a territorial militia, armed with the most modern rifles of the day (new, one-piece ammunition that packed powder, bullet, firing cap all in one paper cartridge, allowed the Sharpes rifle to fire ten times faster than the muzzleloader being used by the enemy.)

Thousands of the Sharps rifles, pistols, barrels of gunpowder, a few small canons all managed to slip in under the nose of U. S. Army scouts.

Shortly after Sam and the girls arrived he built a house large enough to accommodate a few boarders, then volunteered to fight in one of Lane's companies. Leaders, most with experience in the recent war with Mexico (that brought Texas in as a Slave State) suddenly materialized to lead these six or seven companies under "General" Lane. Money and supplies continued to flow in from the North. By August Lane and his well-organized companies…on the march…began to oppose for the first time the pro slavery element and for a few months of 1856 the violence on both sides sharply escalates. The pro slavery forces for the first time get badly beaten. But Lane, too, pays a price. The U. S. Army intervenes and captures two of his companies including Sam's, and incarcerates them in a P.O.W. camp run by a pro slavery squad, leaving Lane with six companies in tact. As a result of Lane's successful summer campaigns, those anti slavery settlers finally begin feeling that they might be able to stay without being continually harassed. Indeed, in just one year, maybe a year and a half, enough Northern immigrants came in to balance and then out vote the pro slavery population. But the Missouri "bushwhackers", now more angry than ever, continued their sporadic raids and dire promises.

After spending several cold months in the P.O.W. camp, Sam and his company get a presidential parole. He reunites with the girls in Lawrence and begins planning a dual career of founding several small towns well beyond the voting districts that remain controlled by pro slavery legislators and becoming a delegate to represent the new district of Butler/Hunter County.

By spring 1858 Sam begins selling city lots in Eldorado. He builds a two-storey house, assembles steam-driven sorghum and sawmills on the banks of the Walnut River and makes frequent trips East to the Legislature where he is also on the Committee to write the State Constitution Banning Slavery.

The territorial establishment and legislature remains controlled by pro slavery delegates. Now, however those legislators who are elected by Free Soil/abolitionists are allowed to attend legislative sessions without being arrested. As the ranks of Northern immigrants swell and vote, soon the anti slavery legislators, gain a majority with Sam Stewart among them, representing the new voting district #17, which he and the Eldorado cofounders established.

News of Lane's success in the field and the growing majority of anti slavery voters in the territory reverberates through the pro slavery ranks all the way to the U. S. Senate and the White House, who in the end must approve or fail to approve the new state constitution calling for no slavery.

For the first time the notion that Kansas might not come in as a Slave State via the political contrivance of the popular vote becomes a serious threat, maybe a reality.

In November of 1858 in pursuit of a stolen horse and absent a sheriff Sam Stewart is killed by the thief but his murder smells of a conspiracy to be rid of an ambitious abolitionist-trouble maker. His Southern killer is arrested and indicted but escapes justice and resurfaces in Texas to brag of his deed. The girls are without a father and Eldorado is leaderless.

Augusta's constant concern about her distance from the altar, compared to others her age, is relieved by her marriage in January of 1859 to the same young Yankee carpenter who she met after he was released (early) from the P.O.W. camp. He had followed her to Lawrence, and then out to Eldorado…the town's first wedding.

When Augusta and Chase marry, Adda moves out to accommodate their privacy. But restless Adda moves back to Lawrence, where there is more social life, paid employment and the promise of romance.

Although Eldorado was founded on land free of Indian claims, during the summer of 1859 a large tribe of Indians swept into the valley: the U. S. Army at Fort Riley fails to come to their rescue. (Why should they bother with an abolitionist settlement anyway?) Eldorado is abandoned but in a week or so the Indians moved on and the citizens return to their largely undamaged claims.

In 1857 the economic balloon, inflated by speculation and investment in all sectors of the railroad business breaks, creating a depression that ultimately embraces the whole country: banks close, bankruptcies and unemployment increase. Those unemployed provide thousands for the 1857 gold strike in the Rocky Mountains. Jacob Chase and others from Eldorado join one of these mountain-bound "outfits" passing through Eldorado. A few of Augusta's friends return having done very well. Chase returns empty-handed but was involved in naming the settlement they laid out as Denver.

Sawmill business is slow due to a lack of cash though Augusta will gladly saw wood on credit.

In the autumn of 1859 Chase takes sick. Even though he has no pain, he is treated with two doses of morphine in less than four hours. The second dose kills him. Augusta is a widow…a pregnant widow, which puts her into a personal depression that will take her four or five years to overcome.

Augusta's introspective entries in volume III contemplates the reality that she is a widow with a business so slow that she is no longer an active employer and added to all this the whole territory is hit with a cyclic drought that ruins prospects for a harvest needed to sustain the little settlement through the winter. The girls sell their property including the sawmill, and return to Lawrence to become employees. They are able to buy a small-unoccupied house on Rhode Island Street near the river and the ferry slip.

In less than a year our Civil War will begin.

33.

MR. DIGGLE
January 10, 1859, Eldorado

It's a terribly cold day. It's not just the icy temperature; it's the incessant down valley wind. It has snowed some, not much, but the wind has piled up little snowdrifts here and there.

In the afternoon, a stranger knocked at the door. Our neighbors just open the door and walk in, although some of them will shout some greeting, as we do when we visit them. But with the knock on the door I knew it was a stranger, so I became a little guarded.

I no sooner opened the door and he presented his calling card. While the door was open, I couldn't help but notice the black, newly painted, elegant one-horse shay tied up outside. That canvas roof was obviously not from around here. That kind of roof wouldn't last a season out here in our western Kansas wind.

I asked the stranger to step inside. As he removed his hat, exposing a handsome head of prematurely gray hair, I took a good look at his business card: Mr. Randolph H. Diggle, Senior Agent, Corcoran and Riggs Bank, Lawrence, Kansas. He took his topcoat off (which had a brown fur collar of a source unrecognizable to me) and draped it over one of our high kitchen chairs.

I'm familiar with Corcoran and Riggs. Father had some dealings with that bank while Adda and I were in Lawrence. I'm pretty sure he borrowed money from them for the syrup mill. It was my impression that Corcoran and Riggs were originally a Southern outfit but by opening a bank in Lawrence, they had acknowledged that the Free Soil people were here to stay and would probably be the main source of the territory's prosperity, but confirms that the bank will do business with anyone who is worthy of credit.

Mr. Diggle wore an Eastern business suit that included striped pants, a buttoned-up vest, which sported a heavy gold watch chain that hung on his ample chest in two little catenaries. From the chain dangled a yellowish white elk's tooth. (It was secured to the chain with a heavy gold bezel that contained some engraving that I couldn't read.) Mr. Diggle wore gray buckled-up canvas spats that covered the tops of his laced-up, polished shoes, quite an impressive outfit for a prairie traveler. I couldn't imagine him going any farther west in this costume. In fact, I wondered what sort of dandy would come even this far dressed like this.

Adda asked Mr. Diggle what had brought him so far west.

With an air of studied politeness that made it obvious he had no intention of revealing his mission to a mere female, he said he had some financial business with Mr. Samuel Stewart, President of Eldorado. "Have I found his residence?" he asked.

I didn't want to explain to Mr. Diggle that Father is dead. Mr. Diggle was entitled to know that, but I haven't come to the point where I can bring myself to say it. Just when I think I've accepted Father's death, an inquiry about him, like Mr. Diggle's, brings up renewed pangs of grief and a choking emotion and I realize that I'm not over it. Adda doesn't share this problem, but she sensed my reluctance to tell a stranger that Father wasn't alive anymore. Maybe she felt it wasn't any of his business, 'least not until we got to know him better, so she remained quiet for which I was grateful.

"Yes, this is the Stewart claim," I managed, "but Father isn't here just now. Won't you sit down, Mr. Diggle, and warm-up." To change the subject, I suggested I make a pot of tea.

Adda went to the sideboard, got three cups and saucers and arranged them on the table.

Mr. Diggle glanced around the room. While surveying our cabin, he busied himself with smoothing down his gray leather gloves, one glove at a time, one finger at time, as if he expected to coax something out that had traveled with him in the glove, perhaps a small mouse, a little toad, maybe a pet cricket. Nothing detectable came forth.

Adda asked Mr. Diggle if he was "westbound."

"Oh my, no, I have to take care of several business transactions in Emporia, Chelsea and some of your other towns out here, then I plan to return to my offices in Lawrence. He asked Adda if she would oblige him by putting the feedbag on his horse. "You will find it under the seat of my shay. I bought the oats yesterday in Chelsea and the bag should be at least half full." His request was polite, but left no doubt that it was an instruction he expected to be carried out. Adda sprang up to locate her jacket and cap with earflaps to carry out our imposing guest's wishes. As she stood in the doorway behind Mr. Diggle, she looked at me and raised both eyebrows and grinned.

It wasn't all that late in the winter's day but it was already starting to get dark.

I invited Mr. Diggle to stay for supper, telling him that he'd have to take potluck. But I felt rather smug about the invitation, since I knew that I had several stuffed sage hens roasting in the oven and a few minutes before his arrival, I had put into the back of the oven a dozen or so sweet cornmeal muffins of my own recipe. Chase likes the little pieces of fried smoked ham rind I grind up and add to muffins. I give them some little "color" with a pinch of ground sweet red pepper, one of many cooking tricks I learned from Aggie Rourke.

While Adda was outside, I poured Mr. Diggle and myself a cup of tea and offered him some sugar and cream, which he accepted. He seems to possess such fine social graces.

To satisfy my curiosity, I approached the subject again of the reason for his visit. Shortly after we learned of Father's death, Adda and I had discussed the possibility that we might have some debts to contend with. Though Father spoke of shareholders in the sawmill, he never mentioned what it or the syrup mill cost and whether we owed money on them. I said to Mr. Diggle that this January storm might detain Father, glad that Adda wasn't in the room; I didn't need her disdain for this "white" lie.

"This tea is most satisfying," he said, avoiding my question. "I would prefer to discuss this matter personally with your father, who is the payee of the bank's note that I'm here to see him about."

There was a long pause. I didn't know how to respond and didn't want to follow up with some questions that would force me to talk too much about Father. Mr. Diggle solved the problem by volunteering the reason for his visit.

"About a year ago, in February, your Father borrowed some money from Corcoran and Riggs to purchase a sorghum mill. My bank," said Mr. Diggle, "made the payment directly to the factory in Pennsylvania, and I have come to inquire about the debt."

Well, we cleared up that mystery!

"I understand your father represents District 17 in the Territorial legislature. Because of his position, I have come to speak to him in private about this matter. Both the note and the interest payments are overdue."

Adda returned and began to pay a compliment on the high style of Mr. Diggle's rig. I interrupted her to tell her about the promissory note, which cleared up the question of whether money was owed on the syrup mill though we hadn't given it much thought, certainly not in November and December, when we were worried about Father.

Adda asked Mr. Diggle how much was owed. He didn't give her an exact figure but responded by saying that the bank was more concerned about the lapse in interest payments than about the note. He explained in bankers' jargon that when interest payments become too delinquent, the note becomes a liability. This financial concern goes away by bringing the interest current.

"Well, we can solve that problem, Mr. Diggle," said Adda. "I'm sure we can cover the interest payments from the money we are making from the syrup we are selling. We can't produce it fast enough. We made four batches in October and November and sold every last quart through the two stores we have here in town." She got up and opened the stiff little clothbound account book where we keep our sales records, presenting it to Mr. Diggle for his inspection. She moved the coal oil lamp so close to the account book I was afraid it might singe his hair.

Mr. Diggle was so pleased he closed the ledger.

"According to these accounts, you have enough to pay up the arrears on the interest." He waved his hand as if he were brushing away the account book, that his inquiry in this matter was now closed.

The three of us had several cups of tea. I checked on the status of my roasting hens and set the table.

I heard Chase's wagon, quickly got up and put on Adda's jacket, which still had little drops of water on it, put a shawl over my head and shoulders and stepped outside. I wanted to explain to Chase about Mr. Diggle but out of his earshot, and I did it outside.

The four of us enjoyed the supper. My cornmeal muffins and the prairie hens came out just fine.

I invited Mr. Diggle to spend the night, though I didn't think he would accept. He seemed too dignified to climb the ladder and undress in the loft. Dignified or not, he stayed and filled the cabin with snores, which woke up Adda during the night. Using a broom handle, she thumped the underside of the loft, which did interrupt the snoring, but not for long. I think the snoring was worse than the wind!

The next morning, before our "star boarder" awoke, Adda and I put our heads together over the ledger.

We both agreed that we should first pay up the interest. To pay off the bank note, we'll use the proceeds from the lumber mill, though collections are rather "spotty" now, because we have trouble getting paid for several jobs. But it's my opinion that the sawmill is a more reliable and steady source of income than the syrup mill and will increase as the valley grows.

I've been having second thoughts about the wisdom of keeping the syrup mill anyway. We only get use of it for about two months out of the year. The balance of the year it is not only idle, but various parts of it rust, and paint is hard to come by out here. Last fall, after we took some sorghum syrup to McWhorter's store, one of the brothers came over and was poking around outside, looking at the sorghum mill. I recall that it was a warm day. I went outside to find out why he was inspecting the mill, and he asked me how much we would take for it. I said he'd have to speak with Father. As he got back on his horse, he remarked that it was a shame we weren't making rum as well as syrup. His comment made me think maybe I should put aside my feelings about alcohol: Perhaps the sorghum press has more value as a mill for alcohol, though we would have to buy a still to coax the alcohol out of cane-mash and a condenser to collect it. All that would require the services of Mr. Eastwood again.

To figure out how much we could pay Mr. Diggle, Adda and I totaled up how much money we had and how much was owed us. We had about seventy-five dollars in cash, plus the seventy-five dollar Army scrip that we got last August from the teamsters. Mr. Conner owed us thirty-five or forty dollars for our sorghum syrup he had sold and the McWhorters owed us about the same amount, maybe more. Adda and I agreed we could afford to pay Mr. Diggle one hundred dollars if we could collect a little from the stores and we decided to do this after breakfast and get a receipt. Adda left to pay a visit both stores.

About 8 AM, Mr. Diggle stirred. I called up to him in the loft, "I have some scrambled eggs and spiced hominy for you when you're ready." He asked if I would be so kind as to heat up some water, saying he wanted to shave before heading back.

While Mr. Diggle was having breakfast Adda returned from Mr. Conner's store with twenty-five dollars, commenting that he still owed us fifteen. I asked Adda, "What about the McWhorters?" She said they weren't up yet.

I asked Mr. Diggle if he would take scrip for part of the intended payment. I explained how we came by the scrip as a means to insure its value to him in lieu of currency.

"Yes, I can take scrip," he said, "but I'll have to discount it steeply." Well, I had no intention of discounting that scrip, so after breakfast, Adda and I counted out one hundred dollars and gave it to him. He drew from his traveling valise a rather large clothbound book, a formal bank ledger that contained blank checks and receipts. He wrote out a Riggs' receipt for the moneys paid, adding a note written at the bottom that the interest was now paid up through February 1859 and put his initials along side it. His penmanship was almost as good as mine.

About 9 AM he bundled up, and gave his horse some more oats. Adda had broken the ice in the trough out back. She said his poor horse drank like a camel. The last we saw of banker Diggle he was headed east in his one-horse shay, its canvas roof shaking and flapping as if it would be off downwind before he reached Emporia.

I said to Adda, "Our friend Mr. Diggle is very interesting. He is obviously a Southerner, but not from the Deep South." I wondered out loud if he was proslavery, and if so, why would the Corcoran and Riggs Bank send him to collect on a note owed by an abolitionist?

OBITUARY

Sam Stewart

1818-1858

Caught up in the abolitionist zeal of the day, Sam sold his sawmill and general store on Lake Erie south of Detroit and in the summer of 1856 bought a covered wagon and with his two daughter, Augusta and Adda, went to the Kansas Territory to add his vote to bring Kansas "in" as a state Free of Slavery.

Within weeks of their arrival Sam joins "Gen." Jim Lane's Militia, fought several battles against pro-slavery elements. ("Bloody Kansas") was captured by the U. S. Army and put into a P.O.W. camp until Sam and the remnants of his company was paroled on New Years Day 1857. He was thirty-nine years old.

He organized a group, raised money and with a small party went far enough southwest of Lawrence to form a new voting district that became Eldorado and several small settlements nearby.

Sam was elected to the territorial legislature, representing District 17, Butler County.

In the late winter of 1858 horse thieves stole his prize horse. Absent a sheriff, he and a young companion pursued the thief, captured him but in a moment of carelessness they were both killed by him.

An affidavit of details appears in chapter 29 of volume II.

34.

THE MARTINS' SUPPER PARTY
January 12 to January 19 1859

Mr. Conner came by our claim today to drop off some mail and a book on carpentry for Chase. Mr. Conner's store has become the unofficial post office. The book was a long awaited one that Chase had ordered while Howland was still here. It came from England, sold through a bookseller in Philadelphia.

Chase has been glued to his stool, poring over the book, which teaches English-style house framing (Chase says that in the States it's called the Chicago style.) There is a chapter on roof framing: how to assemble mill-sawed timbers into connected triangular frames to create an open span from wall to wall to support the roof, then how to connect those roof frames when vertically in place, using diagonal planking that stiffens the roof assembly. This author, Chase says, teaches to caulk between the roof planks with tar or pitch to make the roof waterproof; then page after page of drawings of part names with recommended dimensions. This author, an English contractor who builds homes, claims to be the inventor of the double truss, a system to frame roofs for buildings of varying sizes. By using mathematical formulas, all detailed in the book, the author provides the dimensions required for each truss element for various roof trusses including rafter sizes to provide adequate strength to handle all sorts of roof loads like wind, snow, roof tiles, etc. These dimensions are all arranged in a large tabular summary for each of several ceiling spans.

Chase says this style of framing puts the fireplace in the walls, rather than in the center of the room, where a column of heavy masonry containing the fireplace flue also supports four diagonal roof beams.

The back of the book contains advertisements for carpentry shop machinery: attachments, pages of handsaws, two-man saws, and bucksaws along with details about the number of saw-teeth per running inch of saws for both hardwood and softwood.

One lathe attachment described in the book is for a "spinner," which is really a cutter that yields long dowel-shaped pegs known as treenails or, as the book calls them, "trunnels." The dowels are cut from hardwood lumber clear of knots. This author recommends using these dowels as fasteners, adding that they are the best way to hold together large joints made by mortises and tendons, which Chase cuts now, by hand. The mortise is a deep, rectangular slot chiseled into one member dimensioned to accept a tongue of wood, called a tenon cut on the end of the joining member. The tendon fits snugly into the mortise. The mortise and tendon joint is held together by the trunnel, which is driven in to a hole drilled perpendicular to the joint made by the mortise and tendon.

Tonight, January 19th is the Martins' supper party. I must say that it doesn't look like a very good night for a gathering. It's snowing and blowing a "perfect" gale.

Chase said he would come by for us late afternoon. I think we'll take the small wagon that will give Chase and me a chance to ride up to the Martins' together and have some time alone to talk about our wedding plans. It's so cold I'd better take along the big buffalo robe that Father brought back with him from attending one of his meetings of the legislature.

We left for the Martins' at about four o'clock in the afternoon, the snow had let up some, but not the wind. That old Kansas wind was blowing south and we had to make headway against it. Adda, Mr. Conner and Jerry Jordan were in Jerry's rig behind us.

Chase and I were in the small wagon. Chase was handling the reins. I was seated next to him, wrapped from the waist down in the buffalo robe, with the fur side out and the robe's soft felt lining next to me. The robe draped down far enough to cover my feet. A little pile of snow was accumulating on my lap but I was afraid to disturb it, lest I dislodge the robe from my feet.

The ride up to the Martins' was slow going. The ground was hard and every little frozen clod seemed to rattle the wagon. Kate wasn't as surefooted as usual, though she was a much more reliable horse than Charley. We had sold Charley recently to someone in an outfit passing through, whose horse had been stolen. During the short transaction Adda took me to one side and said, "He needs a horse, so there's no need to tell him about Charley's peculiar habit, so I let her take over the sale." We could use the cash and Adda got $150 for him, which was probably $50 more than I would have had the courage to ask. I wondered how old Charley was getting along and if he was still the big "sleeper" with his new owner?

In spite of the snow, which was beautiful, it was a gloomy afternoon. After some time we passed by the Cordises' place. Light gray smoke was curling up out of their chimney, which the wind quickly dispersed out over the valley, giving a pleasant aroma to the sharp, cold air. Raising my voice so he could hear me above the wind, I asked Chase if he thought the Cordises had left for the Martins' yet. This trip with Chase was so much more pleasant than the walk along the river last winter after our visit with the Cordises'. The recollection gave me a pang, but then I scolded myself for even thinking about it, now that things seemed to be patched up between us and we have set a date for the wedding.

It was a long, chilly half hour's ride and a real relief when we finally got in out of the cold wind.

Despite the weather, the Martins' had a full house. The Cordises were there and so were the Rackliffes and the Weibleys.

The Doctor remained reasonably sober throughout the evening, even though there were ample liquid excuses for him to behave otherwise.

Shortly after we arrived, he proposed a toast to Chase and me, saying a few words in our honor before supper.

To accommodate all of us for the meal, Mrs. Martin had set a large round table in the parlor, which, by squeezing, seated eight. Little place cards assigned Chase and me to that table. Two couples apiece were seated at two small tables, one in each corner behind us. Adda and Mr. Conner were at one of them. They were so close that if I tilted my chair back, I could touch Adda on the arm and I did once or twice for a little sisterly affection. Tom and Elizabeth Cordis were seated opposite Chase and me, near the open entry between the kitchen and the parlor. Mrs. Martin had spread an ivory table tablecloth, made of lace and linen, on our table. I recognized some of the fine utensils that were part of the tableware Mrs. Martin had set out. I think she must have borrowed Mrs. Weibley's table service. Four polished candleholders made everything look so elegant in the flickering light. I wondered if they could possibly be of silver, like the candleholders I'd seen in magazines depicting city life in London. It is quite obvious that Mr. Martin is an ambitious man: Their household furnishings, which they had brought over from England, are among the best in our settlement.

Observing all of this splendor I contemplated for a few seconds the assertion frequently put forward by contemporary newspaper journalists that we pioneers are always so poor. Well, certainly none of us here is poor, though I'm sure we all hope for more prosperous times.

A large cast-iron cubical stove stood in the corner of the northeast wall of the parlor. It seemed to be consuming a prodigious amount of wood to keep the room warm, yet their parlor still seemed drafty. I thought it was because there was no door between the kitchen and the parlor and the stove wasn't big enough to heat both rooms. Tom Cordis had appointed himself fire monitor and, I must say, he was very generous with the Martins' wood. He must have gotten up three or four times during the meal to add more wood to the stove. The guests on the stove side of the table said they were quite comfortable, which I took to mean they were warm. But it was cold where I was. Chase and I were seated opposite the stove. I could see our reflections in the looking glass of the Martins' chiffonier, against the wall across the room from us. I whispered to him, "I can feel a cold draft over my ankles and knees. Do you think it would be all right if I got up to look for a robe?" Considering how tightly packed together the chairs were, I thought I might disturb the others.

He whispered, "Pull your chair over closer to mine." As I wiggled my chair, he put his hand on the inside of my knee, well, really a little above the knee, and drew my leg against his. He looked at me, smiled and gave me a little wink.

This intimate gesture transcended just helpfulness and was so unusual for Chase, especially in such social circumstances, it took me by surprise. Yet I didn't move away, even though I could have. I was holding a stemmed water glass, which I quickly put down for fear I would spill the contents. Somewhere from the depths of me arose a pleasant, warm sensation. I couldn't seem to catch my breath. I thought my neck and cheeks must suddenly be flushed and hoped no one would notice. I was sure Mrs. Weibley was staring at me, so much as to say, "Remember, Augusta, I warned you about being too generous with your feminine charms."

My old sense of propriety seemed to have abandoned me. Without knowing why, I dropped my right hand under the table, but the little ring that I had chosen to wear for this special evening, caught in the lace of the tablecloth. Panicked, I tried to free my hand but that pulled the tablecloth toward me. Afraid I'd knock over my water glass, I stopped trying to untangle my ring from the lace. Chase's hand was still there pressing my leg against his. I stole a sideways glance at Chase but my eyes couldn't focus.

It felt as if they were closing, a pleasant sensation I didn't want to go away.

A vision came to me like a genie from the lamp. Mrs. Gates seemed to materialize in one of the candle flames nearest me. The auburn of her hair mingled with the flame and wreathed around her beautiful features. But she didn't speak, she smiled. She was wearing her low-cut red velvet dress; the one I thought had exposed more of her than necessary. It was hard to bring her face into focus. She was looking at us intently, like I had looked at her so many times, except her gaze was one of approval. I thought I heard her say, "Augusta, sweetie, you've got your heart's desire", I waited for her to finish the sentence, to give me some instruction. After a pause she finally said, "Augusta, you'll know what to do. It's in our nature." She faded back into the candle flame.

I hoped no one else in the room was noticing. There was a time, and not long ago, when a gesture of this nature would have flustered me, and I would have run from it, but Chase's touch, pulling me close to him, seemed so natural and affectionate that it overcame my concern, and since I have remembered this episode for such a long time and with such pleasure, I suppose that even though I was embarrassed by this intimacy, I was more pleased than troubled by it. That we could have this little secret between us while others around the table were eating, smiling to each other, making small talk, oblivious to our little prenuptial romance, added to the joy and satisfaction of this moment. I had forgotten all about the draft on my legs. Finally I freed my ring finger from the lace of the tablecloth and found Chase's hand. Our fingers intermingled. My hand seemed moist. I looked again at Chase. This time I could bring my eyes into focus. We exchanged glances and quick, conspiratorial little smiles. I really wanted to rest my head on his shoulder and maybe I did. I just don't recall. I'm not sure I finished what was on my plate.

Just before dessert Chase put his hand gently on my arm and with his other hand clinked his glass with a spoon. As the room grew quiet we could hear the wind sweeping down the valley, buffeting the trees that stood between the Martins' house and the creek, reminding us it would be a cold ride home, even with the wind at our backs.

Chase said he had an announcement to make. As he paused, I could hear the draft in the stove cause the damper to flutter in the flue.

"I am happy to announce that with Mr. Conner's help I have arranged for a preacher to officiate at our upcoming wedding. We had planned on having it near January 22nd but it will have to be on the twenty-third or the twenty-fourth because those are the only days Reverend Perkins will be available." Mr. Conner, who was seated with Adda behind us, spoke up. By turning my head slightly I could see him in their looking glass. In his delightful Irish brogue, he explained that the Reverend had dropped into his store in recent days, was staying in Chelsea, was scouting out the area and was considering locating a new congregation in the county. Two of the ladies spoke at the same time asking Mr. Conner if he knew the Reverend's denomination.

"I think he is with the United Brethren Church" With a chuckle, he added, "Of course, I had given some thought before Reverend Perkins came by of offering to bring a good Irish Catholic priest out to officiate."

Adda, sitting beside him, said, so all could hear, "Ian, you're funny, but not *that* funny," which produced a short, barely audible, titter in the room. We weren't being impolite towards Mr. Conner. We were laughing at Adda's humor.

"What time will the wedding be?" someone asked.

"Late in the day," said Chase, without consulting me. "I think 4:30 PM would be about right, but you should all be at the Stewart claim by 3 o'clock in the afternoon."

"Augusta, if you get married January 24th, won't that be a Monday," remarked Mrs. Rackliffe. "Are you sure you want to be married on a Monday? Sunday would seem to me to be much more appropriate." Mr. Rackliffe coughed and tried to show a smile to everyone, but said to his wife, quietly, but still loud enough that we could hear, that she should mind her own business.

"I would prefer to have the wedding on Sunday too," said Chase, "but the Reverend will be preaching in Chelsea on Sunday and might not be able to get down to Eldorado until Monday. Between Mr. Conner and myself we'll work it out with him and let you all know."

We cleared off the tables, and put away the two little corner tables, removed two leaves from the big table. All this made a lot more room within the parlor.

Chase, who was standing in a small circle composed of Adda and Doctor and Mrs. Weibley, said he wasn't feeling too well.

"Anxiety, just anxiety," said Mrs. Weibley with a giggle. "You are nervous about the wedding, Mr. Chase." And looking at me, she added, "Augusta, I want you to give Mr. Chase some tea of kava root between now and the wedding. It will calm his nerves. I'll send some over tomorrow. Doctor Weibley has been prescribing it for years. Captain Cook, the English explorer, describes the medicine in his journals."

She said to Mrs. Rackliffe, who was nearby, that they had better have another session on my dress, so they could finish it in time. Mrs. Rackliffe readily assented.

Elizabeth Cordis asked me if I wanted some help with the task of getting "Something old, something new, something borrowed, something blue." Before I could answer, Mrs. Martin and Adda agreed between the two of them that they would take care of it.

Mr. Martin came into the room, bearing a wine bottle and a small, elegant silver tray containing several short glasses. He said he wanted to propose a toast to the couple that would be the "first to marry in Eldorado, maybe the first in the county." He distributed the glasses to one and all, pausing to pour a little wine for each guest. "My, my, where in the world did you get a bottle of Madeira?" asked the Doctor. But I didn't hear Mr. Martin's answer, because I was humorously distracted by Doctor Weibley's quickly downing his glass, rubbing his mustache and, before Mr. Martin could pass on to the next person, putting his glass on the tray for replenishment. Adda, standing next to him, said in mock reprimand, "Doctor Weibley, really!"

"Well, these are the smallest wine glasses, I've ever seen, Adda, I'm a little nervous tonight." He pretended to make his hand shake. "I was afraid I would spill my allotment before I could get it to my lips, and as you know, 'there's many a slip twixt cup and lip.' What the proverb means is that there may be a long interval between what we plan and hope for and what we actually get. Many things can happen between the cup and the lip, so we have to make the most of it. This is a metaphor for my life, there's been so many slips twixt the cup of my youth." Mrs. Weibley said, "Yes, yes, dear, no more proverbs now please."

35

Eldorado - Blissful Days
January 1859

Today, the very day after the Martins' supper party, Chase was able to contact Reverend Perkins, and they came to a quick agreement about the date and time we could hold the wedding. The Reverend said he could perform the ceremony late Sunday afternoon. That will give him time to preach the Sunday service in Chelsea and, if the weather isn't too bad, get down to Eldorado with time to spare. Between Adda, Chase and me, we'll spread the word that the date for the wedding is now set for Sunday, the twenty-third.

Though the last couple of days since the Martin's dinner party have been blissful, they have gone by like the scenery we had viewed from our railroad car after we left Detroit: we could see it fleetingly but were not part of it. Though I have made my journal entries punctually, I seem oblivious to details that I normally would have noticed and described. I am fortunate to have such attentive and considerate neighbors, particularly Mrs. Weibley and Mrs. Rackliffe (though we had some small differences over the design for my dress, a spat that was diplomatically settled by Elizabeth Cordis; I was relieved to let them sort out the details.)

As the wedding approaches, I am not entirely reconciled to Father's death, though the agony is not as acute. We've only known about it for a little over a month. Of course, in recent days I'm buoyed-up by the prospect of marrying Chase and I try to set aside a few minutes each day to reflect on my good fortune, count my blessings and make plans for the future. After two years or so of uncertainty with Chase, and fits of what seemed like mutual indifference, we have now come to a period of serenity.

In the next three days, I will have to get my dress ready and clean up the cabin.

Tom Cordis brought some mail from Connors Store for us today. In the pack were two letters from Frank Robinson: one for Chase, another for Adda, two books and some magazines ordered from Brooklyn, New York so long ago I'd forgotten them. The protective inner wrapping for the books was the year old May 29, 1858 edition of the *New York Times*. One of the minor headlines was a death notice of General Persifer Smith, the old pro slavery despot up at Fort Leavenworth, who had been in-charge of the military for Kansas Territory when we arrived in the summer of 1856. The article gave his birth date as 1798, so he was only sixty years old when he died. I knew he'd had an illustrious military career, particularly in the Mexican War, which of course brought in Texas as a Slave state. But I had no idea he'd died. I can't wait until I can tell Adda. I remember how badly General Smith and those under him treated Mr. A. C. Soley, a leader of one of the Massachusetts outfits that came in the same summer we did. I've lost track of Mr. Soley after he was interred in the P.O.W. camp with Father. He was in the Lexington Company. And it was General Smith that "sat on his hands" when the Missourian Raiders burned Lawrence earlier that spring.

The news article says he died at Fort Leavenworth a few days after "assuming command of the Utah Expedition." I wonder why I didn't see an obituary from a Leavenworth or Lawrence paper. The article says he will be replaced by General William S. Harney, who also distinguished himself in the Mexican War. His sentiments, like his predecessor, are probably pro slavery; otherwise he wouldn't have gotten the post.

The letters came from Lawrence, which was a surprise because when Frank left last August, he'd announced that he was heading for the goldfields. (Someone should tell him he's gone in the wrong direction.) Making that sort of a mistake is what I've come to expect of Frank, but I mustn't say it. Adda doesn't want to hear any criticism of Frank from others. Yet I think my sister shares my misgivings. When he was here, she enjoyed his company and was with him much more seriously than in Archer, but she nevertheless had discouraged him from having any long-range plans for the two of them. That's why he left.

Frank's note has made my sister morose and melancholy, two conditions very rare for her. But it's better if I mind my own business. If Adda wants to discuss it, she will bring it up.

The mill has been operating off and on. The river is frozen. That makes floating logs downriver to our mill impossible. We have had two or three loads brought down on large sled-wagons working about as well as winter conditions will allow. People are either ordering timbers cut to order from wood we supply, or they are bringing in their own wood and having us saw it for them. After Tom Cordis brought in the mail and warmed up a bit, he went down to fire up the boiler. He had some sawing he wanted to do and said he would begin to get the water hot and try to find Chase or Jerry Jordan to come help him do the sawing. Tom is adding a house to his cabin, that is, the addition will be bigger than the cabin, though the two will actually be connected. In the fall he, Chase and Jerry Jordan built a foundation for the house, using thick slabs of sandstone pried and quarried from the riverbank. And they dug out a large opening deep enough to stand up in for a room that will be a combination of a root cellar and a storm cellar for protection when there are tornadoes. Floor joists and a trapdoor in the kitchen will cover over this room, and it will also be accessible from the outside.

Adda went with Tom. She's learning to operate the boiler. It takes several hours for all that water to get hot enough to make steam. As it is wintertime, we have taken several precautions, explained in the sawmill's operating manual, to prevent the water from freezing solid, which can crack the boiler shell. Every two or three days we build a fire in the firebox, not to make steam but to prevent freezing. Because this chore is merely to keep the boiler in good shape and we have to do it even when we don't have any sawmill orders, it's a nuisance, which causes us, I'm afraid, to neglect it.

After Tom and Adda left, I read Frank's note to Adda (perhaps I shouldn't have, but it was not in a separate envelope but in with the letter addressed to Chase.) In his note Frank says he wants "desperately" to come back if Adda will "have him." He misses her *terribly*. It is a rather sweet note. I suspect a professional letter writer wrote it for Frank. The note contained phrases totally outside of his literary capability.

By midafternoon, I'd expected to hear the saw commence to whine. Adda and Tom Cordis had left quite awhile earlier. But it was quiet, so I decided to walk down to the mill to see what was going on.

When I arrived, I saw that Jerry Jordan had joined them. Adda had taken Kate to fetch Jerry to see if he cared to help Tom saw up his logs and he had come back with her. But, it turns out, her invitation had been premature: Jerry, Tom and Adda had figured out that it would be a long time before the water would be hot enough to produce steam. The three of them were huddled together under the open shed roof, waiting for the water to begin heating up. "It has taken three hours just to get a good fire started, it draws so poorly, and everything is so cold including the firewood." Tom told me. In reply, I mentioned that the manufacturer recommended to remedy this problem by building an iron or brick smokestack ten to twelve feet higher than the smoke stack provided by the manufacturer. Father planned to do it, and was going to use bricks from that new brick factory in Leavenworth, but never got around to it.

The boiler's short chimney was now belching out swirls of black smoke, little sparks of sawdust and small chips of ignited bark, all part of the fuel we use. Jerry said, "We opened an access hole on the boiler's top and couldn't believe it. We found a big, thick chunk of ice floating in the water, which must weigh 500 pounds. That explains why the temperature is only about fifty degrees, even though Tom's had a fire going for three hours. All we're doing is melting that danged ice." A few minutes later, Chase came driving up in our utility wagon. "I saw the smoke," he said, "and was concerned."

Tom seems very determined to get steam up. Chase and he have assembled five or six large double trusses at Tom's place, using long timbers from the mill. These frame roof trusses are shaped like the letter "A" and have a fifteen-foot span with a vertical member in the middle that is about seven feet tall. Tom will need fifteen of these double trusses for the house he's building. Now is the time, he says, to work on his house, since his blacksmithing is so slow.

When he heard about the ice, Chase laughed and said, "We'll have to keep that fire going for a long time to get steam up." Jerry and Tom nodded in agreement. Chase added, "In this kind of weather boiler water temperature only rises about one degree every ten minutes and you started with a cold boiler with ice in it. We'll be lucky to have usable pressure by day after tomorrow. Remember you've got about one and one half tons of cold water in there. We'll be able to check the temperature every few hours," pointing to the large clock-faced thermometer on the front of the boiler.

Adda said to the three of them, "Don't count on me to be a party to this all night fire tending, I need my beauty sleep, but you're all invited to stay with us, which will make your watch standing easier." Reluctantly, they agreed. Adda spoke up again, "By the way, you better make sure you've got enough firewood." Chase, Jerry and Tom were talking about that when we left them.

Adda and I walked back to the cabin alone. On the way and with some hesitation Adda said she would like some advice. She told me that she had received a very sweet letter from Frank and didn't know how to respond. (Adda doesn't know that I read the letter.)

She seems to be longing to see Frank. Her athletic new friend, Dick Taylor, has gone to the Mountains. Adda was certain that with a little encouragement Frank would come back. He said so in his letter, she said.

I thought to myself, "Well, he certainly won't get any encouragement from me," but thought better of saying it. Adda seemed so (unusually) serious, there's no need to offend her, particularly with my opinions.

What I said was: "Adda, you should be careful not to encourage Frank to come back to Eldorado with promises you don't intend to keep. You could say that you'd certainly like to see him again, that you miss his companionship, etc., but that marriage is not in your plan just now."

Adda did write the letter. I saw the envelope before she posted the letter over at Conner's store, but she declined to show me what she wrote.

The dress got finished on time and, I must say, looks elegant. Mrs. Rackliffe helped us clean up and arrange the house for the wedding, which is tomorrow. Mr. Rackliffe came over with Chase late this afternoon. They all are staying the night.

36

Eldorado's First Wedding
January 23 to March 2nd, 1859

About 2 PM today, Sunday, January 23rd, the Reverend Mr. Perkins arrived with his one-horse rig. He had stopped by Mr. Conner's place for instructions on how to get here. Mr. Conner closed his store and joined the Reverend for the ride. When they came into the cabin, Reverend Perkins brought his Bible in and put it on the old chiffonier we have in our front room, then he said he wanted to take a spin in the neighborhood, adding that he was trying to make up his mind where to locate his church. Mrs. Weibley and Adda volunteered to show him around. I was a little uncomfortable with that arrangement. I thought some last-minute thing might come up and I would need Adda here to help. So, I mentioned my concern and she agreed to stay, but sent Mr. Conner and the doctor's wife with Reverend Perkins.

About 3:30 PM guests started arriving, but no sign of Reverend Perkins, Mr. Conner or Mrs. Weibley. I was getting a little nervous.

Mr. and Mrs. Martin came and we made pleasant small talk about their delightful supper.

Prior to our guest's arrival, I draped a double flannel sheet in the loft, to create a separate dressing space. A little after 3:30 PM, Mrs. Martin, Elizabeth Cordis and I retired behind the sheet and they helped me with my dress, though I really didn't need the help. But with very pleasant insistence and some sisterly fussing, they "got me" dressed.

I heard the Rackliffes come in with Mr. and Mrs. Carey. Mrs. Rackliffe knew perfectly well where I was, but I could hear her talk to Adda, "Augusta, I have something for you, dear," she said, and popped her head behind the curtain. She came over and pinned a small, lovely cameo on my dress. She whispered in my ear, "That's something 'old,'" and then stepped back to admire it. All the ladies praised it.

A little before 4 PM, Chase arrived and just then the Reverend Perkins came back with his "tour guides". Mrs. Weibley immediately pulled her husband away from the group of men who had assembled around the punch bowl. I'm sure she didn't want the doctor drinking to excess at my wedding. Adda and Mrs. Martin had made a sweet punch, mostly grape juice, and where they had gotten a dozen or so small punch glasses, I don't know, but everybody was gathered around the table, though the men folk seemed to be clustered by themselves, and the women likewise.

About 4:30 PM, Reverend Perkins moseyed over to one wall, stood facing the rest of us and cleared his throat. Someone at the punch bowl clinked it with a glass and the room became very quiet. I thought it was strange that he didn't beckon Chase and me to come towards him but he didn't.

He began a sermon and must have preached for fifteen or twenty minutes. But it was very nice. I wondered what we could do to get him to locate in Eldorado. He preached about the history of marriage, the sanctity of the institution, and its importance in our culture. Afterwards, the singing of two old familiar hymns calmed my nerves. Adda was standing next to me. Chase, who had been with the other men, was now standing on my other side.

Reverend Perkins smiled at me and beckoned the three of us to approach him.

There was a long pause and he seemed to look beyond Chase and me and said, "Dearly beloved, we are gathered here in the sight of God" … I had waited so long for my turn.

He avoided asking, "Who gives this woman?"

Perhaps Mr. Conner explained things on the way over.

He whispered to Chase, "We'll do the vows now. Do you have the ring?" And referring to our names on a slip of paper laying on the open bible he was holding he began, "Do you, Laura Augusta, take this man…to have and to hold, from this day forward, for better, for worse, for richer, for poorer…'til death do us part." Then it was Chase's turn.

When Chase said, "I do", he looked at me with a faint smile.

Reverend Perkins gave a little prayer of benediction, looked up, smiled at us both and said, "I now pronounce you man and wife."

Finally, after such a long and odd courtship, Chase and I are man and wife.

The neighborliness of the rather humble event made it, for me, a sweet wedding. We were the first couple to marry in Eldorado and though we don't have a newspaper, the Chelsea paper printed a small announcement. *

Here it is mid-February and I seem to be adjusting well to married life. I've never known such happiness nor have I had such confidence in our future. I'll confess I had some apprehensions and curiosities and was glad I could share them with Elizabeth Cordis. I learned that she had the same concerns before she married Tom. I suppose they are peculiar to all females as we approach the marriage bed but none of my worries materialized. I'll

---

*The announcement was reprinted in the *Kansas Historical Quarterly*, Vol. 21, p. 451, which includes marriage notices published in the territorial newspapers. The notice was also recorded in the annals of Coffey County (Coffey County and Otoe County were later merged and became Butler County).

admit some relief came from discoveries about marriage that is contrary to what I'd been told to expect and different from what I had read in a few English novels.

One English novel Adda and I had read, for instance, described a proper lady who, prior to her upcoming fashionable wedding, was advised by an aunt to expect to make certain physical sacrifices, and to forego personal privacy, in order to provide her husband the satisfaction he needed. This, the aunt advised, was the price ladies pay for the social arrangement called marriage.

I also recall a troubling conversation that I had last summer with a lady who had come out here in July of 1857 with Howland, the Bemis family, the Careys, the Martins and others. She was a middle-aged widow...except we soon learned that she really wasn't a widow: her husband had left her in Illinois.

Last summer I bumped into her outside Howland's store, when he was still here in the Territory. My conversation with her couldn't have lasted more than thirty seconds but its contents have stayed with me. She asked me if I was the engaged Stewart girl and before I could answer, she clucked her tongue reprovingly and warned me, with a certainty derived from experience, that it's a rare female who gets any pleasure from the marriage bed, and those that do, she said, have questionable moral integrity.

In my case, all those worrisome predictions were simply wrong. Chase and I have become much more compatible than I ever thought we could be. He is a more affectionate husband than I expected, judging from his courtship. I intend to love him all the days of my life. By loving him with all my heart perhaps I can atone for some of my own behavior, which I'm sure contributed to our unusual engagement.

With timbers from our own sawmill and certain parts, like window frames Chase has brought in from other jobs in the area, including one in the town of Augusta, we have most of the materials we need for an upstairs addition. It's turning out to be more complicated to build than we thought but it will be lovely when finished.

To increase the ceiling height to eight feet Chase had laid down on top of the house's original logs three layers of planking each a foot wide and three inches thick of walnut that Chase said we'd sawed so long ago, he was sure it was "cured". Each of these layers, which he calls a sill, encompasses all four walls. The upstairs flooring, also walnut, Chase will lay on the existing ceiling joists, Chase has stretched canvas out on the upstairs floor to serve as a roof until he gets the second storey roof trussed up. I must say that the original maple floor joists and flooring upstairs are so good that we have had very few leaks while we were getting the new roof up.

We will have four upstairs windows: one on each side. The balance of the outside walls is made of diagonal planking nailed to the vertical joists, called studs.

Capping the top of all the second storey studs is another horizontal sill. Double A-shaped trusses, which Chase built exactly like those he and Tom Cordis made for the Cordises' place, will rest vertically on these upper sills. Roof planking, one inch thick of softwood, which Chase is nailing on the diagonal, connect all the roof trusses. He said this adds to the stiffness of the whole roof.

Knowing that the wind blows mostly north south in the valley, Chase wanted the wind to be deflected by the roof's angle, so he has made the roof beam point east west.

We put the stairs in the corner previously occupied by the loft. By the way, we've used all the old loft planks. Father had a good idea not to nail those planks down.

Chase has had to interrupt his carpentry to build a coffin for Mr. Andrew Gordon, who has just died. His widow has asked Adda and me if we would dress Mr. Gordon properly.

If there is a constant nagging concern, it is unexpected sickness. Every day in our settlement someone is sick, and we have already had a few deaths.

I wish I didn't have to do this. Must I wash the body? I'm never anxious to be around a dead man. Maybe what killed him is contagious and lingers still with him and around him. Why must I be the town nurse and undertaker? What about Elizabeth Cordis and Mrs. Weibley?

After breakfast on March 1st, Chase began making some drawings of roof trusses for another job he's working on. He put down his instruments and asked me what I thought about him getting into Territorial politics. This is not the first discussion Chase and I have had about his political ambitions. He believes he can be elected to Father's spot in the Territorial Legislature. He also thinks he needs some recommendations, endorsements he calls them, from the "elders" in Lawrence and plans to go up there to seek their counsel and to do some politicking before running in the next county election. My advice was to visit each of the original founders and discuss openly with them their ongoing financial interests in our settlement and what he could do to aid those interests.

He plans to leave soon for Lawrence, with Mr. Whittier and several others, to attend some political meeting.

When he leaves, I think I'll ask Adda to come down for a few days. Since the wedding, Adda has been staying off and on with the Cordises, but she has said to me wistfully a couple of times that as hospitable as they are, there's no place like home.

I've asked Chase to visit the Corcoran and Riggs Bank, while he's up there, to explain our side of the story on the syrup mill loan and why we went into default. Maybe we should make another payment on the interest since what we just paid took us through this February.

Adda was here briefly yesterday to pick up her mail and was a bit touchy. She has a felon on one of her fingers again. She received a letter from Frank Robinson in Lawrence, probably in response to the one she wrote him in late January. In his reply he said he wouldn't stand for her "jilting" him a second time.

Today, March 2nd, Chase and I we were joined at our noon meal by Tom and Elizabeth Cordis (who is with child) and Dr. and Mrs. Weibley.

We had a big discussion about the small exodus from our town. Adda's new friend, Dick Taylor, and Calvin Kinner have left for the goldfields and I hated to see them go. On the other hand, I won't miss some of the others who are leaving. The McWhorter brothers have closed down their store and have packed up their merchandise and gone, also headed for Kansas gold. Well good riddance. I blame them for all the rowdiness we have had ever since they got here. I contend that their making whiskey available by the glass helped drive Mr. Howland out of business and has had a bad influence on our men folk. They also sold shoddy merchandise: flour for bread that wouldn't rise, cornmeal with weevils, and inferior oil for our lamps. They claimed to sell that new Pennsylvania smokeless coal oil called *kerosene* and charged a few more pennies per gallon for it. I don't know if it was from Pennsylvania but it certainly wasn't smokeless. It stinks like every other coal oil I've ever used. And on top of everything else, the McWhorters skipped town owing us forty dollars for our sorghum.

Doctor Weibley said, "I will miss the McWhorters and their bare knuckle championship fights they sponsored," and he laughed. "I have patched up more than one of those contestants after ten or fifteen rounds." I asked him who paid for the doctoring. He said, "The McWhorters."

He claimed he was "instrumental" in getting the fights limited to ten or fifteen rounds, though some of the Irish toughs from Baltimore and the Pennsylvania mines wanted the bouts to be longer, bragging about their fights back "in the Old Country" that had lasted twenty or thirty rounds.

Directing his comment to Tom Cordis, the doctor said that although the McWhorters sold whiskey by the glass from small barrels, they also sold a higher-quality whiskey in pint and quart-sized square bottles, put up by the Booze Brothers somewhere in the East, and he intended, he said, to see if Conner's store would stock it. I suppose if there were a whiskey authority in Butler County, it would be the doctor.

Mrs. Weibley said she wouldn't miss the McWhorters because after Mr. Conner opened his store she had taken all of her business to him anyway. "At his store I can order special things like seeds and cloth and fancy utensils out of his catalogs."

It was Doctor Weibley's opinion that the McWhorters were typical Irish. Apparently he and Mrs. Weibley had met a number of them when they still lived back in the States.

Mrs. Weibley is quite proud that they came out in 1855 with the first wave of serious abolitionists from Massachusetts. After leaving Philadelphia, the doctor was practicing medicine in Baltimore during the time when the Irish were escaping the famine and coming into Boston and other East Coast cities. Baltimore had by then a large Catholic community and was attractive to the Irish. Some came into Canada, she said. "The fare from Ireland to Canada was five or six pounds. English companies in Canada offered to pay two pounds of the fare from Ireland to Canada, which made going to Canada cheaper than coming to the States. But most of the Irish tried to avoid going to Canada, knowing that it's an English colony.

It's her belief that the Irish are much different culturally from the Yankees. First they are staunchly Catholic and have already brought into Boston and other Eastern cities hundreds of starving Irish and the priests. They don't observe the Sabbath with the strictness expected by the Boston Calvinists. They believe in miracles. And their allegiance is to Rome, she added. "The men are pugnacious and brawl amongst themselves. The women are much more civilized and, in my opinion," she said, "they are brighter and much more ambitious. They will accept domestic work and are reliable. If they find work as a maid or get a job in the mills, since food is so much cheaper in New England than in Ireland, the men use that as an excuse for not working."

Mrs. Weibley said that it was her opinion that the men were ambitious enough but when they found work in the mills they would have to face the prejudice the old guard Yankees felt towards the Irish, an attitude brought over by their English forefathers. "Irish men are too proud to put up with that and choose to work and they work very hard with their own kind on the canals and in the Pennsylvania mines," she said.

"When we left Baltimore in 1855," she said, "New England was enjoying prosperous times, but the factories preferred to hire German or English labor over the Irishmen."

LAURA AUGUSTA STEWART

Original Author of the three bound volumes of her journals began in 1856 and her last entry about 1900

37

ELDORADO'S FIRST ACCIDENTAL DEATH
Spring 1859

Mr. Conner came by about midmorning with some mail. Among the letters and packages what got my attention was an envelope closed with a wax seal, which is becoming unusual, since many envelopes now have a layer of dry glue on the flap that you moisten with your tongue.

This envelope had as the return address "Corcoran and Riggs Bank, Lawrence, Kansas." Since that was the bank that Mr. Diggle represented, I opened it, half expecting to see a polite (but tardy) thank-you from the banker for our hospitality.

It was quite the contrary. The first sentence of the letter, addressed to Mr. Samuel C. Stewart, stated that the bank loan he had initiated in February 1857 is in default. According to the letter, no interest had been paid since October of last year.

That was a surprise but not the scary part. The second paragraph said the bank had the right to seize Father's assets and garnish his salary. "Unless we hear from you by return post," the letter said, "action will be taken."

Assuming my most indignant attitude and wondering just what action the bank could take, knowing that I was holding a receipt for $100, which paid-up the interest on that loan, I began a letter to them, saying that only recently we had paid interest money to the banks' agent, Mr. Diggle, during his overnight visit here January 10th and that we were capable of and ready to pay down the principal, even without the bank's threat of seizing assets. Before signing "Yours truly," I added: "Give my cordial regards to Mr. Diggle." I signed my name Augusta Stewart Chase, implying I was Father's assistant. I couldn't bring myself to write a simple sentence acknowledging that Samuel Stewart is deceased. I hope that omission doesn't break some Territorial banking law.

As luck would have it, the Fort Leavenworth stage came through Eldorado this afternoon. The driver was more than willing to carry the letter to Lawrence on his way.

Since Chase is leaving for Lawrence in a few days, to participate in the political meeting that he, Mr. Whittier and some other men from Eldorado are planning to attend, I've asked him to visit the bank while he's there and explain our side of the story on the syrup mill loan.

A couple of days after Chase left, a second letter from Corcoran and Riggs arrived, and this time the envelope was fatter, but still sealed with red wax. There was no good news in this letter either. In fact, it contained even more disappointing information.

Accompanying the letter was a folded-over sheet of paper with a printed likeness of Mr. Diggle, except it turns out that is not his name.

The letter listed several names for him and noted that it had been some months since he had worked for the bank. "During that time," the letter added, "he has been involved in embezzling customers of this bank and others." The letter then included the following list of statements

- He has defrauded others in the territory.
- He claims also to represent banks in Missouri.
- You have made your interest payment to a fraud, however you will be relieved to learn that Territorial officers have apprehended him in St. Louis: They will keep us informed.
- If any of your money is recovered, it will be applied to the interest owed: Otherwise the loan status is as it was described in the bank's letter of February 27th.

Today is March 10th and quite cold. After having a fire in the sawmill boiler all last night, Jerry Jordan and Adda, who are running the mill in Chase's absence, got up enough steam by noon to start the saw. My, how it whines in this cold air. But I'm getting accustomed to the sound. When we first set up the mill, I was very apprehensive about its safety: Whenever I heard the whine, I knew hands and arms were in jeopardy. But we have had it running for nearly a year now and have not had a single accident.

When Chase gets back, he plans to stock up our lumber inventory. Now that he has had so many months of experience with the mill, he says, he knows what size timbers are most likely to be called for. After finishing an order for the Rackliffes, he intends to saw wood for inventory and has already laid bark down on the ground...planks he calls dunnage...on which to pile the sawed timbers, categorized by size. Now, he says, we'll have a regular lumberyard. It will be fun naming our lumber company.

Chase got home the next day, which was March 11th, from Lawrence.

I'm so happy to have him back. I'd heard from Mr. Carey that he'd be home today, so I'd planned to have a nice quiet supper for the two of us. Adda took a lot of her "stuff" in the old steamer trunk (the one Colonel Cooke's soldiers thought might contain weapons three years ago up in Plymouth) over to the Weibleys, where I think she'll be staying for some time. She is much more tolerant of Doctor Weibley's drinking than I am, and she rather likes the old sot. She occasionally does some kind of nursing duty for him. Mrs. Weibley is like a mother to her. Adda seems to get along with Mrs. Weibley better than I do. I know that and it bothers me and I wonder why that is.

At supper Chase said, "Well, I suppose by now you've heard from the bank. When I visited with them, they admitted that your Mr. Diggle had worked for them and they gave me a poster identifying him as a crook. When I assured them we were able to clear up that debt, one of the managers questioned me about our ability in the absence of your father."

"So," I said, "they know about Father's death."

"Everybody in Lawrence" Chase said, "that knew your father, knew he had been murdered. I wasn't with Mr. Gates five minutes and he inquired how you and Adda were getting on and he said the two of you had a job at the Cincinnati House anytime you pleased. It seemed lost on him that the two of us were married."

Chase brought down from Lawrence an unusually long letter for me from Mrs. Gates telling me all the news about her "boys," particularly those I knew. Her letter confides that Frank Swift (captain of the Mount Oread Rifles in Captain Cracklin's absence) had told her that he was somewhat disappointed to learn I'd married, though, she added, he was most happy for both of us. Apparently Mrs. Gates is making plans for a big addition, either to the Cincinnati House or to her residence, and spoke with Chase about it when he was in Lawrence. As much as I care for Mrs. Gates, I'm not sure I want *my* husband working on a carpentry job at her house. But I don't know how to explain it to Chase without appearing jealous. I wonder if she is adding onto her "boudoir?" I shouldn't have said that.

And in the mail Chase brought from Lawrence was a separate note for me from Frank Swift.

There is a rumor that Hildebrand is in and out of the neighborhood. He was seen with his son Ben crossing Walnut Creek. A neighbor reported that Hildebrand made inquiry if the Stewart sisters still lived on the old claim; he said he had a score to settle with us. If Adda hears about it, I'm sure she will arrange a lively reception if he ever comes around.

Bad news travels fast. Before the day was out, Adda dropped in for "a little visit." She's wearing her vigilante costume, and I suppose her little pistol is well pocketed and loaded. I've heard from others that occasionally, while she's running the boiler at the sawmill, and has time on her hands and thinks no one is watching she will pretend to be surprised by some adversary (I suppose by Hildebrand.) She will whip out her pistol, take aim at a nearby stump and fire off four shots in quick succession, killing her make-believe foe.

Yesterday, April 27th, a gang of us raised the new Cordis addition. Actually the real work was done by Tom, Chase, Jerry Jordan and Mr. Carey. The rest of us cheered them on, occasionally handing up a tool or block of wood.

Chase is the chief carpenter on the job and he's up at the Cordises' place again today. There's plenty of work remaining on their addition. All we did yesterday was to erect fifteen or so double trusses for the roof. I noticed how careful Chase was about making each truss vertical; upright..."plumb," he called it. I'm so proud of my sweetheart. He is so hardworking and gets along so well with the men.

Friday, April 29th, who should pay us a surprise visit but Mr. and Mrs. Eastridge and their handsome son, Jerome, who appears to be a year or so younger than me. Last year after Mr. Eastridge and Mr. Young had assembled our sawmill, they went back to their homes in Iowa. Mr. Eastridge said they plan on being here several days, waiting for an Iowa group's arrival about mid May to leave with them for the goldfields, so they will be here about two weeks.

It's a year ago, to the week, since we started up the sawmill, thanks to Mr. Eastridge and Mr. Young. Mr. Eastridge's visit is a delightful reunion of old friends. He and Mr. Young had assembled the sawmill in contract with the boiler factory in Pennsylvania. The two men took almost all their meals with us and lived in the shed by the saw. We debated about charging them for their board, but considering the importance of their work to our town and us, we decided against it. Mr. Eastridge was more than a contract worker on the mill. He was a shareholder and during this year we've occasionally sawed logs for him at a discount to our normal charge, a discount Father wanted accorded to shareholders. His lumber was loaded on wagons he'd sent from Iowa, but this is the first we've seen of him in person since a year ago May.

I thought it was strange that he planned to be here two weeks before his group would arrive, but he soon cleared up that mystery.

What he wants to do while waiting is to saw up two, maybe three, wagon loads of timber, some 10,000 board feet for buildings he has planned near Denver and since we have plenty of raw logs on hand, we quickly arrived at a charge of $25 pr 1,000 board feet, paid in cash, assuming that he and Jerome would be available for help.

As soon as the lumber issue was settled, Mr. Eastridge suggested that we take in-trade his stock in the sawmill for our syrup mill, which he says he would dismantle and move to the Mountains, planning to reassemble it near Denver and freight in the sorghum cane, probably from Nebraska.

As Mr. Eastridge and I talked, we walked down to the shed that covered the syrup mill and its little boiler. He asked if Chase and I would fire it up for his inspections sometime before he leaves.

"Well, of course," I replied, but I really hadn't planned on selling it until you suggested it just now, and I would certainly need to get Adda's opinion.

Here we are, a year later, with no change in his appearance, which I can detect. His bushy reddish-brown mustache still protrudes over his upper lip by at least an inch and drops down over most of his mouth, so I've never gotten any help figuring out his thick Scottish brogue by watching his lips, but I'll manage, since it's such a pleasure to see him again.

As we walked back up to the cabin, he became very serious us as he expressed his personal condolences over Father's death.

Before he left, he asked about Adda and I said she was visiting Tom Cordis' wife, who he remembered. I said, "I'm sure Adda will be around while you and your son are sawing wood."

His response was that he had been telling Jerome about "my sister." Ah, ha! So that's it…the old engineer thinks he might be a matchmaker.

Outside our place I asked him how soon he wants to start sawing and how much help will he need? He said he will use his team (horses) to drag the logs from our inventory over to the saw, and could use two more men beside himself and Jerome to help. I said I thought Chase would be here most of that time and I was sure I could count on Jerry.

Tuesday, May 2nd, eighteen wagons are delayed from crossing the river, which is swollen from recent heavy rains. As a result of their delay, we are getting some unexpected business. In spite of the rain Mr. Eastridge and his son began sawing this morning, Jerry Jordon and Mr. Rice are helping. I'm glad now we built a shed over the saw and the boiler.

Three days after Mr. Eastridge started sawing logs, several outfits and thirty-five wagons, 100 yoke of oxen are milling around, making terrible muddy ruts while they wait to cross the Walnut.

At noon a man stopped in for some lunch and said that the road west was covered with wagons from here to Fort Gibson on the way to the Mountains, "all", "going to see the elephant." I'm really getting rather tired hearing about the elephant.

Sunday, May 8th, Augustus, a young recent settler with his mother and sister came by to say his mother has died and wondered if we could keep his little sister this summer. Chase was working on a job elsewhere and Adda wasn't here either, so I said, as a family we'd need to think about it.

Yesterday thirty wagons passed through Eldorado. Wondering where they were from, I talked with a few of their people, and learned that they too are headed for the goldfields. These travelers are all Easterners; that is, Kansas is not losing its population in such numbers, compared to the States, though Lord knows we are also losing some. From what I can tell in listening to these people from Chicago east, business is very slow. Farm prices are down because the farmers have produced too much of everything. Jobs are scarce, mostly because railroad building has almost halted and that has affected everybody, including people who supply the railroads. Unemployment is up. Lots of banks have closed, having loaned in good times too much of their depositors' money.

This group must be grocers or butchers. They have about a hundred head of cattle. With all the rain we've had lately, they've made muddy ruts all over the place, not to mention the manure.

We heard from a neighbor that Hildebrand and his son, Ben, were seen with this group, and camped fifteen miles west of town.

I guess married life takes some getting used to. Four months into our marriage and Chase seems to come and go and is reluctant to tell me if he will be home for supper. He went off this morning, didn't say where he was going. But I know he went "uptown," to J. D. Conner's store. They are becoming fast friends. Chase said he'd be gone a half-hour, but three hours have passed and no husband. The temptation to socialize with locals and travelers seems to be more than he can resist.

Several more hours have gone by. It is late at night and I'm lonely for my husband as I make this entry. I suppose the joy and happiness of our honeymoon days spoiled me. His explanation is that he says he must be sociable to get carpentry jobs and if he does run for political office, he'll also need the men's votes. I guess that makes sense.

A few days have passed. It's now May 10th, the rain has let up and the sun is out and we've plowed up about two, nicely moist, acres for a garden that will begin near the house and go down toward the river. I've had a huge sack of seed corn waiting for this spring planting. I ordered it months ago from a garden supply house near Sidney, Iowa. Adda and I "dropped" corn all morning long. Chase followed close behind with a hoe, quickly covering each hill. There were all sorts of curious birds around, some after worms from the freshly plowed ground. I hadn't realized the prairie supported such a variety of birds. The crows were making a terrible racket and were unusually cheeky and aggressive as they try to scare off the smaller birds. We knew if we didn't get the seed covered up, they'd get it. I've never worked so hard. And it's hot. I suppose I'll need to be thinking about putting up some scarecrows, as much as I hate to think about it.

The best scarecrows are dead crows mounted on tall beanpoles set up in various parts of the garden. Why a dead crow scares off live crows is a mystery to me, but it's common practice. We saw scores of them put up in this fashion when we came through Iowa. I hate to use the shotgun for a single crow. That old gun kicks so hard; it hurts my shoulder, particularly when I have to aim upwards, which is usually the case.

I've yet to put in a patch of potatoes, probably they'll be the first potatoes ever planted so far west. Two years ago, Father's exploring party planted the first crops out here, mostly corn. I'm glad Adda and I decided to stay here and fulfill Father's vision for the settlement, yet so many people are leaving for the west.

Early Saturday morning, May 14, Mr. Eastridge and his son dropped in before going to work and Adda and I invited them to breakfast. During the two weeks or so that we have been sawing wood, Adda has had several occasions to be down around the mill and has had ample opportunity to socialize with Jerome. I've heard from others that Jerome is taken with Adda, but if she has any interest in him, I haven't seen it.

With his brand of humor Mr. Eastridge began criticizing Father's shortsighted use of the syrup mill's boiler, which in his opinion is uneconomic. "It's a sorra business," he said, "to see all this 'bra heat' go wafting off into the prairie wind without getting all the work out of it that we're entitled to. 'Tis bordering on a crime, considering this is the last stop for 500 miles before a body could replenish his supply of spirits. Oh, what a lost opportunity," he said. "Foosh how could he have been so wasteful?" I told him our two cows have never produced such milk as they do when we feed them the cane-mash. He ignored my comment.

After breakfast, we all walked down to the syrup press. Chase and I had agreed to steam up the boiler for Mr. Eastridge's inspection. "I tyke it Muss Steewart," looking at me with a touch of reproach, "that you and your family remain teetotalers?"

"Yes," I said, trying with all my might to conceal a smile.

"The reason your cows are so contented is, that mash is already a little fermented."

Mr. Eastridge walked over to the warm boiler and ran his palm affectionately over its surface, saying, more to the boiler than to me, "Oh, ye pair, oonfortunate thang that your labors are soo oonproductive, all because of this national disease of tee totaling."

Mr. Eastridge and I have "danced around" a price for the syrup mill, but we haven't concluded our transaction, yet. First I wanted Chase to go over the numbers. I know what Father paid for the mill. We've only operated it one season and it worked just fine, so I don't see a need to reduce my price too much from what we paid for it, though I don't know what Mr. Eastridge paid for his share in the sawmill either.

In justifying a more favorable price, I hinted to Mr. Eastridge that I've known all along that the mill could be used to make rum from the cane pressings. He smiled and said, "Muss Steewart, I'm a Scotsman, if you 'aven't noticed. You Americans think the first steam boiler was used by its Scotch inventor, James Watt, to run his wee locomotive. Foosh, James Watt was first a whiskey maker and learned about boilers and condensers from his first trade. Scotch boilers, pumps and locomotives came later."

Mr. Eastridge said that when his family left Scotland, they first went to Canada, settling north of Toronto, where there was a community of Scottish Presbyterians. Those Scots, he said, had brought their own grain, called rye to Canada. "And it wasn't for making wee cookies, I'll tell you. We lived there for several years before coming to Iowa," he added.

On the walk up to the house, much to my surprise, Mr. Eastridge began reciting an old Scottish ballad he thought was by Bobby Burns but he couldn't swear to it. The poem was about what happens to a man named John Barleycorn. "I don't remember all of the stanzas," he said, "but here are my favorites."

He recited several stanzas about turning Mr. Barley corn into whiskey. As usual, I didn't get all of the words due to his

Scotch brogue, but the poem was obviously about making alcoholic spirits, so rum or whiskey was part of his plan for our syrup mill all along.

Right after Mr. Eastridge left, I sent a note to Adda at the Weibleys' about Mr. Eastridge pestering me about our selling the syrup mill or, as he has suggested, our taking his single share of the sawmill for it. I suggested that we have a farewell supper for the Eastridge's after his wood is all sawed, loaded-up and I invited her down.

A day later, as I was throwing some dishwater out the back door, I noticed Adda was down by the saw talking to Jerome Eastridge. I waited a few minutes, walked down to the shed and asked Adda if she could spare me a few minutes today.

We hardly got into our discussion on the syrup mill when it became apparent that Mr. Eastridge had beaten me to it. Adda simply said Mr. Eastridge thinks you've already decided. Well, I knew that was self-serving to Mr. Eastridge and he was craftily using it to influence Adda. I didn't know which aspect to respond to first. I detected in Adda a bit of irritation with me that I'd made this decision without asking her, yet I was also mildly put off by her question. I suppose I was jealous of the sole right to make the decision, but I quickly realized that not only did Adda have an interest here, for after all she owns half of it, but that I would probably gain from her opinion.

"Ya', that's because you like Mr. Eastridge" Adda said.

I said, "Adda wait. I haven't made a decision. Don't you see, the old coot is trying to make his job easier with this… prevarication."

"No, it is that the sawmill operates all year round, where the syrup mill only operates in the fall when we get sorghum cane. The rest of the time parts of it rust."

Adda summed up the situation perfectly, "The trouble is if you don't get cash from the sawmill and you can't collect on the jobs done for credit, we really get more cash from the Syrup, never mind that we only run it a month or two."

Adda was right about the cash. I said again that I had not made up my mind, that Mr. Eastridge was using her to influence my decision and suggested we both think about it, but I'd like to have it settled one way or the other before our supper with them on Thursday."

Much to my surprise Adda said, "I've been thinking about going back to Lawrence this spring, so whatever you decide to do with the syrup mill will be all right with me, and it's all right with me if you take back the share of the sawmill ownership, but get the certificate from him."

Adda's decision to go back to Lawrence was more disturbing to me by far than what to do about the syrup mill. I've never been without Adda around.

On Friday before our supper for them he and Jerome dismantled the syrup mill and boiler and packed it in one of their several wagons. Later, he handed me a stock certificate for one share in the sawmill and paid me $250, in cash for 10,000 board feet of lumber. I was relieved that there was no last minute haggling over money, though I suspect that there's at least an extra 1,000 board feet of sawed lumber in his wagons. And the old coot always selected the very best logs we had in stock, almost all hardwoods and most of that walnut. Directly after they left Adda and I had a pot of tea and I said, I thought we'd clear at least $200 on the Eastridge lumber sale, since we had the inventory. I proposed we split net profit 50/50. I can certainly use the cash for groceries this year and it will give Adda a little cushion when she gets back to Lawrence.

They all left early on Monday, the 16th, in the rain. Since the 6th of May it's been raining on and off. On several occasions the river has been so high wagon trains accumulate and have had to wait up to three days before they could cross, of course that's been good for local business and Adda and I have enjoyed the extra income from feeding an unusual number. Two weeks later, except for two days of sunshine, which allowed us to put in about half our garden, it's still raining. Last night it rained almost through the night.

This morning, May 16, about noon we saw a large westbound wagon train stopped on the other side of the river. They must have twenty-five or thirty head of cattle and twelve wagons of varying size.

The wagon boss came over and asked Adda and me where the best place was to cross the river. Before I could answer, Adda said, "If you had any brains, you wouldn't cross anywhere along the Walnut today, probably not even tomorrow. The river is up, way up. For two weeks we've had lots of rain here and north of us in Chelsea. The river is usually low enough that you can walk it, since the bottom out there is mostly sandstone, particularly if you cross up there, above the falls. But the river must be up four or five feet above normal."

The fellow listened carefully as we spoke, then he said, "I still think we can make it across today. We'll divide our outfit and our cattle into two groups."

"Can you swim?" I asked him. He nodded. "Then why don't you take a long stout stick to poke for the sandstone bottom, and to see how far out into the river you can walk and still stand up? The sloping bank's pretty soft in places, but I'm afraid by the time you are eight to ten feet from the shore on your side, it will be too deep to stand and the current will try to sweep you downstream. Since you can swim, you will be able to fight the current but it will push you back to the east bank, because of the bend in the river. You shouldn't underestimate the force of that water."

Adda joined me in offering him some advice. "There's a big bend in the river here, but don't go too far upstream to avoid it, or else the current will push you back over to your side," she told him. She then advised him to round up his horses that are the best swimmers. "Get them over here first, before you start crossing with the wagon teams, tie ropes from the horses on our side to the teams crossing and let them pull each wagon out of the current, then up the grade. The grade on both sides will be muddy."

The man scowled at Adda, put both forearms up with his palms facing her in a very offensive gesture and said, "Lady, do you think this is the first crick or river I've been up against on my way out here from Ohio? All I wanted to know was the best place to cross the river."

In a huff, he turned and walked off towards his wagons. "What an ungrateful and conceited bird. He acts like he knows everything," Adda said in a low voice. "Just wait, he'll be back here wanting to borrow something. I'm going to put on my raincoat and see what they intend to do." I joined her.

The rain had let up. We walked down towards the river and watched the men on the other side as they started to herd the cattle, dividing them into two groups.

They roped half the cattle together, one after the other in a single file. The men asked if they could use our little rowboat to row to the other side, which they did, pulling a loose rope end with them that they could use to pull the cattle over to this shore. Once two of them got to the other side, the man on this side began pulling on the rope and one by one the cattle were guided into the river by him. This scheme worked well enough, but it took at least an hour, maybe more, just to drive across the dozen or so animals.

Jerry Jordan, who was working around the sawmill, came down to the river to watch. He told one of the men on our side to call for the rowboat advising that, "Once you're over here, find Mr. Rice's place. He has two oxen. I don't think your horses are strong enough to pull your wagons up the riverbank. It's too muddy over here. But with the help of his ox team, you should be able to manage it."

I wonder if he would have been as willing to take that advice if it had come from Adda instead of Jerry.

In the middle of the afternoon, the other half of their party began making preparations to cross. The river had continued to rise. Some of the riders dismounted and led their horses out into the river, then allowed their horses to pull them across the water. One fellow insisted on staying in his saddle. Jerry yelled that his weight could push the horse under. The man said he couldn't swim and slowly spurred his horse out into the swollen river. Not twenty feet into the river rider and horse began a side-to-side rocking motion. On one of those "rolls" he and the horse failed to return upright, and the rider simply slipped off the saddle, but he must have held onto the reins because we could see his head bobbing up near the horse. Now that the rider didn't weigh down the horse, more of the horse's body was visible. The horse continued to swim toward shore, except the current was carrying them both downstream. After fifteen minutes or so they both, somehow, reached our side.

"First time I ever saw a horse save a man's life," Adda remarked.

Jerry asked the train boss if their wagon beds were watertight. "Some of them are," the man answered. Jerry suggested they put more of their load into those wagons and tie some softwood logs to the wagons that were apt to leak. He said if they leak too much loaded, they will sink before you get them to this side. Lashing a log on each wagon side will prevent that. Jerry said that he could provide the cottonwood logs but he wanted fifty cents apiece for the use of them and another fifty cents for any log you lose. "We're in the lumber business and I want the money after you've made up your mind how many logs you'll need." I thought that was a smart idea on Jerry's part, though it produced some grumbling from the wagon boss, but he reluctantly accepted Jerry's offer. The boss ordered the teams that had the most watertight wagons to begin first. The men assigned to those wagons all swam or held onto ropes attached to the wagons. Five wagons made it fine. But when the sixth wagon got out into the middle of the river, a large pack of drifting logs, well over a dozen, came rotating down the river.

"Those are logs I cut some weeks ago," said Jerry. "I piled them on the riverbank several miles upstream. When the river rose, they must have washed off the bank."

Very slowly the log pack surrounded the wagon, causing it to commence rolling over in midstream. The horses also got tangled up in the logs. One of the drivers jumped into the water. I suppose he intended to free the horses but he landed on a log and bounced into the water, and we lost sight of him. Just then the wagon turned completely over, and continued to roll over very slowly three or four times. The current in the bend of the river began to push it back toward their side. The wagon was upside down. We could see all four of its wheels still slowly rotating, as the current made the wagon dip and sway. Those horses somehow got free of their traces and were able to swim out of the logs and make it to this side. The wagon finally wound up downstream on our side of the river, coming to rest on its side part way up the soft, grassy bank.

Later in the day it started to rain again. Two men went down stream on our side with a yoke of Mr. Rice's oxen and pulled the wagon a few feet higher up on the bank, but with main strength alone, they could not right it. They eventually just left it there, and it lay on its side several hundred yards down from our property.

Four wagons still had yet to cross. One of the men began to load things, including two or three rifles that had been piled on the ground into the front of one of the remaining wagons. As he climbed up into the wagon with one of the guns, it discharged.

The bullet struck one of his companions, who was working nearby in the loading process. From where I was standing I could hear the shot. The bullet went through the victim's chest, they said, instantly killing him. The first thing I wondered was if they would just leave him here and we would have to bury him, but they quickly lifted him up into one of the wagons and that's the last I saw of him.

All the ingredients for an accident were there: The gun was obviously loaded and the hammer was probably full-cocked.

The gun must have gone off because he had either tried to unload the gun or uncock the hammer at the same time as he was climbing up into the wagon.

It's a tricky maneuver to uncock a loaded Sharps. You have to use the fingers of one hand to restrain the hammer, while pulling the trigger with a finger on your other hand, keeping it pulled back as you rotate the hammer slowly from the cocked position to the half-cocked or safe. Holding back the hammer requires considerable strength, because it's cocked against a spring powerful enough to make the hammer strike the bullet's cap with enough force to ignite it.

Father used to tell Adda and me that, whenever we needed to uncock a loaded Sharps to use both hands and always point the gun either down at the ground or up at the sky, keeping the gunstock some distance from our faces. If the gun is inadvertently discharged with the stock close to your face, the kick could break your nose or jaw.

The Sharps is a powerful gun and should be handled only by someone who knows the damage it can do. This fellow, no matter how strong, should not have tried to uncock the hammer in the process of stepping up into the wagon, especially in the rain. He probably used one hand to get up into the wagon, and thought he could manipulate the gun with the other. Or perhaps the wet gun simply slipped from his grasp and the trigger was pulled by accident.

Now, in addition to all of the other confusion caused by the stubbornness of the wagon boss, who had insisted on crossing the river today, we might have a dead man on our hands, if the other wagons can't get across to the our shore until the river goes down and that might be three or four days.

There were seven women in this party and they were all on the other side when the accident happened. I wondered but didn't ask, if the fellow that got shot was the husband of one of them.

By late afternoon, it was obvious that the remaining wagons weren't going make it to our side by nightfall.

As Adda and I walked back to the cabin, one of the men followed us to inquire about an evening meal for six of them, who had been handling things on our side of the river including the wagon boss.

At the end of the day, four of their "leaky" wagons, along with their teams and two or three head of troublesome cattle were still on the other side of the river. The men had worked until dark, pulling Jerry's flotation logs back over to their side in order to reuse them for the remaining wagons tomorrow, and that was no easy chore.

Fortunately, I had a good supply of food at home and could provide them with a hearty meal. A month or so ago Chase and I came by a 100 pound sack of Army-quality small white beans by trading with a westbound military freight wagon train some smoked turkey and fresh milk. Even the Army calls these, "navy beans." Two days ago, I heard a faint rattling in the bean sack and upon inspection chased four or five mice out of my beans. I wondered if they were regular Army mice from Leavenworth, or just locals. I really don't begrudge them a bean or two, but I don't like their habit of defecating in among the beans. Luckily their little hard black deposits float to the surface when the beans are washed. The night I discovered the mice I washed and soaked about three pounds of them (the beans!) This morning, after I saw the wagon train, I put the beans on the stove to simmer so that they would be ready should some of those travelers need a meal. I figured we'd get some business from this outfit. I had a small six-pound ham hock with the bone and knuckle still in, and a thick fat rind still on. That, and some carrots, as well and two or three onions, have been simmering with the beans all day, and I'll make cornbread. That ought to hold them.

If it rains tonight, and I predict it will, looks like I'll also have some overnight business. I hope I won't have to do anything more for these visitors than give them supper and lodging. I told

Adda I don't intend to do any undertaking work tomorrow. "Let's hope the rain stops long enough so they can get across tomorrow and take the dead man with them."

"You betcha" she replied. "An' when that bird from Ohio comes to supper. I'm going to ask him how things went today."

It was almost dark before the wagon boss and five more came in for their evening meal, wet. They were very somber and one of them just went on and on with his blessing. Adda avoided her question. I had hoped in vain that Chase would be back by suppertime.

38

Eldorado
An Intriguing Offer from Texas
Late Spring 1859

The day dawned bright and sunny, a welcome relief from all that incessant rain, but the beauty of this spring day is an inadequate antidote for my loneliness. I miss my husband who is away on a carpentering job. Just as I turned to the almanac to plan some spring planting Adda came in and that cheered me up.

I told her I was lonely and so glad for her company. She mumbled an acknowledgment but became absorbed in looking on my bench and elsewhere for some writing materials and a notebook that she believes is here because it isn't with her things at the Weibley's.

I jumped up to make a pot of tea. The teakettle was still on the stove, hot from breakfast.

When the tea was ready, Adda sat down for the first time since she came in. We exchanged pleasantries. I asked her how things were at the Weibley household and she said they were very pleasant, "but it's not like home. I know you and Chase need your privacy, but I just don't like living in somebody else's house. If I can't live here," and she waved her arm in a sweeping motion, "then I might as well go back to Lawrence. I know I can get a job with the Gates at the Cincinnati House and it would be fun to see Aggie and the old gang and to earn a little money for a change."

"Where is Chase?" By putting the accent on "is" she displayed a little exasperation in her voice. Rather than telling her where he was, I thought I would tease her in a sisterly way and said, "Oh ho, you're not here to see me, but my husband," but I didn't carry it off.

She said she'd spoken to Chase a few days ago. He said he was going up to Lawrence soon.

I asked if she'd made up her mind to go, hoping she'd say no.

She said, "Well, on Monday I think I'll go, but on Tuesday, I think I'll stay, but if I thought Chase was going up there, that would tilt my thinking in favor of going. Do you know if he plans to go soon?"

She got up and rummaged through one of the drawers of the chest and gave a little squeal of satisfaction, as she waved the old notebook at me, then asked, "What do you think, Augusta?"

"About what?"

"My going back to Lawrence."

I knew it was a rhetorical question, for when Adda makes up her mind to do something; she's beyond opinions to the contrary.

No sooner had she located her notebook, a few other things and the cup of tea, she made motions to leave.

I said, "What's your hurry? You haven't been here an hour.

As she put on a light jacket she said, "There's no hurry. There's just nothing else to talk about." And she made gestures of leaving.

I thought I could detain her so I asked, intending some humor, "Well have you shot old Hildebrand yet?"

She laughed, "No, but that's only because I haven't seen the old asshole. I think the word got to him that he'd better not tangle with this Stewart daughter."

I said, "Adda, are you less angry now than last winter?"

"Yes, but I'm a better-shot now." and she left. The lonely quietness that I simply can't abide filled the house. I felt so bad about my marriage creating this problem for Adda. I'm sure she feels she's been displaced. She's old enough to understand it. After all she volunteered to move out, but I could tell today she doesn't like the consequence. All of her boyfriends are gone, so she doesn't have that as a pleasant distraction. I think I'll speak to Chase about our asking Adda to move back in with us. I know he will say yes but I know he will view it as an imposition on him by two sisters, one's his wife. He has this notion that two women in a married household can be a source of irritation. He'd told me on more than one occasion that having his father's mother living with them, when he grew up, was a source of frustration to his mother.

Chase came home two days ago, on the 24th from White Water where he's been working on a house. He was upset because Nudge and Old Gray, two horses he's recently bought, are missing from the pasture at the Rice's place across the river. He said he wanted to go to Lawrence next Friday and would need those horses for the trip. Now, he told me, he would have to waste his time looking for them, and if he didn't find them, he would have to buy others and maybe delay the trip. I intended to ask him if Adda had shared her plans with him, but didn't.

Before we went to bed, I said, "Well, if you think you've had trouble the last few days, let me tell you about a terrible thing that happened while you were gone. I think it's the first accidental death in Eldorado."

And I told Chase about the tragedy here during the rain spell the day the river was at its peak.

Still upset over his missing horses, Chase left again yesterday to continue looking and was gone all day. He came home last night empty-handed and disappointed. He went out again after breakfast this morning. I felt so bad for him, particularly when he said he thought Nudge would colt in a month or so. In a few hours he returned to say that he had found Old Gray but not

Nudge. I asked him where or how he had found Old Gray but he was in such a hurry to go back out I didn't get an answer.

Chase came back in the mid afternoon saying he'd spent most of two days and had searched as far as he thought prudent. He had stopped by Conner's to pickup the mail, since Mr. Conner had just returned from Lawrence. There was no mail for us. He said Mr. Connor did bring back a barrel of whiskey (all important to the men around here) adding that Mr. Conner had also brought some new pipe tobacco, which he was anxious to try even though he knows my attitude about tobacco. After he had filled his pipe, every time he tried to light it I would playfully blow out the match. At first, as we chased each other around the table, he thought my pestering was fun, but soon tired of it, claiming I was trying to cheat him out of his smoke with the first good pipe tobacco that's been available for months. So I stopped teasing him and returned to my chores and speculated about whether he and Mr. Conner had also sampled the new barrel of whiskey. Is there no vice that my husband can resist?

On Sunday, May 29 Mrs. Brooks and her baby came by for a visit. We made small talk, remarking on the number of eastbound wagons that were passing through town, full of disappointed gold seekers returning from the Mountains. It was quickly apparent to me that she hadn't come to see me but was here to talk to Chase about a trip to Lawrence she and several others are planning to make. This was all news to me. Chase seems reluctant to include me in these details. When she came in Chase was out again looking for Nudge. A neighbor thought he saw her west of here. Mid afternoon he returned but without Nudge. From what he said I'm afraid that horse is gone for good. Well, Mrs. Brooks was still here, so she and Chase began to discuss their plans. It looks like they will all go up to Lawrence next week.

During a lull in the conversation I said to Chase, "You know, I would really like to go along if you're not going to be gone too long. I need to do some planting, but I can put it off for a while. How long will you be up there?"

"I don't know, but you are certainly welcome. I simply hadn't thought to ask you."

"Well." I thought, "That's flattering."

Despite what he said, I could tell by the tone of his voice and his manner that he would rather I stay here, but was too embarrassed in the presence of Mrs. Brooks to say so.

Since Adda's not staying with us at the moment, I can't inquire as to her plans, but I have a feeling that Chase has already spoken to her about the trip and that she will be joining them. "Is Adda going with you?" I asked him.

"As far as I know."

Well, that was another reason for me to go. There was something special I wanted to tell her and I knew I'd have plenty of time on the trail.

After an afternoon of give-and-take about whether I should go, and how welcome I would be, it was obvious that he wanted me to decide for myself, but my attitude was I didn't really want to go if he didn't want me along. By suppertime it was agreed that I would stay home. I was really disappointed with the outcome of this protracted discussion.

I'm afraid I was not very hospitable yesterday to Mrs. Brooks. I was feeling "unwell" then and this morning, so I tried to take a nap this afternoon. I've been married a little over four months. My, how time flies.

Well, they all got away early this morning, June 6: the Brooks, George Rice, Chase and Adda. They wanted to leave yesterday, but things kept coming up.

During the hustle and bustle of their packing I was not feeling well, but I was not going to tell them that. But now they are gone. Things are so quiet; I'm suddenly lonely and not feeling any better. Mrs. Rice has proposed to stay with me until her husband returns.

Now, two days later, I'm making my entry in an unusual posture. I'm writing in bed and it's broad daylight. I'm simply not feeling well, or I'd feel guilty about being in bed.

I hope I'm feeling better tomorrow. The Almanac says tomorrow is the best time to plant radishes, lettuce, citron, potato eyes and tomato sets. Some weeks ago, I planted some tomato seeds under a double layer of cheesecloth (stretched out about 6" above the ground.) The sets are pushing up against the cheesecloth now, so I'm anxious to transplant them.

Oh yes, I did the same thing with cabbage seeds and now have almost 300 cabbage sets for transplanting. I see the crows circle menacingly around those little sprouts out on the garden's edge. I guess I'll have to get those scarecrows up or lose some garden.

I'm glad I have the gardening to look forward to, not that I'm without chores, but I miss my husband. I am so lonely without him. It was a mistake for me to have given in and not joined them. It was my own pride and vanity; after all, Chase said I was welcome if I wanted to go.

A week has gone by. Chase and Adda aren't back yet. I heard yesterday from the neighbor who had sold Nudge to Chase. He was returning from a buffalo hunt forty miles west of here and said that he saw her with her colt. Some Indians had her with several other horses…probably stolen.

A youngster came by midmorning, handed me a note and stood in the doorway. When I looked at him "sideways," he said he was supposed to wait for an answer. The note read:

Monday, June 13, 1859
Dear Mrs. Chase,

A visitor from Texas, named Doctor Crabtree, is acquainted with one of your relatives, a John Wesley Stewart, * an uncle of your father's who wants to know your whereabouts. May I bring him over later in the PM?
y.o.s.   Conner

There was enough room at the bottom of the note for me to add my response, so I simply wrote:
"By all means on second thought, please come to supper.

y. t.   Mrs. J. Chase"

Towards 5 PM, the two gentlemen arrived in Mr. Conner's little one-horse, two-wheeled singletree. I was happy to have the company.

Doctor Harold Crabtree was the first to come through the door. I'd say he is almost, if not, six feet tall, in his mid to late fifties, and distinguished: He has a thick shock of wavy gray hair, nearly white. He is not a handsome man but has an air about him that makes one pay close attention.

He took my right hand into both of his. They were the soft hands of someone who certainly didn't chop wood for a living. He looked at me until it became a little embarrassing.

"So you are Augusta Stewart."

My first reaction was, "How did he know my maiden name? Mr. Conner must have told him."

---

*This is the first and only reference to Captain John Wesley Stewart in Augusta's journal. This incident is also mentioned in a book of Adda's reminiscences collected by her daughter, Memories of Addie Stewart Graton by Alice Graton Kincaid, now in the archives of the Kansas Collection at the University of Kansas Libraries, Lawrence, Kansas. Captain Stewart's offer is also noted in the Stewart Clan Magazine, a genealogical publication, Volume number 12, June 1924, and pgs 93 – 95

"Yes, except I'm married. I'm Mrs. Chase now. I am the daughter of Charles Samuel Stewart. I'm sorry to say that my father was killed seven months ago in the Cherokee Nation."

"Yes. I know about it; indeed your father's death is one of the reasons for my visit. I handle certain business matters for Captain John Wesley Stewart, an elderly gentleman in Texas. He had a much older brother, Charles Stewart who lived near Flint, Michigan. He believes that brother was your father's father. Did your grandfather take his family from Onondaga County in New York to Michigan in about 1834?" I nodded.

"It seems to me to be a very unusual coincidence that in Texas the Captain could become acquainted with a man who claimed to have killed your father. The captain heard a fellow named Worldy brag that in a dispute over in the Cherokee Nation, claimed he killed Samuel Stewart, a Free State politician and was the founder of Eldorado, an abolitionist town in the Kansas Territory."

I remembered that Chase had wondered, when he came back from the Lynch ranch, if the escorts who had taken Worldy to the court at Van Buren, Arkansas might have allowed him to escape, since they were all fellow Southerners. If Worldy were in Texas now, he probably would never pay for Father's murder. Texas was a proslavery state and wasn't likely to turn him over for justice.

I found this discussion very disturbing. To compose myself, I got up to prepare some refreshments.

I asked the gentlemen to have a seat and poured out three glasses of lemonade. To impress them (and please myself) I had put a thin slice of lemon in each glass, letting it float on top of the lemonade. Mr. Conner took a sip and said, "Mrs. Chase, where in the world did you get fresh lemons?"

Trying to be debonair in front of the stranger, I said, "Oh, a friend of ours in Lawrence sends them regularly." I had fibbed about regularity, but two days ago I had received the lemons in a package from Aggie Rourke, not in the post but carried by a teamster. Aggie simply asked him to carry it out when she heard he was headed for the Santa Fe Trail and would go through Eldorado. Most of our mail gets delivered that way.

I needed a little time to think about these disturbing revelations. Why couldn't Chase and Adda be here, so I could include them in all this? To give myself some breathing room, I made an excuse to tend to our supper I took the roast out of the oven and put it on a large platter with some Missouri potatoes that I'd purchased earlier from Mr. Conner. Though the rolls needed more time in the oven, the gravy was ready and had really turned out well. I know Mr. Conner loves "his gravy and potatoes." When I can get it, I like to use small amounts of cornstarch to thicken the gravy, rather than wheat flour. Tonight I had used cornstarch. Aggie Rourke once said to me that it takes a cook five years to learn how to uses cornstarch properly.

I also pried the wax off the top of a small glazed terra-cotta jar of raspberry jam that I'd put up a month ago and asked the gentlemen to have a seat.

I asked Mr. Conner if he'd slice the roast while I checked on my rolls. The flour I had used to make them hadn't looked all that good to me. Though they rose in the pan nicely, they should have been done by now, and it distracted me that they weren't.

Doctor Crabtree seemed anxious to continue. He said, more to Mr. Conner than to me, that the Captain had given him $500 * to carry up to Eldorado, with instructions to see if we were indeed his nephew's daughters. I couldn't imagine anyone paying such a princely sum to satisfy that curiosity. But I didn't voice that opinion. What I said instead was: "Doctor Crabtree, my father never spoke of an uncle by the name of John Wesley Stewart. I do know that my grandfather had brothers. He also had twelve children in Massachusetts, all from his second marriage. My father was the youngest of those children. The Captain's connection to my family does seem to be more than just a coincidence of names, but I have no way of knowing for certain if we are related. I am

---

*According to the Stewart Clan Magazine, the sum was $300.

flattered beyond words, however, that he would send someone so far to make inquiry about us and offer to be of such gallant help. He must be a very generous soul."

"Well, he can afford to be generous, Mrs. Chase. He has been very successful but I think his intentions go beyond just simple generosity. He operates two large plantations near Austin, one devoted to cotton, the other to cattle. I don't think I'm breaking any confidences by saying that Captain Stewart feels his family in the States had not done right by him when he needed help before the war. * He has a son, but the son's dissipated habits will soon make an end to him, so Captain Stewart is anxious that his holdings go to someone who will respect and husband them properly. If this meeting convinces us all that you girls are indeed related to him, there's little doubt in my mind that he intends to consider passing his property on to you two. Doctor Crabtree added that the Captain had learned about us from Worldy himself. This shocked me, until I realized it was possible that he could have known about us since we know now that (the stranger) Worldy spent a few days at Hildebrand's cabin before the theft and knowing what a blabbermouth Hildy is. "Hearing that you two girls are now orphans worried my partner, and it was from that concern that he asked me to come this distance. I've been instructed by Captain Stewart to invite you and your sister to come down and live with him in Texas."

I said nothing in reply and managed to hide my amazement at this unexpected offer. To let it sink in and to quiet myself, I assumed a detached tone and began to talk about Worldy, discussing Father's death with far more dispassion than I really felt.

"It's very interesting, isn't it, that my father's murderer knew that he had two daughters. We never knew that he was so well informed. But it confirms my suspicion that he and a local pro slaver by the name of Hildebrand were part of a conspiracy."

---

*Since John Wesley Stewart lived in Texas, this reference is probably to the Mexican War

Augusta's Journal - Volume III

I related the whole episode of the horse theft and Father's murder, and read him parts of Mr. Bell's letter, including the part where Worldy was caught on November 30th and taken to Van Buren, Arkansas for trial. "If he is in Texas now," I added, "he's escaped punishment."

"It looks more and more," said Mr. Conner, "like someone paid Hildebrand and that other scoundrel to kill your father, stealing the horses was only part of it."

"I'm on my way to California," said Doctor Crabtree. "It's my job to give you and your sister this money with instructions on how to get to Captain Stewart's claim in Texas. This money is yours if you decide to go."

I had something important to ask, but I didn't want to be offensive. I knew I was talking to a Southerner, though an old-fashioned chivalrous one.

"Since Captain Stewart owns two large plantations, am I correct in presuming that he is a slave holder?"

"Yes. Would that affect your decision about accepting his offer?"

"Oh yes, the main reason my father sold his sawmill and store in Michigan and brought us out here in the first place was to help outvote the existing proslavery element in this new territory. Knowing the sacrifices he made, not to mention what the three of us have gone through, I don't think I could be comfortable in a proslavery state." What I thought, but didn't say, was that if the country came to war over the slavery issue, which seems to be the common opinion, and if we were living in Texas, we'd be involved in fighting in favor of slavery. I couldn't abide that.

As the supper conversation went on, I related several episodes about our life in the Territory, starting with Plymouth. It was flattering that he would ask me to speak about our abolitionist experiences. The whole story, including Father's incarceration at the prisoners' camp, the presidential pardon and finally Father's election to the Legislature must have taken twenty or thirty minutes. By the time I finished, both men had put their knives and forks down. They had eaten all of their roast and potatoes. They seemed "full" and pleased with my meal. In mid-recitation I remembered the hot rolls. When I brought them to the table with butter and raspberry jam they made a nice, but unintended, dessert.

About half past eight, the gentlemen decided to leave. I inquired where Doctor Crabtree would spend the night, as he was more than welcome here.

"Doctor Crabtree is going to stay with me," said Mr. Conner. He added, with a conspiratorial smile at the doctor, that they might have a little libation and some "politicking" before bedtime.

"Our visitor has some Chicago papers, which we were discussing on the way over here. The Republican Party has nominated Abraham Lincoln from Illinois as president. They had their big convention in Chicago in mid May. There's not a single plank in their platform for abolition, which seems strange for a party that's been invented around anti slavery sentiments."

I said, "Well, almost anybody would be better than Buchanan. What about the Democrats? What are they up to?"

Dr Crabtree spoke up, "Although they got started in April, before the Republicans, there seems to be a real problem for us. They met in convention in Charleston and immediately squabbled over the unintended consequences of Douglas' contrivance of Popular Sovereignty, which you people know all about…and he laughed a little as though it was an acknowledgment that the abolitionists had won that one even if most of them are Republican. Southern Democrats say it doesn't matter how Kansas votes, anyway, since the Dred Scott decision had already legalized slavery in the territories. The Southern Democrats want nothing to do with Douglas. Nevertheless after a week of debates and arguing, the platform nominating Douglas was carried by a slim majority…probably provided by Northern Democrats. Immediately eight Southern states, I don't remember all of them, but Alabama, Louisiana, Texas and five more * all walked out. They reconvened elsewhere and nominated John Breckinridge from Kentucky". I said I'd never heard of him, but I was really impressed that this gentleman from Texas was so well informed about National politics and a little irritated with myself that I was learning this from him.

"Tell me again, who did those Democrats in Charleston nominate?" Mr. Conner asked.

"Stephen A. Douglas, Senator from Illinois."

As the gentleman walked to the door, I said, "That splits the ticket for the Democrats, doesn't it? And that ought to be good for our side. When you are done with those newspapers, I'll trade you an evening meal for them."

As they prepared to leave, Dr. Crabtree asked me if I needed some time to think over his proposition. "I am in no hurry."

"Thank you," I said, "but I have made up my mind. As flattered as I am by the captain's offer, I want to stay here and see if we can make a go of the sawmill and of our farm, I can't speak for my sister. She is working in Lawrence and is very independent for her age. My husband is a house builder, though that business is spotty out here due to a shortage of cash and credit, and he's spoken of running for the Legislature in my father's old position." I asked him to give me the captain's address before he left for California, so that I could write him a note, and he agreed to do so.

I said more to Mr. Connor than to the Doctor that this visit was the only pleasant thing that's happed to me while Adda and Mr. Chase have been away in Lawrence. Otherwise I've been rather lonely and I thanked Mr. Connor for bringing Dr. Crabtree for supper. I was so hungry for company that I invited them both over for breakfast.

---

*The other five were Mississippi, South Carolina, Florida, Arkansas and Delaware. They represented a population of about 4.3 million people out of a total of 9 .1 million.

I'm planning, the very first thing tomorrow to write this all up and get it to Adda. With her spirit of adventure she might want to become a Texan.

39

Eldorado Abandoned to Indians
Summer 1859

Chase received a rather terse letter from his brother today relating some bad news from home. The letter said: "Mother is very sick and unless you can arrange to come back, you may never see her again. Little Frank is also very sick and not expected to live." (The letter included a likeness of his brother.)

After considerable discussion dealing with the extreme distance to New Hampshire, the potential dangers en route, whether we should both go, the cost to undertake this travel and the lost business during his absence, which we expected to be at least six weeks, he decided he would leave on August 3rd, five days from now. I will stay here.

Chase left today, riding Old Gray to Lawrence, where he plans to sell the horse. From Lawrence he'll try to book passage on a riverboat to Kansas City then to St. Louis and take trains from there.

Late Wednesday, well after Chase left, a large tribe of Indians came in to Eldorado. Many Indians come out here for buffalo, but I don't know enough about their dress to identify their tribe. Some said they are Osages. Others in town aren't so sure. Their intentions are unknown to us and their numbers considerably exceed ours. That's frightening.

On Thursday, we heard that they cleaned out Conner's store of whiskey and anything else they could lay their hands on. They didn't harm Mr. Conner but they made a mess of his store. After they raided the store, one of the Indians got stabbed by one of their own, who ran off. Someone in town helped them take the wounded one and his squaw up to Doctor Weibley.

At three o'clock Monday morning (August 8th) some stranger banged on my door, and in the process, pushed it open it yelling, "The Comanches are coming!"…And left.

Well, that woke me up. I lit the coal oil lamp hanging nearby, got dressed quickly put a saddle on Kate, and rode her up to the Cordises', arriving before daylight. Tom was gone. Elizabeth (who is with child) and I didn't spend much time talking things over, except we both wondered if the recent new arrivals were really Comanches. "What's the tribe that's already been here for five days?" I asked her. "I didn't know there were any Comanches in this area.

Elizabeth Cordis had also heard about the tribe that had come in on August 3rd, so we wondered if the Comanche alarm was simply someone mistaking the Indians already here for Comanches.

Elizabeth had a small poster card put out by the Territorial Commissioners for Indian Affairs that listed the Kansas Indian tribes by general location: Indians west of Fort Riley, those north into the Nebraska Territory, those east of Fort Riley to the Missouri River; no other information, just the names of the tribes. She said, "Let's consult this before we leave." She read out loud tribe names: east of Fort Riley to the Missouri River: Cheyenne, Kaw (Kansa), Apache, Kiowa, Arapaho, Shawnee, Otoe—and there it was, Comanches.

"There are four or five more tribes," she said, "but that's all we need to know for now."

"Aren't the Osages on the list?"

"Maybe, I was only looking to see if the Comanches were on it."

Before we got all excited and worried, we decided to ride down to Mr. Conner's store. We knew others would be there. Perhaps some of them would know whether these Indians were menacing or not. We soon discovered we were not alone in getting the alarm. Even though it was 8 AM, a dozen or so people had already gathered at the store. Most of the men were armed. I was relieved to see that: I'd left the house in such a "toot" I'd forgotten to grab our carbine, but Elizabeth had remembered to bring that long-barreled revolver of theirs and I noticed how dexterous she was as she popped open the cylinder to make sure it was loaded.

Conner's store was still disheveled from the looting the Indians did a few days ago. Odds and ends were scattered all about. I noticed a strong odor of cinnamon and cloves. No doubt they got into the spice jars, but there was no major damage. Mr. Conner was quite composed. In fact, he was in a rather jocular mood. I remarked to him that I didn't find this situation as humorous as he apparently did. "Mrs. Chase," he said, "when you've survived the Potato famine, the English hatred and disdain for us Irish, their success in driving us off our own land, an ocean voyage in steerage from Belfast to Boston, then more English discrimination in Boston, a few Indians hopping around are an easy accommodation."

There were clots of four or five men carrying-on about what should be done. It was my opinion that we lacked leadership. These groups of men would dissolve and reform differently, but the men didn't seem to be coming to any consensus, nor was Mr. Conner, who had been appointed sheriff during the Hildebrand trial, taking charge. Even though he had the authority to draw up an armed posse, he wasn't doing it.

If I had to flee, I didn't want a few show-off braves to vandalize my home or ruin my garden. The parts for the sawmill are so massive it's hard to imagine the Indians could do much damage there; however, the Indians are known to set prairie fires, so it's conceivable that they might set the sheds on fire and pile-up wood around the boiler to set fire to that, as well.

By 9 AM, another dozen citizens had congregated at the store. Some rode horses to get here, a few walked and two or three families came by wagon.

Recent arrivals from down valley said some Indians had come up from the south and had stolen some cattle and broken into Careys' cabin on the way up here yesterday. "Was anyone hurt?" someone asked. Luckily, it appears not.

A consensus seemed to be forming that we should leave Eldorado and go to Chelsea. Well, I was not impressed by that idea. "For heaven's sakes," I said to J.D. Conner, "with a little effort you could round up at least twenty men, see to it that they had good horses and were well-armed, rig up a heavy wagon or two, and confront these savages." But Mr. Conner argued in reply that we shouldn't assume that the Indians came here unarmed, and he pointed out that they outnumber us five to one. "Still," I said, "we need to put up some resistance." I told him about the incident with Mr. Beerop's mules. "When Father reclaimed the mules from the Indians, he used a show of force. That scared the Indians and made it unnecessary or him to use violence and he came home with the mules."

"We've all worked hard to improve our claims," I said, "and if we don't defend ourselves, the Indians will conclude that we won't fight to protect our property." But there was such commotion and agitation in the store; I couldn't get Mr. Conner's, or anyone else's attention long enough to state why I thought we should stay and fight. In retrospect, I should have gotten up on an old prune box. If Father had been here, or Adda, for that matter, they would have rallied those people and we wouldn't be scurrying off, leaving our homes and possessions to the mercies of God knows what.

Someone else reported that Indians had without resistance taken cattle from settlers south of here. So there were definitely more Indians and they could be intent on harm. We started for Chelsea, hurrying off in scattered disorganized groups. What a surprise awaited us: Hundreds of people from miles around had gotten the same Comanche alarm and had rushed, like us, onto the river road to Chelsea.

Mr. Conner rode up with our group, as an armed escort. As soon as we found a place to camp, he left again along with Mr. Carey and widower Smith. They said they were going to ride back down the river and do some scouting to see if the Indians were going to stay in Eldorado or if they had already moved on—and if so, in which direction? If Mr. Conner reports back that the Indians have broken up Tom Cordis' blacksmith shop and the Martin place, it will mean that the Indians are moving upriver.

In the afternoon, Mr. Conner rode back up to our Chelsea camp, along side the Walnut River. "I didn't see Comanches," he said. "I think they are Osages. There are hundreds of them, and they are all over Eldorado. He thinks they have gotten it into their heads that we've abandoned our houses, which, of course, we have. Perhaps they view us as nomadic as themselves. Mr. Conner reported that they were helping themselves to household goods and anything else that was not nailed down. I hope they spare our livestock and chickens and my garden. I've worked so hard on it.

Since so many settlers from the surrounding areas had come to Chelsea, we had enough armed men and wagons to mount a good defense if the Indians were so fool hardy as to come up this far. By nightfall, we seemed to be better organized to protect ourselves. Hoping that the Army could come to protect our property, several men formed a committee and dispatched Pete Gilespie on a fast horse to Fort Riley to summon assistance, even though we knew that the fort's commander under General Persifer Smith, the proslavery general headquartered at Fort Leavenworth would take his sweet time coming to the aid of us "stinking abolitionists."

So it will be very interesting to see if he will send a company of mounted dragoons. I'm certainly not going to hold my breath.

Well, what a day this has been, and what a disappointing way to celebrate my twentieth birthday. I'm not apt to forget this August 8th—no birthday party. I'm worried about leaving our claims to the Indians and I'm so lonely in this camp without my husband. I can't believe we've been in the Territory three years.

The next few days we spent settling in, waiting to see how long the Indians intend to occupy Eldorado. I decided to visit Jerry Jordan at Hayworth's mill, who has come up here to work full time for them since we haven't had a lumber order for weeks. I spent one whole day and evening with the Hayworths and marveled at the progress they've made with their gristmill. This also gave me an opportunity to talk with Jerry Jordan, who seems to be adjusting nicely to Chelsea. One of the reasons certainly surprised me.

We are still camped out in Chelsea. That's going on a week now. Chelsea has two stores compared to our one. I'm sorry to report, though, one sells whiskey by the glass.

I'm now so compulsive about writing in my journal, I brought volume number two with me and I'm making this entry in camp, so I could jot down events and describe the people while those impressions were fresh.

Another Indian scare early this morning, August 12th, but the raid failed to materialize, so most of us are planning to return to our claims.

A little baby died last night here in this makeshift camp. The mother is not well and the family has decided to bury the poor thing here in Chelsea.

Early the next morning dozens of us left Chelsea for Eldorado.

We're now home and a dreadful looking place it is. The Indians really didn't plunder much. What they did take was more a nuisance than real mischief. No Eldorado buildings were burned.

I was fearful as I headed to our claim, but what I found has left me simply astonished. My garden is as I left it, though it needs weeding, the cabin and the sawmill and sheds are standing untouched and it looks like the livestock are safe. The Indians took all the indoor food they could find. They ignored the furniture but stole some of our bedding and my medium-sized cast-iron stew pot is gone. It was on the stove, warm and full of a thick bean soup flavored with smoked ham rind. They took beans, pot and all. They didn't disturb my writing materials on the long bench or take my supply of medicines, even though the bottles weren't hidden. But some other items are missing, knives, forks and spoons, all gone. They spilled sugar and cornmeal all over the place and the ants have found it, not to mention some large ground bees. A tin of green coffee beans was undisturbed, as well as a peck sack of red beans. I believe the Plains Indians don't like beans. Some of them must have slept indoors when we were gone. One or more of them urinated in the kitchen wood box and, I suspect, more than once. My, they must have thought that was hilarious.

One of our possessions I did worry that the Indians might damage or steal was our old but well-crafted chest of drawers. It was made of seasoned Midwestern walnut and really belonged in a bedroom, but even after we built the upstairs we preferred to keep it in the main room of the cabin It was a wedding present to my mother and father from Uncle Ransom in Trent. It was made by a German cabinet maker living in Michigan,'What's so special about this piece of furniture is that only one drawer can be fully-opened at a time and when a second drawer is pulled out, the other open drawer somehow magically closes.

When we were very young, Uncle Ransom explained that all this happened because a very thin person lived inside in the back of the cabinet and saw to it that when our one drawer was pulled out any other drawers would magically close. He said the person in the chest was named Sir Chester Drawers.

On more than one occasion when Adda and I were much younger we would bring our neighborhood friends in and show them this piece of magic furniture. Nobody we knew had <u>anything</u> like it. '

It was so well made that we have it here in Eldorado and it continues to work perfectly…and the Indians didn't touch it. The Indians are gone, but where did they go? My guess is they came up from and went back to the south.

The Weibleys are both fine. They hadn't gone up to Chelsea with us because Doctor Weibley had chosen to remain here and take care of the Osage who had been stabbed the night the Indians raided Mr. Conner's store. He figured the Indians would not harm him if he was doctoring one of their own and he was right. Mrs. Weibley stayed with him. I admire her courage! I must ask her if she and that squaw of the wounded Indian had anything to talk about.

It's strange but not all of the Indians have left. I saw some of them still around town. At least ten to twelve of them are down by our sawmill and boiler. I don't think they are actually camped there; they are just loitering about. There are two very unattractive, dirty-looking squaws with them. And I'm worried that when the Indians see me around the cabin, they'll come up and want me to feed them. I'd have to shoot some game for that and I'd prefer not to. With Chase on his way to New Hampshire and Adda in Lawrence (she has found work at the Whitney House), I decided it would not be prudent to spend the night alone, particularly since the Indians who stayed here stole the Sharps carbine we had hanging over the door. So I camped with several neighbors, including a new family named Etter, in a tent on this side of the river. There must have been ten of us in that tent, not counting several children. It was quite a welcoming episode for the Etter family.

Well, it rained hard all through the night and the wind came up. I had heard, if you touch the inside of a canvas tent while it is raining, that spot will start leaking, but hadn't believed it, I discounted it as a superstition. I can now testify that this is not a myth. We were so crowded in the tent that as we moved around, we rubbed up against the tent and by midnight we had standing puddles of water everywhere. Some of the people slept through it all. Well, I didn't sleep a wink and as people shifted to avoid the puddles, I ended up in a sitting position. Long before daybreak I was soaked through.

At dawn, some neighbors came over and built a beautiful fire. Where they got the dry wood, I'll never know!

I could hear them outside talking as they made the fire. I got up, gingerly, trying to avoid stepping on anybody. I went outside and found it had stopped raining. I got both my bonnet and the skirt part of my dress dried out by fanning them against the fire. The rest of my clothes simply dried on me. I smelled smoky, like an old side of bacon. If my husband were here, I'm sure he would find my new fragrance alluring.

I persuaded Pete Gilespie and Mrs. Frame to come with me to our house. The three of us began cleaning-up. As we tidied up the damage left by the Indians, Pete told us what happened when he went to Fort Riley. The men in our town had dispatched him the day we went to Chelsea to get help. "I made it to Fort Riley but the Colonel who was in charge of the fort told him that half his troops were on patrol out west, so he could only send one company of dragoons, and even that commitment he made only halfheartedly." I'm not surprised. In fact, I see no signs that they ever came here.

Even though we cleaned up the house, I didn't want to stay there by myself at night until all of the Indians were gone. For the next week, my friends and neighbors invited me to spend the night at their places, and I willingly accepted their hospitality.

I'm still reluctant to stay here alone and it's now August 21st. The Osages camped down by the wood pile have dwindled down to five or six, including one squaw. I spent last night with Mrs. Rackliffe. I'm afraid I bragged a little too much about my garden. This morning, to convince her of my farming prowess, I invited her to come and pick some cantaloupes. We came down in Rackliffe's little wagon. As we prepared to leave, I suggested she put a side arm under the seat. She thought that was a good idea, but was surprised that I had proposed it since I had made my feelings towards guns well known.

My! I can't get over my own change of attitude. A few months ago I was so disturbed with Adda, when she told me how she intended to use her little revolver on Hildebrand. But now I can see what a nuisance the Indians can make of themselves if we don't put up a show of force. Perhaps I'm coming around to Adda's point of view, which was Father's too.

"Augusta, would you actually shoot one of those redskins?" Mary Rackliffe asked me. Well, since it was my idea to bring the gun, I owed her an explanation.

"Certainly!" I said. "If I had to shoot in self-defense." Then I wondered with a bit of humor if I should ever admit this to Adda. Lord, I'd never hear the last of it!

I told her that I'd raised some cantaloupes, called Hearts-of-Gold, from seeds of melons we had been given while crossing Iowa. I had already planted some of them two years ago, when we were in Lawrence; growing them in a little plot of garden in the back of the Cincinnati House and in a small garden I had made for Mrs. Gates at her farm outside town.

What melons! Too bad we don't have a county fair. I'd win the melon contest outright.

I sent Mrs. Rackliffe home with a large wicker basket of cantaloupes and ripe tomatoes, as well. Before she left, I made us some breakfast. We had fresh fried tomatoes dipped in cornmeal along with some bacon. I'd forgotten how good fried tomatoes could be.

I'm rather puzzled that the Indians didn't bother the garden. I have a variety of squash and some not-yet-ripe pumpkins and I know they like those but they ignored them. I don't think they pulled up so much as a single carrot!

I checked yesterday on my potatoes. They're not ready to be dug yet but they are already the size of a hen's egg. That's good news for this winter.

I've got to get out there and worm the cabbage. Large fat green worms, some almost two inches long are helping themselves to my cabbages.

I'm surprised the robins and other birds aren't eating the worms.

While I was in Chelsea, I read a rather dated edition of an Eastern newspaper—*The Philadelphia*, as I recall, —that had a report about an infestation of caterpillars that was threatening the famous apple orchards of the Hudson River valley. A visiting agricultural expert from Germany, a specialist on apples has brought over some sparrows (called spatzie) known for their affinity for apple-tree caterpillars. The article said his first experiments with the sparrows in the orchards had been successful. Maybe I should contact some of my relatives in Onondaga County. They raised a famous apple named after a town in Cortland County. They might know how to get rid of cabbageworms, since there are a lot of Dutchmen in that area and they love kraut and other cabbage dishes, perhaps they've solved the cabbageworm problem, maybe by a special bird from the Alsace.

40

CHELSEA - THE GLENNIS BEMIS STORY
August 1859

At midmorning, I was still cleaning up the mess that the Indians made when I head a commotion and opened the front door. Who should be outside but my beloved husband and Adda. I could barely contain my elation. As I rushed toward the wagon, I shouted, "I can't believe it! I thought you were on your way to New Hampshire. What happened?"

With a "whoop" Adda was first off the wagon and almost knocked me over. As we exchanged a boisterous hug, she was craning her neck and twisting her body. "Where are all the dead Indians?" she asked.

"Dead Indians?"

"Yes, Chase had a Leavenworth newspaper claiming a big battle out here with over 100 Indians killed and one white."

"Well, we did have an invasion of Indians, about 500 of them, but we all left and went up to Chelsea and camped there a week or so with about 1,000 settlers from counties around here."

Looking at Chase, I asked, "Is that why you came back?"

"Yes, getting a friendly riverboat out of Lawrence is not so easy for a Northerner."

"If they don't block us from getting on, the rumor was that proslavery passengers would take care of us, en route."

"You had Old Gray. Why didn't you just ride her to Iowa City and catch the train?"

"I didn't think that horse would make it that far. It took us five days just to get to Lawrence. I tried to buy a seat on the Davenport stage, but they were so booked I was put on their waiting list. Mrs. Gates wanted to see me about some carpentry, so I went out to see her while I was waiting. They didn't have enough lumber to do what was wanted, so I drew up a schedule of lumber sizes they'll need. Lawrence still doesn't have a sawmill, so they'll need to get it from Leavenworth. The day I was at the Gate's place I picked up the Saturday edition of the *Leavenworth Evening Transcript* (a proslavery newspaper) and saw the front-page article that Adda just mentioned. I rode over to the Whitney House, showed the paper to Adda, rented this rig from Sculley's livery and we left early Sunday morning," Chase said.

"The Indian troubles were two weeks ago," I said, "and, I might add, the U.S. Army from Fort Riley never to my knowledge ever put in an appearance and they were asked to help. Well, let me improve the accuracy of the article you read," I said. "I'm a qualified reporter since I was here. There was no battle. They simply came in like a herd of buffalo, but over several days hundreds of them. Yes, one Indian was wounded, not killed. They looted Conner's store and took all of his whiskey. Two of them got into an argument over plunder. One Indian stabbed the other. He was treated by Doctor Weibley and hung around their house for a week, eating all his meals there. Not a single citizen of Eldorado or our county was injured nor did we kill a single redskin.

I learned when we were camped in Chelsea that both Fontanel and Origano were so threatened that those settlers abandoned their claims. Some of them removed to Eldorado first, and then went with us up to Chelsea." For the next quarter hour I described what had happened when the Indians came and how we all removed to the camp in Chelsea by the river.

I mentioned that five or six Indians and a squaw were still here, camped among the logs down by the saw. Adda said, "Well, we'll put a stop to that. If you let them hang around long enough, they'll soon believe they have some rights to the place."

Later that day Adda, Chase and Pete Gilespie went down to the sawmill, conspicuously armed. When Adda came back, she brought back my cast iron stew pot unharmed. I asked Chase if he had run them off. He said he didn't want to get physical with them. His plan is to get some locals needing lumber to fire-up the boiler and start the saw. He figured the noise of the saw and all the commotion would be enough to scare them off.

"With the Indians around before you left weren't you concerned about your safety?" Chase asked.

I assumed a pretentious, perhaps haughty, pose and said, "A little. I was alone when I got the alarm. I quickly rode up to the Cordises. Tom was gone but Elizabeth grabbed that long-barreled revolver of theirs before we rode down to Conners, where everyone was congregating."

Adda grabbed the bait, "You two had that long-barreled revolver, eh? Well, well, well! What a change has come over my big sister. It was only yesterday you were hectoring me about my hostile aggressiveness; how uncivilized I was to plan on shooting poor old Hildebrand, even in self-defense, and now you tell me you and Elizabeth Cordis had a revolver. A loaded revolver, my, my, my! I guess if you had come across any hostile redskins, you were you going to civilize them with that revolver, hey?" By now my little sister was up, doing a little jig and pointing her finger at Chase, pretending he was an Indian and she was shooting him, and I realized how much I missed these shenanigans even when she was poking fun at me. Adda found so much humor in the change in my attitude that her appreciation of it totally interrupted and distracted their questioning. Of course, I didn't want to tell Adda in the presence of Chase that now I was pretty certain that I had an additional reason to think about defending my home.

As Adda teased me with such welcome humor and congratulated me on my new readiness to use a gun, then gloated about my "conversion" to her Old Testament religion, I noticed listlessness in Chase and wondered what the reason was. Normally Chase joins in and adds a little humor to these conversations. But today he was quiet. I went over and gave him a little hug and detected a fever. "Chase, you've got a fever. Have you been ill?" I asked.

"Yes, in Emporia I came down with it and the shakes, sometimes accompanied by chills." Those are symptoms of ague and that's cause for concern.

"Well, if we are finished with the Indian report and whether or not I'd shoot one, I have some very interesting news, and information that begins to answer some questions we had about Glennis Bemis while she was here," I said.

"When we all fled, I took volume two of my journal with me, so I could jot down events and describe the people while those impressions were fresh. While we were all camped by the Walnut River in Chelsea waiting to see how long the Indians intended to occupy Eldorado, I decided to visit Jerry Jordan who has been working full time at the Hayworth's mill, since we hadn't had an order to saw lumber for months. I spent one whole day and evening with the Hayworths and marveled at the progress they've made with their gristmill. This gave me an opportunity (twice) to talk with Jerry Jordan, who seems to be getting adjusted to Chelsea. One of the reasons will surprise you.

"In addition to Jerry, who do you suppose I accidentally bumped into in Chelsea? Almost the last person on earth I expected to see. Miss Glennis Bemis! I hadn't seen her since she left for the gold fields with the Dempseys and the rest of the Irish outfit last June.

"Adda, you remember she broke Howland's heart by going off to the mountains without saying good-bye to him last summer.

"Glennis told me that all Irishmen found work in the mines out there. Many of those mines now have been taken over by major mining companies with eastern money. They were starting to dig and tunnel and that's what those Irishmen had learned to do in the Old Country and they were so good at this type of mining, that they were in demand.

"Glennis said that they lived in a crude mining camp near Pike's Peak called by them, Terryalt, after one of their secret societies back in Ireland. Living conditions were terrible. Prices were outrageous. The mining companies were using timbers and any other available wood to shore-up mine tunnels so even firewood was scarce. There were too many families in the camp for whatever stove wood was left. All that time they lived in tents: no cabins.

"I told her about Howland's leaving for the Cherokee Nation. You'll recall, when she and her parents were still in Eldorado, she and Howland had been pretty thick with each other. Whenever Howland learned that she was boarding with us, he would spend as much time as he could at our place to be with her, starting with breakfast. And she'd often visit with him at his store, helping him wait on customers, unpack merchandise and so on, sometimes spending the night at Howland's store. Of course, they were both considerably older than the three of us and their personal lives were really none of our business, except we certainly didn't want any gossip or scandal, though we wished them well.

She said on their return to Chelsea several months ago she'd been in Eldorado for a few days making inquiries but couldn't bring herself to call on us. She knew I'd expect to have things explained and she wasn't ready for that then. Perhaps I was gone. Anyway, she said, she talked with Mr. Conner and learned that Howland had left and that news had disappointed her but the way she said it, I think she meant it was *very* disappointing. It sounded to me like she had intended to rekindle that old flame. On the other hand she didn't know that I had married or that you (Adda) were working in Lawrence.

"I got the feeling that Glennis didn't stay out there the whole year, in fact I doubt that she stayed through the winter, for you remember how much she disliked 'camping.' Just when she returned, I didn't ask. Nor did I inquire if she was living with her parents up there. Since it was noontime, we decided to take a meal together at a Chelsea boarding house familiar to her. Except for being more introspective and more open about her private life, she hadn't changed a bit, still as talkative and as beautiful as ever. Though she's six or seven years older than I am, I've always felt that she's had far more experience in these matters of the heart. Gingerly, I asked her about her feelings toward Howland. I asked, when she went out west if she discovered that she missed him, and if in hindsight had she thought that their romance could have blossomed. I told her there was no doubt in my mind that he loved her and was devastated when he learned they'd gone and I told her it was my opinion that her departure contributed to Howland's decision to leave the Territory.

"We continued to chat most of the afternoon. We both reminisced about the good times we'd all had, the good singing sessions, the Bentons' housewarming, etc. We even remembered the funeral of Mr. Curl when she sang so beautifully at the gravesite. We both wondered what had happened to his widow and those five children. She grew wistful when she remembered the dinner party at Benton's, the pot luck dinner with more food than we knew what to do with, the evening of poetry and singing was the nicest time she'd had since coming here from Ireland. For that brief while she said it not only helped make her forget her troubles in the Old Country, it seemed to be a promise of hope, of how much better her life might be over here.

"Rather naively I asked what the Old Country troubles were she had referred to, thinking she'd explain them in terms of their famine, as other Irish I had met, did.

"That's when her entire past sort of tumbled out. She had come over here by herself when she was twenty-two or twenty-three years old but not to escape the famine. That would make it about '54 when she arrived and I suspect that her parents were already here."

"Without reluctance and as though no time had lapsed since we had last seen each other she explained how she had been happily married in Ireland, wed when she was nineteen.

"I harbored some suspicions as such when she was with us. Her behavior was much more worldly than ours; for instance, after we'd returned from the Benton's housewarming, the way she had slowly and enticingly took down her hair in front of Howland that night, the way she bared her shoulders and arms to him by removing her shawl. No single girl, even a twenty-six or twenty-seven year old one, would ever take down her hair like that in front of a man who was not her husband. Heavens, we can hardly show a bare ankle or shoulder without rebuke.

"She told me that in Ireland her husband had gotten into some very serious political trouble and had to flee. She said they left for Wales one step ahead of the English sheriff. While they were there, he found work in the mines. Her husband, like many of the other Irish political exiles, continued to be involved in the movement to free Ireland from English oppression. As she spoke, I began to see similarities between their struggle for freedom from England and our abolitionist movement: the same zeal, the same willingness to relocate, to fight and die for a cause. The many more who can't or won't move or fight, donate money to support the cause. She claimed there are thousands of them in this struggle. In the winter of '52, he and four like-minded patriots went back to Ireland or were sent back by their organization intending to blow-up courthouses in Limerick and Clonmel where

Irish dissidents were routinely either sentenced for Transport* or condemned to death. They succeeded in blowing up at least one courthouse and they all managed to escape the scene. But none of the original party returned to Wales or the mines because the timing of their absence would have been conspicuous. Most of them eventually came one by one to the States, except her husband who was later caught in County Clare. She didn't discover until she got to the States that the English had hanged him on the spot. She believes while he was hiding in County Clare, he was betrayed. The English were clever in enlisting informers among the locals, and especially the Prods.

"I asked her as delicately as I could how she found out that her husband was dead. She said she learned the truth one piece at a time. Later there were newspaper accounts of the escapade. Those who did the bombing had spread the word about their success but even they didn't know what happened to her husband. When they regrouped at a safe house in Wexford, before they started for the States, all they knew was that he was missing. Then newspapers published accounts of the bombing and reported that he'd been captured, so that is when she learned he'd been arrested. She said he was very resourceful and had money enough to bribe his way out of jail. But she knew he'd never go back to Wales because that was too dangerous. But, she said she was sure she would see him again. I could understand that sort of hope because I had felt it for Father, I believed one fine day he'd come walking in and we would discover that Worldy had shot someone all right but it wasn't Father.

"One day, while she was in Wales waiting for news of her husband's whereabouts, she was taken to the police station and questioned by people who were not local Welsh policemen, but English detectives who were working for the Government and weren't in uniform. They wanted to know what she knew of her husband's political affiliation, if she knew whether any of the

---

*Transported to English penal colonies in New South Wales (Australia)

Irish miner friends of her husband were also members of those organizations.

"She told me she knew that her husband was involved in the movement to free Ireland but she was kept in the dark as to any details and didn't know of the plot to blow-up the court house until months later and even then wasn't sure her husband was involved in it. She was kept uninformed so she would have nothing to reveal, if apprehended. During the interrogations the English authorities wanted to know where her husband and the others got the guns. Glennis said that there was constant communication and travel between Ireland and America and wherever else the Irish exiles were. So she knew the guns had probably come from the States or Irish sympathizers in England or Europe. Then the detectives wanted to know where her husband and others got their blasting powder. Well, she said that was a stupid question: powder, fuses, caps, punk all that stuff are tools of the miner's trade. That question, she said, was the first time she began to believe her husband might be in custody. Later in the day, in desperation she asked why they were questioning *her*, they came right out and told her that her husband was in jail but wouldn't reveal where. At that time she believed he was still alive, they never let on that he wasn't.

"Glennis said, they didn't hold her overnight because she had not been charged with anything, though she was told she'd need to return in the morning. They were still trying to link her with details of the bombing. In that way they could charge her with aiding and abetting. She said they had jailed hundreds of women in Ireland on that charge and in many cases, for good reason, they were indeed often aiding their men folk.

"She said that night she bobbed her hair, dressed up in her husband's mining clothes and left town, posing as an itinerant powder monkey. She explained that she had taken this disguise because if she were questioned, she knew the miner's "lingo" and could pass herself off as a powder monkey, knowing she was too slight to pose as a miner. Before she left that night, she collected enough money from others in the Free-Ireland movement for boat fare to the States. She was to be questioned the following day, so they all knew it was to the benefit of the cause to help her escape. She said she had no trouble getting from Cardiff to South Hampton, where there were friends of the movement. She bought passage to New York, continuing to pose as a man. It was only in New York Harbor in the confusion of getting off the boat that she changed into women's clothes. When she got off the boat, she presented herself to the immigration authorities as a simple Irish widow, a victim of the Famine. She was detained at the harbor and given a little pink card with W.O.P. at the top, which meant that she was 'Without Papers.' But the immigration officer, who was an Irishman, soon remedied that. He sent word to some of his friends in the Fourth Ward and she was released to their care.

"Glennis said that she finally learned of her husband's death in New York when she saw some Irish newspaper clippings, which reported that he had been hung.

"She stayed in New York for some time, had no trouble finding work but getting a place to live was more difficult. She usually roomed with friends from County Clare, where her family was from.

"Glennis told me about Irish politics in New York, echoing many of the comments I had heard from the Dempseys last year. She said the Irish in the Old Country and in New York "backed" Zachary Taylor, when he was President, because he favored independence for Ireland. Many Irishmen found employment by joining President Polk's Army to fight in the Mexican War, so they liked him as well, she said, but President Buchanan was controversial. Some Irish Whigs didn't like him because he was the Ambassador to the Court of St. James and they thought that any friend of the enemy is an enemy!"

"The Irish Democrats, on the other hand," she said, "think well of Buchanan. He likes easy immigration and easy voting rules, knowing that the quicker he could get immigrants naturalized and registered to vote, the quicker they will vote Democratic.

"She told me that the issue of American slavery was not a major concern of the Irish. Those Irish Democrats who pay any attention at all to it, favor slavery, because Buchanan and most of the Democrats support it.

"I asked her how she handled being a widow, a young attractive widow. I had been wondering about this in light of her successful but charmingly deceptive behavior when she had pretended that she had never been married last summer.

She said she never thought of herself as a widow. By never allowing herself to see herself that way, she thought she would get over her husband's death sooner. She learned about his death so much after the fact that it had also helped soften the blow when it fell.

"She told me that she had found it difficult to be around her husband's old friends. Some of those who had done the courthouse bombing with him had escaped to New York and were living in the fourth and sixth Wards, which is where most of the Irish live. Whenever she would go to see any of them, if they mentioned her husband's death, she'd either deny it, or if she was getting sympathy and felt like accepting it, depending on her mood at the time, she would acknowledge it. But by not wearing black and not by being conspicuous about mourning, she thought that would help her handle his death better.

She said that she went to church, made novenas, said her confessions and prayed for help, but church and prayer provided no answer and no comfort. She said one young priest had the gall to congratulate her husband's courage for being willing to die for Ireland. He even praised her for her strength. Pretending that she was unmarried, a free, blithe spirit, had helped her cope, she told me, but on several social occasions, particularly at social gatherings, she felt she hadn't always been able to carry it off.

"Since I had engaged in some small deceptions myself when mother died, and again recently because of Father's death,

I didn't hold her imposture against her. Glennis, though, does seem to carry it further than I do, and maybe she even conceives of deception as necessary and right.

"She thinks Christians are too obsessed with the truth. Other cultures she believes aren't so hobbled by the truth. Digressing, she launched into a political monologue about truth and slavery. The gist of it was that slavery would only be solved by bloodshed, as in Ireland. She thinks that the truth is that Ireland should be free but won't be without bloodshed. And with a strange clarity she pointed out that blood on both sides had already been shed in the Territory for the freedom of the slave. She also thinks that slavery stems from a desire for possessions, like England, where they think of Ireland as a vast plantation, to be possessed by them, and see the Irish as nuisances. She believes John Brown is a lot more right than Harriet Beecher Stowe, who, she thinks would have been a lot better off if she had published her book in Ireland than in England, as the English don't give a hoot about freedom. She said that everywhere they plant their flag, they suppress the people. In fact, she believes if there is war here over slavery, the English will come to the side of the South.

"I realized, as the afternoon progressed, how girlish and superficial were my earlier questions about her romance with Howland. I was embarrassed about having asked them and apologized.

"I asked her if she thought she would ever get over her husband's death and she said until she met Mr. Howland last year, she thought she was over it. She said Howland wanted to get married. He proposed, but she said she never gave him an answer or told him about her husband. She didn't think he'd understand her husband's activities. And she was afraid that Mr. Howland would always quietly wonder if she were also involved in the political movement. Another reason she didn't tell Howland of her past was because of shame, shame that she'd been married before, and wouldn't come to him as a vestal bride. She said she didn't trust love to absolve her of that shame.

"When she realized that she wasn't willing or ready to reveal all of these things to him, she knew she wasn't over her husband's death. She said she can't shake the mantle of shame, shame that her husband was hung, though hung for a noble cause, shame that she's a widow, a poor widow, shame she is childless,—she thinks the Irish carry shame around like they do their accent. They can't get rid of either.

"As soon as we got word that it would be safe to return home, I began to fret as to how I would get back to Eldorado. In the afternoon I walked over to the boarding house where Glennis and I had eaten earlier in the week, thinking it would be nice to take supper there again. I bumped into Jerry Jordan, who was also there for the same purpose. I considered asking him to carry a wagonload of us back to Eldorado but decided against it as the evening wore on.

"I mentioned to Jerry that I had accidentally seen Glennis Bemis and had such a pleasant reunion. I asked him if he remembered her. He put his knife and fork down and began talking to me as if I was his little sister, not someone to whom he'd twice proposed marriage."

"Of course, I remember Glennis Bemis, Augusta, next to you I thought she was the nicest thing that existed in Walnut Valley," and he paused and frowned and said he was offended when the Bentons had their housewarming, and he'd not been invited. He reminded me that the housewarming was a few days after he'd proposed to me, adding that he had sawed as many timbers for the Bentons' house as Chase and David Upham, yet none of us considered inviting him to the party.

"I interrupted him to say it was the Benton's house and only proper that they did the inviting, but I knew he was right. Any one of us could have brought old Jerry along, but we didn't and he still nurses a grudge about it. Jerry was also apparently upset that I encouraged Howland's monopoly on Glennis. He said he was just as disappointed as the rest of us when her outfit went to the gold fields. He complained that before and after Father was killed his feelings were never seriously considered in our household, adding that Adda and I treated him like a handyman, "Go chase the cows out of the corn, Jerry. Don't forget to cut some more stove wood before it snows, Jerry," he said in a mocking voice.

"Then after a long pause, he allowed a small smile, as though he had a secret that gave him great pleasure to keep to himself. But he didn't keep it for long, deciding it would please him even more for me to know that, yes, he had been seeing Glennis Bemis pretty regularly since she had returned from Pike's Peak. That's when I put *my* knife and fork down. Jerry said that just as she would occasionally visit him at our sawmill last spring, now she visits him at the Hayworth's gristmill and sometimes helps Mrs. Hayworth with the bookkeeping.

"I asked Jerry if he knew how to get in-touch with her, as I didn't know where her claim was. I said we'd all be going back to Eldorado in a day or two and there is something urgent I needed to tell her before we leave.

"The next morning someone came over and said a lady was looking for me. I knew it was Glennis and that Jerry had carried my message.

"Everybody in Chelsea knew where *we* were. Heavens, there were upwards of one thousand of us camped by the river, but Glennis was still able to find me without trouble.

"I told her that I'd had supper with Jerry Jordan the previous evening and that he'd explained that the two of them frequently saw each other. That provoked a slightly bowed head and a knowing smile I said, 'Glennis, I want to give you some advice. Jerry Jordan is a fine man, sober and hard working. He likes you very much. For your mutual happiness, tell him about your husband. Jerry will understand that. He came out here from Illinois to help abolish slavery. Like your husband, Jerry was also captured and imprisoned. He spent time in Lecompton with my father, both charged with murder, so Jerry will understand that.

But for your future happiness, perhaps Jerry's as well, drop this pretense of being unmarried. Be proud of your past that you've quietly suffered and survived.'

"She smiled, thanked me for what I had told her and promised to come down to Eldorado for a visit.

"I told her what a pleasure it had been seeing her again and to know she was back in the neighborhood."

41

ELDORADO - ADDA RETURNS TO LAWRENCE
August and September 1859

About noon, the Rackliffes came by for a visit. After awhile, Mrs. Rackliffe took me aside and said she thought Chase was pretty sick and needed bed rest and suggested that maybe I should send for the doctor. She agreed to stay with us while I nurse Chase. Pete Gillespie had already volunteered to help me out in the garden, first by making some scarecrows in exchange for having all the fresh vegetables he can carry home. He borrowed a shotgun yesterday and killed eight or ten crows; don't know where he got all the shells. He's off now looking for some ten-foot saplings he can use to make beanpoles. He's gutted the crows and will place them on the poles. I'm glad he's doing this chore. I've been avoiding it, and now the crows are getting into my cucumbers and are starting to peck at the sweet corn. Between the worms and the crows, it's nip and tuck who gets the corn.

But I'm exaggerating. We have more sweet corn and vegetables than we can eat. I told Adda that if she wanted to take some of our produce to Mr. Conner to sell on our behalf, she was welcome to the proceeds. My potatoes are doing so well I'll have all I need for the winter, and then some.

If I can keep Chase in bed and can get three or four days of fresh vegetables into him, I'll have him back on his feet in no time. I've handled patients with ague before, and pulled them all through. He just needs rest, maybe some quinine pills, good food, and my tender loving care. I'm so happy to have him home; he'll get plenty of all three.

I was not feeling well when I woke up this morning and I'm sure I know the cause. Mrs. Rackliffe spent the night, but when we saw that Chase's fever was down, she thought she'd better get back to her own household. Chase and Adda agreed to make breakfast. Mrs. Gates had taught Adda to make French toast the way it's made in the Parker House, a fancy new hotel in Boston. When the Gates had their hotel in Springfield (Massachusetts), they hired a chef from the Parker House, who brought with him some of the hotel's recipes. Adda looked for some bread to make the French toast. She had to make do with some brown bread in the "tin," which the Indians had missed and which had gotten quite hard. She soaked the bread in a concoction of cream, fresh eggs, fresh ground nutmeg and a "splash" of vanilla until it got soft. I had made some raspberry conserves, and we used a small crock of that. The toast was just what I needed. It was a marvelous breakfast, just the three of us together.

It was wonderful hearing all the latest news from Lawrence. I'm just overcome with joy that my husband is home.

As we talked, I learned that Adda has some news that is mildly surprising and disturbing in a complicated way I'll try to explain.

While she was in Lawrence, she'd been working at the Whitney House, which she said was not only a good job, but also an interesting and exciting one. Since I knew a little about the Whitney House and some of the people who frequent it, like

John Brown and the abolitionist journalists, Richard Hinton, William A. Phillips, James Redpath, all who write for the Eastern press, I was concerned about my sister's safety.

"If I'm not gone too long," she said, "I'll still have my job at the Whitney House, when I go back to Lawrence. Those were the terms when I asked for permission to come back out to Eldorado to see how you and our neighbors had faired with the Indians."

As calmly as I could, I asked her how soon she needed to go back.

Adda looked at the floor, not out of shame, but because she knew her answer would disappoint me.

"Well, I just found out that Mr. Smith is going to Lawrence and I asked him if I could go back with him."

"When is he leaving?"

"Tomorrow."

"Tomorrow?"

"Yes, that's when I can get the first ride back. I just came to make sure you were all right but now I need to go back"

Adda, did you say Mr. Smith? Do you mean widower Smith?"

Adda sensed my sisterly concern but didn't acknowledge it, avoiding the implication of my remark. "Yes," she said, "what's wrong with that?"

"That you are leaving so soon is a terrible disappointment and I'm not at all comfortable with the knowledge you will be traveling alone with a widower for four or five days. Heavens, Adda, what will all those boarding house owners say when you appear with a widower? You know, most of them knew Father and they know you and me?"

"You worry about the unimportant stuff," she said.

I asked as casually as I could, if Frank Robinson was in Lawrence. Adda didn't respond, so I suppose the answer is yes.

Another disappointment. I had hoped she wouldn't see him anymore.

"I was counting on your company for a while. There's lots of local news and I thought you and I could do some visiting, maybe see the Martins and you could help in the garden, with all the produce now ready for picking." And I thought to myself how very much I wanted Adda to stay so I could tell her about my baby and spend this precious time with her. Even as young as she is, she will revel at the notion of being an "auntie." And, by her knowing of my condition, when my time comes, I was so hoping she could be here. I know I'll have help, but Adda and Chase are now the only family I have.

I said nothing about this, but asked her instead why she had decided to work at the Whitney House. I just assumed, I told her, that if she were going back to work, it would be at the Cincinnati House with Aggie Rourke and the Gates. "The Whitney House is just too dangerous."

Adda certainly understood what I was saying, but seemed to attach no importance to it. She did say, "Well, the pay is better and I have a little side income that I'll tell you about, that I didn't have at the Cincinnati." But it was obvious that she was going back to Lawrence. She had made up her mind, and, as she says, "That's that."

I wanted to talk with her about my misgivings about her working at the Whitney House, but I just didn't have enough time, things kept coming up. She obviously doesn't want to explain and is determined to leave in the morning anyway; perhaps I can write.

I know something about the Whitney House from my days working at the Cincinnati House. It's nicely located within an easy walk of the Kansas River and owed part of its prosperity to trade that came from the riverboats. Although the Whitney House was a rather small place, it was always bustling, attracting a crowd of excessively zealous abolitionists. Father stayed there occasionally and sometimes also conducted business there.

Richard Hinton, the English journalist and staunch friend of Old John Brown who came through Plymouth the same week we arrived there, uses the Whitney House as his headquarters when he's in town. I knew he and Jim Redpath, the other newspaper fellow, were thick as flies, likewise John Kagi, who has been quite conspicuous in his various antislavery activities including raids, into southern Missouri, sometimes with Old John Brown, to "spirit out" a few darkies and get them started north on the Underground Railroad; that activity, in my opinion, causes more trouble than its worth.

Mary Knowles, a girl from Massachusetts I knew who worked at the Whitney House, told me that John Brown preferred the Whitney house over the other local hotels, as a place to hold his meetings when he was in Lawrence, which was frequently and John Kagi was always with him. Now if I know these things, they have to be common knowledge, particularly around Lawrence.

I have a high regard for all these gents, but I don't want my sister working there if some hotheaded, half-drunk proslavery group decides to even up the score with us abolitionists by shooting up the place or burn it down as they did to Shalor Eldridge's Free State Hotel. They destroyed it because they thought it was an abolitionist headquarters, which it was and so is the Whitney House.

I have seen posters offering varying rewards for John Brown, dead or alive. It will take a very clever proslaver to capture him and to collect that reward money, but I'm sure there are many proslavers who dream of it. I don't want that confrontation to happen at the Whitney House while my sister is working there.

But Adda has always enjoyed a little excitement and she has so much courage and self-possession that I could never simply use fear as a means of dissuading her from working at the Whitney House. I know she is already familiar with some of those abolitionist figures. Jim Redpath was the one who brought the large wagon train into Plymouth when we were there. I know she remembers him and she also knows he's a friend of Preston Plumb. She's probably looking forward to the new adventure. I just hope she doesn't get more than she's bargained for.

Very early the next morning, Mr. Smith, who seems to have recovered from the loss last September of his wife and child, came by to pick Adda up in his rattletrap, two-wheel buggy, only to discover, to his extreme agitation, that she had not yet packed.

Recalling how opposed his father-in-law had been to his daughter marrying an Irishman, especially a Catholic Irishman, I asked Mr. Smith if his returning to Lawrence wasn't a concern. He replied that he thought it was time for reconciliation, even though he knows it might be difficult because his wife's father blames him for her death.

Traveling to Lawrence takes four or five days, depending on the weather. Nowadays, thank heavens, travelers don't have to camp out because there are ample lodging places along the way, but a trip of several days was a rather long time for a young unmarried girl to be "alone" with a young widower. I commenced giving Adda a speech about this concern of mine once or twice but I kept being interrupted by Adda's packing needs or by Mr. Smith's urging her to move along.

Mr. Smith was so impatient to get going I was afraid he would leave without her, which would have been all right with me. He was really quite put out that she wasn't ready. He is so much more assertive now than he was when his wife and child died last year. He just talks all the time. A bit of humor popped into my head as I recalled the famous dinner party last summer when we discussed with such hilarity the subject of phrenology: bumps, irregularities and cavities on the skull's surface. Listening to Mr. Smith rattle on and on, I wondered if he had those little "cavinosities" on the back of the skull that, according to the Lyceum professor, was a sign of incessant talking.

I tried to distract him by asking him to go with me to the garden while Adda packed.

I planned to give them a nice picnic basket of fresh vegetables that they could lunch on most of the way. I also wanted to send along a basket of melons and some tomatoes to Mrs. Gates. And I packed a quart of ripe raspberries for them. Though I sprinkled on some sugar, I didn't pack any spoons. The Indians took them and I've not found replacements. I'm afraid they'll have to eat the berries with their fingers.

Mr. Smith was nervous and so anxious to leave that he wasn't much help picking the vegetables and berries. I don't know what he will say when he finds out that some of Adda's "stuff" is at the Weibleys', which will require another stop on the way. I wonder if Adda will be able to get him to go by there.

Well, Adda finally announced that she was ready. She playfully poked Mr. Smith, asking him, "What are we waiting for?"

As they drove off, I saw Adda point in the direction of the Weibleys, no doubt intent on picking up some bedding and other personal items that she had taken there after Chase and I got married. Paying her no notice Mr. Smith continued on the road east, no doubt headed for the eastbound Santa Fe Trail.

Hours later, that afternoon, some relatives of Nelson Frances came into town asking where his brother's claim is located. The visitors were Nelson Frances' brother and his family. Since it was getting late, I invited them to take supper and stay with us. They can get off to an early start in the morning. Mr. Keyes and Mr. Conner joined us. It seems that my husband invited them without telling me. Well, what with the garden and with all the game in abundance, we are living off the fat of the land this summer, so providing supper was more of a surprise than a problem.

Our fine old yoke of oxen, abolitionists both, Tempus and Fugits who so faithfully pulled us across Iowa and down to Plymouth, and did the plowing for us and for several neighbors, are dead. And that's not all; our best milk cow is dead as well.

It's not just our cattle that have been singled out. This disease has spread up and down the valley as if it was carried on the wind. Though it's called Spanish fever, we don't have the slightest idea what causes it. All we know is that it's very contagious. We had a discussion about how to dispose of the carcasses. I guess we'll figure a way to drag them far enough west out on the prairie that we won't smell them as they putrefy, though I doubt that the meat will stay on their bones long enough for that to happen. I think the wolves will dispose of them in three or four nights. The buzzards and crows will feast on what's left. Maybe if the crows feed on Tempus and Fugit, they'll leave my garden alone!

Chase has been home from Lawrence for about two weeks now. Today is September 7th. I've seen to it that he's had plenty of rest and a diet of fresh fruit and vegetables and a lot of tender affection from me. The diet seems to be working. In recent days he certainly seems much better. This morning Chase felt so good, he saddled up Kate and rode off to Mr. Frame's place to join a turkey hunt. We're getting some small yellow sweet potatoes from the garden now. They will go well with roast turkey.

Mr. Trask, who bought our little utility wagon last June for a trip to Texas, returned in late summer to his claim north of here, which Father and Frank Robinson had surveyed for him. His wife, who, when he left, was early with child, stayed with the Frances family on an adjacent claim while he was gone. Though Mr. Trask learned that Father had been killed last November, he came by today to pay for the surveying. I appreciate his honesty since I didn't know what arrangements existed between the two of them.

He told me that their baby died yesterday and his wife is distraught. I'm not feeling too well myself. He asked me to go up with him to the Frances claim, where they are still staying. He didn't have a team of horses with him and I didn't feel well enough to ride alone. I told him if he could locate a wagon, I'd go.

An hour or so later, he came back with a team and Pete Gillespie's wagon. We arrived about dark at their place. Mrs. Trask was not well and couldn't bring herself to layout the little body. And Mr. Trask was too distraught to do it. We did and sat up part of the night with the Trasks. It rained incessantly and the Frances' house leaks awfully. Between the wind and the rain and the leaks, it was almost impossible to find a dry place to get some sleep. In my condition, which I certainly didn't reveal, I didn't think I could handle the emotion of a child's funeral. Without a casket or the means to build one, the Trasks planned on burying their child in its little white rocking cradle, which is where I found her when I got there. I wanted to say they might have a future need for that little cradle but thought better of it.

The next morning, before the funeral got started, I simply had to leave. All that crying and lamentation was depressing me. I agree with Adda that depression is as contagious as measles; I'm convinced that it makes your body more susceptible to disease.

Mrs. Schaefer, a neighbor of mine, had also been helping them and she intended to come back to town, so the two of us left on foot. I planned to stop at Mr. Conner's store on my way home. I'm still trying to replace the kitchenware the Indians stole. I swear they stole every knife and fork they could find and they found most of them. Mrs. Schaefer and I went into Mr. Conner's. I didn't "cotton" to his selection, or to his prices, so Chase and I will have to get along without spoons, knives and forks for a while longer. But at least the walk to town provided Mrs. Schaefer and me with an opportunity for an unusually nice visit.

Leaving the store, we met Chase coming to get us. By the time I got home, I was feeling even less well than I had earlier in the morning. I've been thinking about how to share my condition with Chase, but I want to feel buoyant, pleased and proud when I tell my husband that I think, according to my *Gunn's Book of Medicine* and Elizabeth Cordis' reckoning, that I'm with child. And when we talk about it, I want him to be well and in good spirits, too. For the last few days he has been vacillating between moderate health and sickness: He'll have four or five days when he's up and about, followed by three or four days of fever, the shakes, etc. and some of that time he stays in bed, which is very unusual for him. It is my opinion that it is definitely the ague. Since he's been back from Lawrence, there hasn't been a day that we're both feeling well, or when we have time to talk. Either someone is here or he is being called off to a job. I know he will have many questions when I tell him about the baby and I don't want to be impatient because I'm not feeling my very best and, anyway, I'd like to write to Adda first, not because she has some sort of family priority but because I could get some practice with my sister before I tell Chase.

More out of curiosity about details of maternity than a desire to share a secret, I discussed my symptoms with Elizabeth Cordis. Elizabeth questioned me like a detective as to exactly when I was sure I had missed what she called the moon curse. We got out the calendar and became very technical in trying to find first the month, then the week I started expecting. But the determinant was my first missed moon curse. With certainty Elizabeth Cordis pronounced that I was "with child," which she referred to as my "condition." She has a handsome son and is "with child" herself now too. The finality with which she makes decisions reminds me of Mrs. Strong up in Archer. When those two women make up their minds, there is no "shaking" them from it.

**ADELAIDE HENRIETTA STEWART
"ADDA"**

*Taken in Lawrence, kansas in November 1859
Adda was 18 years old and working at the Whitney House.*

42.

ELDORADO - JACOB EASTMAN CHASE
September 11 to late September, 1859

It's been some time since I've made an entry because I haven't felt well and I've been so busy. Since the successful turkey shoot on September 7th Chase has had good days and bad. To preserve all that turkey meat, the Frames' and ours, we are slow-smoking all of it, like ham, in a small, enclosed tool shed down by the saw. Mr. Frame comes every day, two or three times, and feeds a small firebox with wet pieces of hickory wood and hickory bark. The smoke goes throughout the shed, so we are not only smoking the turkeys hanging in there but we are smoking all the tools. My, won't they smell lovely when Chase wants to handsaw some molding or use one of his hammers or hatchets! Now that the weather has cooled off, that smoked turkey meat ought to keep for several weeks.

    Though Chase had a slight fever today, the two of us went up to finish framing the Cordis addition. I helped him load the wagon with additional planks from our inventory.

    We had quite a turnout. The men all worked very hard and the women were kept almost as busy fetching the specific planks and tools and nails they needed. I stayed there Sunday and Monday and came home alone today to rest. Chase decided to stay on the job since he's the contractor. Chase and the other carpenters still have to plumb in some windows, nail on all the siding and finish the roof.

He stayed at the Cordis claim until Thursday. When he came home, he ate sparingly and went right to bed. I felt his brow; he had a fever.

Today he's stayed in bed all day. I had some chicken broth with rice and some nice fresh carrots just out of the garden, that I put in the soup. I offered him some but he said he wasn't up to eating anything. I asked Pete Gillespie to go to the store for me. He did and must have told Mr. Conner that Chase was sick in bed, because the two Irishmen have now returned here together.

Mr. Conner is quite worried about Chase. We agreed that it's the ague and I gave Chase some of old Doctor Sappington's quinine pills. We discussed the matter and Mr. Conner decided to ride up and fetch Doctor Weibley.

It's Friday evening, September 16th, and Mr. Conner and Doctor Weibley are both here. The doctor is showing more concern about Chase than about any patient that I can recall since meeting him. He says Chase's condition is not improving and is tending toward congestion and when that happens, it's difficult to reverse or control.

Both Doctor Weibley and Mr. Conner stayed here all night. This morning, it's our combined opinion, or overworked optimism, that my husband has rallied some. Though he has the shakes, he sat at the table and took breakfast with us. He's just bound and determined to fight this thing.

Doctor Weibley wants him to rest. He gave him some morphine earlier this morning, but the morphine seems to be putting Chase into a stupor and a very restless sleep. He gasps for breath. He didn't gasp before the medicine. The fever has not abated and it's my opinion that his pulse rate has increased. He woke up about noon. Conner and the doctor were still here. About one or two o'clock the doctor dosed him again with morphine. I thought they were both rather heavy doses. It's news to me that morphine is medication for ague: Serious pain was not a symptom. Chase was so intent on getting better that late in the afternoon he wanted to go outside for a breath of fresh air. Against my better judgment, I let him do it, but later he was dizzy and flighty again. I suppose it is the morphine that affects him so. Even when he's awake, he gasps for breath and his heart rate is alarmingly above normal, the fever is still with him and he is sweating prodigiously.

He wants me to be with him and seems happier and a little more at ease when I am sitting next to him on our settee or when we lie down together.

Although he slept for two or three hours this afternoon, his pulse is irregular and too fast to suit me, over a hundred times a minute. I've mentioned that to the doctor but got no response. Doctor Weibley didn't tell me what that might mean. Chase wheezes and his breathing is in fitful gasps.

Late today near suppertime old friend Conner came by again. I asked him to stay with us.

I fixed some supper for Mr. Conner but I had no interest in eating. While Conner was eating, Chase woke up. That is, he stirred, opened his eyes, but he didn't know us. His pulse is so fast, it's frightening, and his fever is raging. I'm simply beside myself with worry. I wish Adda were here and I'm so grateful for Conner's company, but it's so frustrating that we seem powerless to help.

Chase's fever continues, and he seems occasionally to stop breathing altogether, which is alarming. It and the fever are most alarming. Toward nine o'clock, I asked Mr. Conner to fetch the doctor again. I was relieved when Doctor Weibley walked in about midnight. He examined my husband and though Doctor Weibley doesn't have much to say, I can tell he's very worried. Part of his concern is that he seems powerless to improve Chase's condition. Four AM, the fever has not subsided. Doctor Weibley paces the floor and wrings his hands. In frustration he runs his hands through his gray hair. I never realized before just how involved he gets with his patients. Perhaps it's this powerlessness that he tries to escape from with alcohol. Now that I'm in his "shoes" I can see that I've been too harsh in my judgment of him.

Doctor Weibley applied mustard plasters on Chase's neck, wrists and ankles. Although we moved Chase's arms and feet, as well as his head and neck, to apply the poultices, Chase slept through all this physical manipulation.

At dawn, the doctor and Mr. Conner discussed leaving, which they postponed an hour or so. Before they left, I asked Doctor Weibley for some assurance that Chase would be all right. Doctor Weibley cupped both his hands under my elbows, but avoided looking me directly in the eyes. "Augusta, get some rest," he said. "Chase will pull through this just fine." I am ambivalent about the doctor's departure. I have an intuitive feeling that he's given up and that he has realized that he is powerless to alter the outcome, so is anxious to return to what does give him relief and comfort, the bottle. Of course he and Mr. Conner are companions in this folly.

On the other hand, I wish, oh how I wish, I could believe him, that Chase will pull through.

I have seen no signs of improvement whatsoever. And the knowledge that they are leaving me alone with my husband, on what I'm so afraid is death's door, is frightening beyond description.

Doctor Weibley and Mr. Conner came into the bedroom to say they were leaving. I was sitting up in bed holding my husband in my arms.

Chase is sweating so profusely his nightgown was wet and my arms are moist from holding him. His fever, coupled with his sweating, has caused the medication in the mustard plaster to run down his neck and off his arms and onto my own clothing. The odor from it is mildly offensive and the odor from Chase's body, as he fights this disease, smells of onions cooked in rancid oil, not the male odor from strenuous work that he usually has and that I know so well and have come to love.

He occasionally emits a short raspy groan, not loud, and not regular. But each groan increases my anxiety. Each groan pierces my heart.

If adoration can save a life, my husband will recover. In my worry and frustration, I tried to make a pact with God. I promised anything, I said I would become a missionary. I said I would refrain from carnal love if that was the price He wanted. To save Chase, I would do anything, including trading my life for his. I explained to God I needed Chase for the father he was about to be.

After the men left, I was still holding Chase, cradled in my arms like a child. The time went by slowly and I drifted in and out of sleep. I hadn't really slept for about twenty-four hours. My mind vacillated between drowsiness and a tenuous, vague awareness, shrouded in a dreaded premonition that something terrible and gradual was happening to us. In one of my lapses into sleepiness, Glennis Bemis appeared as an angel at the foot of the bed. She was singing the Bach "Ave Maria." The ethereal music filled the room with a cloud, a cloud without substance that provided a strange calm and for a few minutes I was at ease. Her voice washed over Chase and me, as it had floated out over the valley at Mr. Curl's funeral.

As a candle that goes out of its own accord, leaving a wispy vapor, Glennis, the Angel of Death, departed.

Just when my husband died, I'm not positive. His fever never subsided and his pulse remained considerably above normal and irregular, and he would discontinue breathing from time to time. I could usually get Chase breathing again by changing his position slightly or gently squeezing him several times. All of those things and his increased heartbeat seem to me to have been aggravated by Doctor Weibley's double dose of morphine yesterday morning.

Sometime early this morning, I suppose it was a little after 7 AM, he died. I was still holding Chase in my arms. Even though I don't know the precise time he died, I am grateful that it was while he was in my arms. Mrs. Weibley came by immediately after Chase's death. She was most solicitous and tried to comfort me. "Augusta," she said, "you will know despair and grief like you've never known it and in your own way you must learn to fight it. Some people will tell you to deny it, not to cry, that it will be a measure of your inner strength if you don't cry. When I was your age, I believed that nonsense. Cry, Augusta, cry! It helps. It's a form of self-pity that you can accept. Condolences from others will be of very little use, though you'll have to put up with people's condolences in order to have their company, which you will need."

"How long will this sorrow last?"

"Well, it depends on many things. We knew a Doctor Schweitzer in Philadelphia, or was it Baltimore who lectured on remedies for grief. He said the pain of our sorrow diminishes in time and lasts for half the time we knew the loved one, except he thought for women the melancholia ended more quickly for biological reasons. He also believed it was possible to communicate with the departed in properly conducted séances, which were just becoming popular then. It's my opinion that it's good to talk about it and write about it. You're a writer. Write an obituary for Chase. Send it to all the Territorial papers."

"The grief you feel will last six months, maybe a year, but as your sweetheart, your first true love, the anguish of that loss, will slowly be replaced by memories of your marital joy and bliss, that will be with you for a very long time.

"I've never told you this, Augusta, but we lost a little girl four years old. Julie died in 1839, exactly twenty years ago this winter. I was with child once and only once and produced an angel. That was in Baltimore. My husband's practice was five years old and thriving. Being Boston-trained, he was invited frequently to give medical lectures to the hospital docents. That's what they called beginning doctors in those days.

"How he loved that child. They would romp together on the floor like two puppies, and fill our house with shrieks of laughter. That summer he bought her a little Shetland pony and a saddle to match. That winter she died. To this day I am convinced she died of something he brought home from that damned hospital. Since that year he's never again worked in a hospital.

When Julie died, he got so drunk he couldn't attend the funeral. I had to make all the funeral arrangements myself.

Since then we've moved, on average, every two years. His drinking has never stopped. He's home now, passed out on the parlor sofa, using his inability to help your husband as his excuse to stay drunk. I don't even bother anymore to try to get him to bed. I love my husband and want to help him but his stupor when he's drunk makes me vacillate between feelings of devotion and disgust.

While he was studying medicine, I think he got it into his head that he and his fellow doctors could cure any disease; that is, if they could name it. But in practice, except for bone fractures and lacerations, they usually can't do much. That knowledge and the bottle are killing him. They work so hard for such little reward. All those years in school memorizing all those body parts and all those chemicals that they've been taught to think are magic potions, and when they come up against a real case, knowing all those words, half of them in Latin and Greek, is worthless. My husband has told me over and over how useless were many of the treatments he learned of in school. Just this morning he said he wasn't even sure if morphine was the right medicine for Chase and her voice trailed off.

She told me more about Julie and the sorrow it had brought them. I think she wasn't really talking to me anymore: She was talking to herself. Before she finished her story of grief, there were tears in her eyes and her voice was hoarse and gravely.

The next day, Monday, September 19th, the day after Chase died, I buried him. We had the service late in the afternoon. Tom Cordis, Mr. Frame and Mr. Rackliffe dug the grave. We had a small ceremony at the gravesite but it is too painful and deeply personal to describe just now.

"For richer, for poorer, 'til death do us part."

Elizabeth Cordis at the gravesite funeral gave me the only comfort I could use, reminding me that I must take care of myself for the baby. She's right about that, of course. But as I heard her talk, I thought, "Chase and I will never know the joy of planning our child's future together, listening to our baby's first gurgles, first laughter, first words."

What tragedy. Adda wasn't here. Only ten months ago Father was killed. And my sorrow is now compounded by Chase's death and by the fact that he didn't know about the baby. I never found a good time to tell him that I was carrying his child. For the first months, maybe three or four, I simply wasn't sure of my symptoms and out of modesty I held back in talking to Doctor Weibley about it. In fact, I've never told him about it.

The house is deathly quiet and lonely. I can't fall asleep. I can't find a comfortable place for my limbs and my body long enough to go to sleep, and now that it's dawn, I want to go back to bed. Nothing pleases me. I hardly ate any supper last night. I have no appetite this morning. I ought to go out and work in the garden. Pete got up eight scarecrows and they work fine to frighten off the crows, but I haven't found anything that is good for scaring away the cabbageworms. There's not a bird in the valley that will eat those green hungry pests, and I don't want to go outside and pick them off. I just don't feel ready to do any chores today.

I can't reconcile myself to my solitariness. I'm a widow, a widow at twenty, impossible. I cannot, except as a remote idea, accept that Chase is dead. When Mr. Smith lost his wife and child, rather than show compassion, I avoided him. I wonder now that Chase is gone how others will react, particularly since Father is also now gone, along with all he meant to this town and all the talent and leadership that he had. Will I be avoided and become a pariah? When Father was killed, the neighbors helped with the housework and tried to comfort Adda and me. My grief was too personal. I appreciated their efforts but I needed to work out my own answers to the sorrow I felt. Some of their advice not only was worthless, it was offensive.

Mary Rackliffe advised me to ask God for help. Maybe that works for others and I'm happy for them if it does, and I know it's the social thing to say, but it's like saying, "take care of yourself."

I've observed one major difference in how I have reacted to Father's death compared with Mother's. When mother died, and still today, a host of little reminders, things like smells, music, food, another person's clothing or posture, an almost endless list of signals could trigger childhood memories of her and those recollections were not all sad, but the mystery of her death remains and I have never found a satisfactory answer for it from my faith.

With Father, that grief has been entirely different. I simply miss him. I'm (secretly) more sorry for him than for myself, because he was cut down in his prime. His various businesses were getting started, his political career had just begun, and the three of us enjoyed such grand expectations. Then his murder brought all that to an abrupt end.

When Father died, Mrs. Weibley said to me that I would never find a replacement for him, so that I shouldn't even try. She told me that when I married Chase, I shouldn't expect him to be my father or to even be like him. "It's a shame," she said, "that our English vocabulary is so limited that it imposes so many uses for the word 'love.' We really need ten or fifteen different words, each expressing a different aspect of love. The love you had for your father is not the same love you'll have for your husband." I think hers was the only good advice I received when Father died. I did get a little comfort from others but very little useful advice. There's a difference between comfort and advice, but you only know it when you need it."

Mrs. Weibley was right. The love I found with Chase was different from what I had felt for Father. The life that Chase and I have shared these past eight months, I know now that it's over forever, was profoundly blissful. Chase was shy and taciturn and occasionally moody, so it took some getting used to, but we became close and very dependent on one another. But now that he's gone, his love for me is gone. I just don't know what to do. I've loved him for a very long time and I will love him for the rest of my days. I wish Adda were here, but if she were, I know all my crying and self-pity would depress her. Adda seems to make these adjustments better than I do and becomes a little impatient with my behavior.

I am still grieving for Father. Just his raw physical absence took, is continuing to take, getting used to. Before he died, people would come to our house for political favors or to give Father political advice. Sometimes that advice bordered on instructions, but he seemed patient, knowing that he represented the whole district, not just his like-minded friends. Some were suggested proposals that he should make when attending meetings of the Legislature. Occasionally they handed him written notes. Father said he was given some excellent suggestions regarding land use, etc. to be inserted in the Free State Constitution. But now all that traffic, all that visiting, all those discussions which would often last so late into the night that the visitors would stay over and Adda and I would serve them breakfast in the morning, all that has stopped.

Some of the men would come here inquiring about the legality of their claims: Were they filed? Would the proslavery scalawags in the Land Office respect the filing of an abolitionist, or would they concoct schemes to cloud or deny the title?

Father was the acknowledged founder of this town, and its surveyor. He could decide whether we would grow north, which, according to his reading of history, was the custom. He used to tell Adda and me that cities grow north and uphill. "Therefore", he advised, "Always invest in land north of the existing city, up hill and away from the river, which will become commercial and cluttered with shipping." Our family was the center of this town and Father had one of its first businesses, the sawmill. Sometimes our shareholders would come to tell Father how to run the sawmill better, how long to dry hardwood, etc., advice he invariably took in good humor. After all, his family had been running sawmills for two generations.

Although Father was gone a lot, because of his work in the Legislature, I knew that sooner or later, he'd be home. Now, there's *no* sooner or later.

I thought perhaps Adda and I could run the sawmill together, She certainly learned, better than me, how to operate the boiler, but I think, now, that was just to be sociable with the men and to prove to them that she could do it. "Except for Mr. Eastridge," Adda would competitively say to Chase or Jerry, "anything you can do, I can do better" and she'd give them as hard a poke as she thought they'd tolerate without hitting back. But she has never really expressed any interest in the business side the mill, so I'll probably have to take a business partner, maybe Jerry Jordan.

It's Sunday, September 24th, and during the night I must have gotten a little cold, or maybe I wasn't cold but was reacting to the absence of the comforting nocturnal habit I'd learned to appreciate since I commenced sharing a bed with my husband. We were married last January, during the coldest part of winter, which, in Kansas, can be very cold indeed, and though the house was usually warm when we went to bed, occasionally I would warm-up the bed by wrapping two hot flat stones separately in pieces of old flannel and putting one of the stones on each side of the bed a few minutes before bedtime. After awhile the wood fire would go out and as the house got cold, our natural response was simply to snuggle a little closer together for warmth. Though we were, I suppose, too shy to discuss it, we expressed our affection in this way and it never seemed to disturb our sleep, just the opposite.

Last night, half asleep; I moved my body towards my husband's. My husband wasn't there and I vaguely recalled a passage from the Song of Solomon. "By night on my bed I sought him whom my soul loveth: I sought him, but I found him not." The starkness of that reality woke me up and I cried for my own loss and I cried for my husband. When I'm wide-awake I can't believe my husband is dead, has been dead a week. I'm sure he will walk in the door with news of one of his jobs or something he must do, yet in another, recessed part of my mind I know I need to get it into my head that Chase is dead. I know Chase is dead and buried. And I know I have to learn to live alone, without him. That may sound like one and the same problem but in my despair I've parsed these realities into several realities. I'm trying to adjust to widowhood and attempting to do it by comprehending fully and without too many self-delusions, that Chase is dead and gone—never to return. I must record for future reference, however, that by denying his death, I get some comfort from it. On the other hand, whenever I accept his death, grief and dark despair enshrouds me. I've discussed this with Elizabeth Cordis. She said she had the same problem when her mother died. She said by visiting the grave, she gradually got confirmation that her mother was dead, but the time at the grave must be "an honest visit," she said, explaining that I couldn't just stand there and mumble the Lord's Prayer. "That won't do unless you totally acknowledge that Chase is down there, horizontal, never to be with you."

Then she made another suggestion, but it's one I simply cannot follow. She advised me to sell his carpentry tools and get rid of his clothes. Get rid of his clothes? I adore his clothes. He has an old brown wool sweater. It hangs on a nail by our bed. I hold the sweater next to my face. I bury my face in it. I can still smell my husband. I will never get rid of that sweater. I've thought about putting that sweater into a small pillow, nobody would know about it. I have his old work shoes under the bed exactly where I put them Saturday a week ago, when he insisted on going out and getting some fresh air. When he came in, exhausted, to lie down, I took his shoes and socks off. He never got up again, on his own, after that. I had put his shoes under the bed on his side. They are still there, right now.

I think it strange that the doctor never comes 'round. Perhaps he is ashamed to face me and is having doubts about the medical treatment he gave Chase.

A week or so after the funeral, I heard Pete Gillespie outside sawing something. I went out to see. "Pete," I asked him, " where did you get that saw?

"It was hanging in the tool shed behind the house."

"Well, you put that saw up right back where you found it and don't you ever touch it again, do you understand?" I turned away from this loyal neighbor and started to sob.

Pete came over and put a big hand on my shoulder. "Mrs. Chase, you've got to get a hold of yourself. I know that's your husband's saw, but whether I use it or not, he's not coming back. He's never ever going to use that saw again."

OBITUARY
Jacob Eastman Chase

Laura Augusta Stewart Chase married Jacob Chase on January 12, 1859 – the first couple to be married in Eldorado, Kansas Territory. He was born on November 19, 1837 in Massachusetts and died in Eldorado on September 16, 1859 only ten months after the wedding. This tintype was taken in Chicago when he was 18 years old and mailed to his mother. He had joined Captain Stowel's Party in Worcester, Massachusetts and arrived in the Kansas Territory that summer of 1856, in time to join the Lexington Company of Jim Lane's Militia. They fought several battles. After the Battle of Hickory Point he and 101 others, two companies, were captured and interred in the P.O.W. camp in Lecompton. Due to their youth, he and Frank Robinson were given an early release but ordered to leave the Territory, which they did. The summer of 1857 they returned to Lawrence in pursuit of the Stewart girls. He followed Augusta to Eldorado, where they married two years later. He became one of Eldorado's first builders.

JACOB EASTMAN CHASE
B. 1837 - D. 1859

43

Lawrence - A Visit with Adda
October and November 1859

Pete Gillespie got back from Lawrence today and reported that he boarded at the Whitney House, saw Adda and that she's fine. Mr. Storrs from Emporia came by late in the day with one of Judge Lamdin's boys and wanted some supper, so I fixed something up for all of us and I'm afraid we talked past our bedtime.

The next afternoon I went up to Mrs. Frame's and asked if she and Mrs. Rackcliffe would go with me to visit Chase's grave. Mrs. Rackcliffe is large with child but is so reticent about discussing it, yet she gladly said she'd go along. She did say she thought she would be "ready" between Christmas and New Year's. Mrs. Frame and Mrs. Rackcliffe were both so understanding and accommodating. It was a sorrowful visit even though it was a fine day. I'm glad I had two friends along, otherwise I don't think I'd have had the strength to leave the grave site, which I'm sad to report had been seriously dug into by some sort of animals. Wolves, I suppose. At the grave, I quietly told Chase about the baby. It's difficult for me to describe the empty loneliness I feel. I'd waited so long for marriage, long past all my other friends. Indeed by the time of the wedding, some of them already had babies. Somehow a God-provided hope outlived and overcame every squabble and disappointment, and finally Chase and I were together and so tenderly and completely in love. Then without warning, he was cut down, still so young. Why? Why us?

I spent the night and the next several days at the Rackcliffes'. When I got home, I learned from Sammy that two visitors had stopped by my place while I was away. Sammy said Mrs. Barrett had come over to see how I was getting along. She's been so pleasantly solicitous since Chase's death. I had invited her to visit, but hadn't been specific as to what day.

The other visitor was none other than our old friend Preston Plumb, who had come by on October 7th. I wonder if he had heard about Chase and had come by to pay his condolences, or if he had some business to discuss.

It just dawned on me: Since we've all known Mr. Plumb since the summer of '56, it could be that he is a shareholder in the sawmill and came by to see what's happening to his investment or maybe he has in-mind some lumber for a building he has in Emporia. I know he has a printing press up there.

Next time I go to Lawrence, I'll stop for the night at Emporia to see Mr. Plumb and satisfy my curiosity about why he had come.

During the next couple of weeks I did my best to come to terms with Chase's death but nothing provides enough balm for my incessant loneliness, grief and self-pity.

October 19th began as a crisp, beautiful dry fall day with a light westerly breeze and stayed that way all day. A little after noon a group of people came by and pounded on the door, yelling about a prairie fire a little south of us. They were gathering folks to fight it. I didn't tarry long at the door but I could see Mrs. Frame, Sammy, Mr. Carver and Pete Gillespie were among this hasty party. They were in two wagons. I shouted for them to go ahead, but asked Pete to wait for me while I gathered some things. I was grateful that he had his wagon. We drove a mile or so south and caught up with the others, who were battling the fire, which was 500 yards east and within sight of the Rackcliffes'. Mr. Rackcliffe and Mr. Frame had gone to Fall River for a convention. (I really shouldn't call it Fall River. I believe it's registered now as Eureka, but most of us locals still call it Fall River. Father was a trustee and did all the surveying and the early Land Office filings.)

We fought that blamed fire until sundown. Several times I felt so exhausted I wanted badly to just sit down and rest but couldn't. The earth was black with burnt prairie grass stubble and in some places quite hot. Although I wore a pair of Father's old gloves, by sundown my hands and arms were black, as well as my shoes and legs. I'm happy I grabbed one of Adda's yellow bandannas before I left the house. I had wrapped it tightly up around my head, and it protected my face and hair.

There were fifteen to eighteen of us fighting the fire. It came very close to taking the Rackcliffes' place, which borders the river, but is a few yards upstream from where the fire stopped.

The fire's appetite for our prairie grass was both variable and voracious but it didn't produce much smoke. What smoke there was, was quickly carried off and dissipated by the prairie breeze. At times it would surge in all directions, occasionally surrounding part of our group. I had no idea the prairie was host to such abundant animal life. Rabbits fled the flames by the score, often making a shrieking noise I'd never heard before; occasionally they'd wait too long and their fur would catch fire. Flocks of prairie chickens would raise up out of the flames, as well as a variety of small birds, some the size of pigeons.

Except for some warm cocoa, I went to bed that night without supper, which is unusual for me. I was stiff and my arms and shoulders ached from pounding that fire with lengths of burlap sack. I was feeling some pains in my back, which is unusual for me. These cramps started in my lower back and sometimes would radiate all around my waist. I suppose I was having them because I was bent over fighting the fire.

I'd like to claim we put the fire out, but it just seemed to burn itself out. The fire was proceeding over to the bank of the river but died down because the wind wasn't blowing in that direction. Thank heavens the wind was mostly towards the river. Had it been from the south, there'd been *no* containing the blaze and it could easily have gotten to our place.

The next day, I had some cramps, more in my groin than in my lower abdomen. Being hunched over fighting the fire all yesterday afternoon had made my muscles and bones sore. I thought if I work in the garden it would loosen up those muscles and relieve the cramps. I brought in several pumpkins and small squash and was thinking about what I needed to do to keep them for midwinter's use when I felt something warm and moist seeping down my legs. In panic I examined myself as best I could.

The bloody discharge continued with mild to severe cramps…I'm afraid we've lost our baby.

Seems to me I've read that physical exertion, even if strenuous and of long duration, by itself usually isn't enough to provoke a miscarriage but I don't know what else to blame it on. I've been getting plenty of rest, been careful about food. I've boiled all my water. I've taken no falls. I have certainly been depressed since Chase's death but I can't see how depression could be a cause. Earlier, I had the usual "morning symptoms," as described in Gunn's book as normal.

I think as soon as I can I'll go up and stay a few days with Mrs. Frame. I've known for a week or so that Mr. Frame plans to go to Lawrence. I spoke with him about going to visit Adda. Maybe he is still away at that convention in Fall River.

Well, I was wrong, Mr. Frame had only stayed at the convention a few days but said he couldn't leave for Lawrence until the third of November and that's when the two of us started for Lawrence on schedule. Although we used the Frames' wagon, I pulled along Kate so as to have some transportation when I got to Lawrence. We arrived at Indian Creek about an hour after sunset and met Mr. Moreton (from Eldorado) three miles below the springs.

Yesterday, we left Camp Creek a little after sunup. This was a sentimental stop, a prairie pilgrimage, for it was from here that my darling husband wrote his last letter to me. I got down off the wagon and walked along beside the wagon, as Adda and I had often done during those beautiful, green July days traveling across Iowa. I looked to the November clouds, the sea of waving brown grass, the vast open Kansas prairie for a solution to my predicament. If God intended to respond, his message was in an unknown language. How I long for some help, some comforting advice, some answer to these profound mysteries. How I envy those who get some form of security from their religion.

I continued walking until well after sundown until we could see a few lights in the cabin windows up ahead. I wasn't sure, but I thought we were coming into Emporia.

On several occasions, both Father and I (often separately) have stopped off here to visit Mr. Plumb who founded the town and asked Father to survey part of it, although I think Alfred Pierce did some of the surveying as well. We had planned to stop and visit with the Pierce family but they had a sickness in their house, so I decided it might not be prudent to impose. Mr. Plumb has been successful in attracting quite a number of Quaker families to settle in and around Emporia. The Pierces recommended we find lodging with one of the Quaker households and we did. I also wanted to see Preston Plumb to inquire what it was that had brought him to Eldorado October 7th, but he was not in town.

There is a "site" under construction here, I notice, and it's not just for a simple residence but also for a large building of some kind. Someone has carefully excavated an entire basement and laid in large slabs of stone for the foundation. Maybe it's intended to be a store…or a church. So, maybe the purpose for Mr. Plumb's visit to Eldorado was to inquire about lumber for this building site. I certainly hope so. We could use that business.

By November 6th, we were on the Lecompton road and we passed directly in front of Father's old prisoner-of-war camp and it brought back the gloomy memories of our visit there on a cold January night two years ago. I would have missed it in the dark, except we saw a few soldiers, guards, no doubt, standing around a bonfire. We pulled up and exchanged greetings. We chatted for a bit. The guards told us that there were still a few prisoners remaining at the campsite, mostly criminals, horse thieves, murderers, etc. The camp site is mostly being used now as a parade ground by the U.S. Army, which has a company at Lecompton no doubt to serve as a guard for the Territorial Governor Medary, * who's proslavery. When we hold our first election for Governor, we abolitionists will have the majority of the votes, and I'm sure it will be Dr. Robinson, who will be elected to that office. The Federal appointee will simply disappear.

From the old Lecompton prison site to the Gateses' place, which is a little west of Lawrence, is about nine or ten miles. We almost got lost finding it in the dark since the main trail east to Lawrence makes a bend to accommodate the river. The path to their place goes straight and is marked by a lone signal post, which I hadn't remembered, just a piece of tree limb stuck in the ground. We located their claim at about bedtime. Thank heavens Mrs. Gates had not gone to bed. We could see a light in the window to the north of us.

Getting to her place so late at night reminded me of our first visit here two years ago, when Father, Adda and I had arrived after having visited the prisoners who were still in Lecompton. Her husband was among the abolitionists still being held at the camp.

Sammy Frame and I went up to the house and knocked at the door. We had a very emotional reunion, Mrs. Gates and I. She was delighted to see me. She was unaware that Chase had died. When I told her, her demeanor changed. Stunned, she put both of her hands on my shoulders and held me at arm's length, staring into my face. "Augusta, I can't believe it. He was here just a few weeks ago and left a list of things for me to order from the lumberyard for our addition." When she got over the news, she embraced me in the warmest possible way. My response was to

---

*Samuel Medary served as territorial governor from 1858 to 1860.

commence sobbing, and she continued to hold me in a motherly hug. When I got myself under control, she became rather curious as to the cause of Chase's death and I explained it as best I could. I told her about Doctor Weibley's futile attempts to save him, but because I was already rather emotional, and wasn't sure I could control some of the resentment I felt towards the doctor because of the medical care he gave Chase, I held back telling her about the morphine and its dire results. I will take Mrs. Gates into my confidence on this matter but in due time.

"You're such a good nurse, Augusta, I just can't believe you couldn't pull him through, like you did for my little Fanny when she had that terrible attack of small pox. I've always been so grateful for what you did for our family."

I asked her if she'd seen Adda. "Yes," she said, "we've been trying to get her back at the Cincinnati House. She's such a steady worker and the boarders all love Adda, but you know your sister, so unbeknownst to her, I spoke to the proprietor of the Whitney House, an old family friend, and asked him to 'keep his eye' on Adda."

I appreciated that. I'm afraid I was too immature in my earlier holier than thou censure of Mrs. Gates, when Adda and I were working for her here two years ago, while her husband was in prison. She was obviously lonely. I've suffered through the loss of Father and have reconciled myself to the certainty that he's gone. And I have now lost Chase. I'm a young widow, who in less than a year of married life has lost her first and only true love, but before that loss I knew a bliss that only heaven can provide. Now I'm all-alone and in that loneliness I seem to be getting piece-meal little allotments of wisdom not to judge too harshly the behavior of other lonely and forlorn women.

Well, while the two of us were reminiscing, poor Sammy fell asleep on her sofa in the big parlor. When Mrs. Gates used to feed the soldiers here at her place, we would occasionally set an extra table in front of the sofa for them...and that's where he slept 'til breakfast.

It was late when she finally assigned me a bedroom. I was almost in bed when she returned carrying a dainty coal oil lamp, a cup of warm milk with a little nutmeg grated on top and two cookies. She had taken down her hair and, I must say, she is as beautiful as ever. I try to obey the Tenth Commandment but it's difficult not to envy that auburn hair, which, as she turned to leave, seemed to glow translucently in the lamplight. It's a fine line God gives us between knowing the joy of beauty and the sin of envying it.

Mrs. Gates insists that I stay here while I'm in Lawrence, and I will lodge with her for as long as I am in town. Tomorrow I'm going to take Kate and ride over to visit Adda at the Whitney House. I hope my presence doesn't breakup some vast abolitionist plot and I hope Adda isn't involved in one, though I wouldn't put it past her.

I haven't been on a horse since I lost the baby on October 21st. That's almost three weeks ago, but I think I'll be all right riding Kate, but I'm wondering if I should tell Adda about the baby. When I was expecting, I was so anxious and proud to tell her, but now that I've lost the baby, I'm not so sure I will say anything to her. Is that vanity, or am I blaming myself for this misfortune, and am therefore reluctant to discuss it with her? Or am I reacting this way because I am afraid that she will, as she has in the past, call it one more of my inexhaustible sources of sorrow and grief?

There's another thing I want to do before leaving Lawrence, I want to look up a doctor who Mrs. Gates might recommend to explain Chase's symptoms before he died. I want to describe Dr. Weibley's treatment, though I won't reveal his name. I'm not satisfied that what we did was the best we could have done and, more importantly, whether the treatment (two doses of Morphine in less than four hours apart) was called for. That's the least I owe my loving husband and I owe it to myself to clear it up, if I can.

I had been planning and looking forward to visiting old friends while I was here in Lawrence and the first person I am going to see is Aggie Rourke at the Cincinnati House, which is on the way to the Whitney House.

Aggie is still the Gateses' chief cook. I learned so much from her when I sometimes served as one of her assistant cooks, first at the Gateses' place when they had the contract to feed the Mount Oread Company out there and later at the Cincinnati House here in town. I often think of Aggie as I prepare meals for our boarders in Eldorado. Aggie loves onions but her fondness for them is more than just affectation. She believes that onions contain some magic power they add to food and consequently to the health of those who eat them. For her "feminine" health she eats some onions every day and encouraged us to do likewise.

There are a dozen diseases, including melancholy, according to Aggie, that respond to eating a yellow onion boiled in sweet salted milk, boiled so slowly that it never loses its shape and has to be eaten with a sharp knife. Every time I or another of her assistant cooks prepared it she would say, "Don't be leavin' the milk."

Aggie also taught me that slices of buffalo liver gave up its gaminess if it's sliced thin, dredged in brown flour and quickly fried with sliced white onions in fresh bacon fat.

Aggie would pickle sliced onions in spiced sweet vinegar for two or three days, to create a dish guaranteed, she told certain male "regulars" at the Cincinnati house with a wink and a throaty chuckle, to improve their love life.

Because of Aggie's affection for the onion she carried about her a fragrance of it. As I came into the kitchen at the Cincinnati House, and the two us embraced, her shiny, black wavy hair, with wisps of it around her moist neck and forehead, and especially her fragrance of onions, all instantly seemed so familiar and so unmistakably Aggie.

I wasn't in the kitchen but two minutes and she already was laughing and recalling all the good times we'd all had together feeding the soldiers, both on the farm and here in town. As we talked, she busied herself making a small crock of tea for the two of us and called me "dearie" and said she was sorry beyond words when she read in the paper a year ago about Father's death.

"You know," she said, "in the depth of the winter before your father was released from Lecompton he and one or two other trustees were allowed to leave the camp regularly to drive a wagon up here to collect food, clothing and blankets for the prisoners. Everybody in town had a relative or friend or two in that miserable pesthole. One of those prisoners was Jason Connelly, who claimed to be from Illinois, but before that he was from the Auld Sod, like me. We was keepin' company pretty regular before he joined one of Jim Lane's companies the summer of '56 and was captured and thrown into Lecompton."

I asked if Mr. Connelly had been pardoned and she replied, "Oh my yes, by February or March of '57 and he came back to Lawrence with Mr. Gates. Don't you remember? He was at the welcoming home party for Mr. Gates. He was a slater and sometimes coal miner in the old country, and had done odd jobs at the Cincinnati House. And we had the pleasure of renewing our acquaintance," and she gave me a little wink, a knowing wink between two grown women.

By spring, he had gone to Pike's Peak with a small outfit that had organized a wagon train here in town.

Each member had to contribute two hundred dollars. I had saved enough to lend him some money. As soon as the grass could support their animals in late June of '57, they left.

I thought to myself, I bet I saw them go through Eldorado.

"Is he still there now?" I asked.

She laughed. "Oh, yes, he's a millionaire now, a big Rocky Mountain gold miner south of Denver." But she said with obvious pride, "He's a deep underground miner."

"It's so interesting, Augusta, the best miners out there are Irishmen, They had learned their trade in the Old Country, often in the English mines. Out in the mines we Irish are 'on top,' Mr. Connelly writes me. He assigns all the muck work to anyone with an English accent. We weren't good enough for the English back home or in Boston or in the States for that matter, oh no. But out here, we're all accepted for what we can do and our willingness to do it, and, that, my girl, is the way it should be."

I asked Aggie if she planned to join Mr. Connelly.

"If he asks me, dearie, if he asks me. I'm hoping, by and by, he will. We write pretty steadily. "As she laughed, I could see that she was continuing to lose teeth. But as my mother would say, she was "no spring chicken."

I had intended to tell her about losing Chase. I had wondered whether she had read an obituary, but we had such a pleasant reunion I didn't want to spoil it. For my part, I wasn't sure I could tell her without getting emotional, so I thought I would put it off.

As we said our good-byes, she hugged me. "I light a candle now and again for your dear sweet fayther. It was he, bless his soul, who kept Mr. Connelly alive in that miserable camp."

"Is Adda around?"

"Adda? Sure, she's around. You won't miss Adda. Augusta, you know your sister doesn't work here anymore. She works at the Whitney house now."

"Yes, yes, I know." Adding with a wink and a chuckle, I see your sister fairly regularly, "We have a little business arrangement between us."

I wondered what sort of business arrangement it was that existed between Adda and this sweet but crafty Irish cook, old enough to be my mother, but I thought that if Aggie had wanted me to know, she'd have told me and she didn't, so I let it pass… for now.

"Aggie, do you know a Frank Robinson? He was a beau of Adda's in Eldorado and is supposed to be living here now."

"Well, Adda doesn't lack for male attention but I don't recall that name. But I have seen her with a young gunsmith, a rather successful local businessman. He rooms here in town and boards mostly at the Whitney House so I suppose he sees Adda there every day."

"Oh, what's his name?"

"Don't know."

"She is popular with the Whitney House boarders but that is not surprising. When you two were working here, half the young merchants who ate here were sweet on your sister."

I took my sister by surprise. Adda was not so busy that she couldn't talk, and so we had time for a visit. Adda introduced me to the proprietor, who became most cordial when he learned we were sisters. He knew from Adda that we were among the first Free Stators in Plymouth and had arrived in Kansas Territory in August of 1856. When I told him we were in Plymouth when Jim Lane started organizing all five of the new settlements up close to the Nebraska line and that John Brown was a frequent visitor to Plymouth while we were there, he almost got conspiratorial with us. He got a big chuckle when Adda told him that John Brown had issued to us and several other women at Plymouth, Bowie knives and said, "Yep, that's Old John Brown." He told Adda to make a big pot of tea and the three of us old abolitionists sat around for an hour prior to the noon meal talking about people like Preston Plumb and Richard Hinton, the journalist. He said Hinton had just been here a few days ago, firing-off another report on the troubles of the Territory for some Eastern newspapers. "He does all his writing right here in this lobby," he said, pointing to a round table by the front door. In fact, I'm holding three letters for him from East Coast papers, which contain, I suspect, checks for his most recent articles."

He asked me if I knew James Redpath. I told him about the time in Plymouth, in September of 1856, Mr. Redpath had arrived in Plymouth and was waiting for Preston Plumb, Sam Tappan and Alfred Pierce to bring in the supplies that Mr. Redpath needed for his party of 300, who were on their way down here. Adda's boss interjected, "Well, that's why I asked if you knew him. I know all about that incident, because after he picked up those supplies in Plymouth, he came directly here. On the way he was stopped in Topeka and had to convince the new Governor that his party consisted of peaceable settlers only and that his cargo was mainly food and food for Lawrence, but the three of us know that wasn't the whole story, don't we? Reverend Parsons, who had a party of fifty or so, all Bostonians, were bringing supplies for relatives and friends here in Lawrence and aided Mr. Redpath in this deception. They joined his group over in Topeka and on the way over here dropped off some food for those poor souls imprisoned over in Lecompton." He paused and stopped smiling. I suppose he suddenly remembered from Adda that Father had been one of the prisoners and realized that this topic might be painful for us. Looking serious, he told us that Richard Hinton had written an article for "the *Boston Traveler* in September of '56 that listed the names of the 107 abolitionist prisoners and where they were from, writing the story right here at the Whitney House. This fact interested me since, of course, I knew about that article, having read it up in Archer. "At about the time," he said, "the proslavery forces surrounding Lawrence were growing in number and we thought we were in for it again, but it turned out we were much better organized than we were in May of 1856, when the pro slavers sacked us. Jim Lane had 600-armed people nearby and, true to his military training from the Mexican War, had 600 more in reserve a little north of us. And my old friend John was south of here, with a company of 100 of his men." He laughed, "At least ten percent of Brown's company were his relatives."

"When Geary became Governor, he saw to it that the U.S. Army would be used to prevent the Missourians from destroying Lawrence a second time, he said. "John Brown occasionally took meals with Mr. Hinton and Mr. Redpath here. They were both part-time reporters and they'd interview Osawatomie Brown, who was always favorably inclined towards them. He knew their articles would help raise financial and moral support for our cause back East.

"He asked us if we knew William Phillips. Since we didn't, he explained that Mr. Phillips is a full-time reporter with the *New York Tribune* who has also interviewed John Brown in this establishment and written about his exploits out here. One particular article that made quite a stir in July of 1856 was about how John Brown and a small group of his men defeated and captured Colonel Pate and a company of Missourians who had been sent to capture the Old Captain. Whenever Mr. Phillips talks to John Brown they hold their meetings upstairs, so they can keep them secret, and they post John Kagi as their lookout. Since this is the major abolitionist establishment in town, and we are well prepared for any problems from the pro slavers, I think all their precautions are a bit overblown and unnecessary."

Well, we had a long tea and just before it was time to serve all the boarders coming in he said, "Adda, when you are done, why don't you take the afternoon off and visit with your sister. But I'll need you again for supper.

He invited me to join him at his table for the noon meal and introduced me to several of the diners as they filed in to take their places. He was such a gentleman and treated me like someone very important.

We were fortunate to have at our table a physician, who, I think, is new to Lawrence. For some reason the proprietor introduced me as Augusta Stewart, Adda's sister, and said I was from Eldorado. Perhaps he didn't know I had been married. Doctor Lewis takes his noon meals here. He seems to be five to seven years older than myself. I asked him if he knew the doctor Mrs. Gates called in when Fanny had the small pox.

"Yes, but he's no longer here." I wondered if Doctor Lamb, the Brooklyn doctor who had so impressed me, had returned home. I asked Doctor Lewis if Doctor Lamb was still in town.

"No, I'm afraid I don't know that gentleman. He must have left Lawrence before I arrived."

There was so much noise at our table that we had trouble hearing each other. Doctor Lewis asked the gentleman next to me if he would change chairs with him. As they switched places, I happened to notice the floor, which was spotted with tobacco juice. We had seen that nasty habit in Chicago, and I guess the custom of indiscriminately spitting tobacco juice has been imported to the new territories.

Doctor Lewis said he was from Ohio and was affiliated with the Methodists. He came out to the Territory in the summer of 1856, but had only recently moved to Lawrence. To get acquainted, we used Old John Brown as a topic of conversation. He knew him, Redpath, Hinton, Kagi, W.A. Phillips and the others so well I wondered since we were at the Whitney House and there are several other places in town, that serve noon meals, if he was involved with some of John Brown's activities. But I knew, even if he were, he wouldn't be telling me about it.

When the meal was over, I was glad the others left the table to fire up their cigars. Their absence gave me a chance to have a quiet, private talk with Doctor Lewis. I asked him if he knew Mr. and Mrs. Gates. He said he occasionally takes an evening meal at the Cincinnati House. I explained to him that two years ago when I was living here working for them that I had nursed Fanny Gates back to health under the supervision of the doctor he knew who had left Lawrence. (I didn't reveal how little I thought of that doctor's contribution to Fanny's recovery.) Then I began to talk about the details of Chase's illness without identifying him. (Doctor Lewis had mentioned that he had never been west of Topeka, so I was fairly sure he wouldn't know anyone as far out on the frontier as Eldorado, but as a precaution, I simply moved all the details of Chase's illness to Chelsea.)

I described Chase's symptoms, and asked if he'd ever heard of using Morphine to treat ague.

"Morphine is usually prescribed to relieve intense pain, such as from a gunshot wound, or a broken bone, particularly a compound fracture.

People, who are suffering with Ague, even in as serious as the case you are describing, usually are fatigued and weak but are not in acute pain. What happened to the patient? How did he react to the morphine?

"He went into a restless and tossing sleep, perspired more and his breath came in shallow little gasps. His fever didn't break, so the doctor decided to dose him again with morphine."

"Again? How many times did he give this patient morphine?"

"Once in the early morning and another about noon, which was about three or four hours after the first dose."

The doctor groaned. "Did the second dose increase the patient's pulse rate?"

His question almost caused me to lose consciousness.

"Yes."

"The doctor took his pulse and said it was over one hundred times a minute."

"Did the patient gasp for air?"

"Well, yes, that's exactly the way to describe it. He simply couldn't get enough air into his lungs." I couldn't bear to tell him that on more than one occasion early that morning Chase would stop breathing for long spells and I'd had to help him start breathing again.

" If a case of ague, doesn't get better," he said, it tends to become consumption, which makes breathing and lung problems even more acute. The heart tries to remedy this by pumping more blood to the lungs. He added that even though ague causes fever, sweating and chills, the patient usually doesn't have any significant pain, so there is no good reason to prescribe morphine. "It's been well-known for centuries that morphine, relieves pain but makes the patient drowsy and will also speed up the heart and respiratory rate. Morphine can put such a strain on the heart and lungs, that the lungs simply collapse."

I could see that Doctor Lewis was tiring of this examination, so I did not try to detain him when he pushed his chair back and prepared to get his coat off a rack on the wall. "Had I been called in to help in this case," he said, "I wouldn't have used morphine at all, and I certainly wouldn't have used it again four hours later."

This statement was so disturbing I became a little dizzy. I wasn't sure I'd be able to get up to bid him farewell but somehow I did and followed him over to the door. "Good-bye, I hope to see you and Adda again. I hope our little chat helps you in the future when you are, as I'm sure you will be, called upon again to be a nurse out on the frontier."

I tried to help Adda clear the tables, but was so terribly distracted by what I'd learned from him that I found myself putting dishes in the wrong place or stopping and staring blankly at nothing while carrying trays full of cups and saucers. What Doctor Lewis had said was so compellingly close to what had happened to my poor husband that I began to wonder if Doctor Weibley had been drinking with Mr. Conner that morning and what little judgment the doctor possessed had become even more clouded by the alcohol. I thought it would help if I explained all this to Adda.

After the noon meal I rested for a half hour or so by the window in the lobby of the Whitney House. I'm afraid I dozed off for a while.

I had intended before returning to the Gates' place to go by the Riggs Bank and clear up Father's outstanding loan and make inquiry about the embezzlement. I had been careful to bring with me the Riggs Bank receipt, showing the fully paid-up interest, signed by Mr. Diggle. But after the troubling discussion with Doctor Lewis, I was still a little shaken, so I decided to postpone the visit until tomorrow.

As planned, the next day, November 9th, I stopped in at the Riggs Bank. I inquired of the manager if the detective who had apprehended Mr. Diggle had recovered any of our $100. The manager said he would give me what had been recovered and fetched an envelope that had the name Stewart/Eldorado marked on it. The gentleman gave me such a reassuring smile as he handed me the little envelope, that I felt sure the amount inside was going to be significant. The envelope yielded $8. I didn't let my disappointment show but wondered how I could pay back the $92 difference. I knew from the letter I had received from the bank in March that I would owe beyond whatever was recovered even though the money had been embezzled and the debt wasn't my fault. For now, I didn't want to address this question with the manager, so I asked him, "When Mr. Diggle left our house, he said he was going to Chelsea, then to Emporia. Did he defraud anyone there?"

"Yes, and in Topeka, Lecompton and several more towns west of here."

I asked about Mr. Diggle's whereabouts.

"As far as I know, he's in the Territorial jail in Lecompton, which is under Judge Lecompte's jurisdiction; we may press charges."

I remarked that Judge Lecompte, was not exactly a friend of the abolitionist cause.

He laughed, "Yes, you have that right and we suspect Judge Lecompte may not keep him in jail. They're both proslavery."

I rode back to Mrs. Gates' house and discussed the bank matter with her. Adda was staying over at the Gates' for the night. I showed her the eight dollars. "Well," she said, "that will more than cover our likenesses at Dagarian's tomorrow." We explained to Mrs. Gates how we expected to have our likenesses made with that new chemical process, called a daguerreotype.

Midmorning the next day, I went back into town with Adda and helped her with the noon meal. We were both excited about our appointment at Dagarian's Gallery that afternoon and we talked about it like two schoolgirls. We were concerned about our hair.

After cleaning up the noon dishes and setting the tables for supper Adda excused herself, saying she had a little errand to run over at the Cincinnati House. I offered to go along but she declined, saying she wouldn't be gone but fifteen or twenty minutes.

When she returned, she was carrying a small canvas bag. She signaled for me to go with her up to her room. I assumed it was to make sure we looked all right for our appointment at Dagarians.

"Did you see Aggie while you were over there?" I asked.

Adda smiled. "Indeed I did. If you can keep a secret, Aggie and I are business partners and have been for some time. Well, I'm a junior partner." "Oh, what sort of business?" I asked trying to be casual. Now I was going to find out what Aggie had been so mysterious about when I had stopped by to see her.

While we were talking, Adda had her back to me. She took something out of her canvas bag and carefully put it on her bed. She turned to face me, stepped to one side, grinned, and pointing to the bed, simply said, "This."

There were three flat pint bottles full of something neatly arranged on the bed.

Without explaining the contents Adda said, "Come over to the mirror. Let's work on each other's hair and I'll tell you the whole story. "Aggie Rourke has had for years a connection with some of her countrymen over in Davies County, Missouri. They make two special whiskeys out of wheat and barley. She helped them get their still started by loaning them the money." Some of the men who stay here at the Whitney House know that I used to work at the Cincinnati House and that Aggie and I are old friends. So occasionally they ask me if I can get a pint or so of whiskey from Aggie. These customers like it better than the other whiskeys offered around here because it is made from wheat, not corn. There's a class of men who look down on drinking corn whiskey. These same men, though, think it's putting on airs to drink European whiskey, even though there's plenty available.

"All I know is that these gents tell me that the whiskey Aggie gets is as good as any of the imported stuff. Some of my customers want Irish whiskey, which is different and they claim much better than Scotch mostly, I think, because they know it's made by Irishmen, but Irishmen over here.

"I think Scotch tastes terrible, but some men like it better than Illinois corn whiskey, which they could buy for between thirty and fifty cents a gallon. Aggie pays a dollar a gallon for her whiskey and we charge twenty-five cents for a pint and fifty cents for a quart, but we don't sell many quarts because we can't get bottles in that size. We get eight pints out of a gallon, so that's how we make our profit. I get half the profit for what I sell over here and sometimes, if he's a passenger off one of the boats, I charge a little more.

"Three guests at noon asked me if I'd run over and see if Aggie could spare a pint. So that's what I was doing just now. But you shouldn't breathe a word of this. Aggie would get fired if Mr. Gates knew that she was carrying on this little business right under his nose, in his own kitchen! After all, he sells imported Irish and Scotch whiskey at the Cincinnati House. He's quiet about it, but he sells it, it's not against the law. But he certainly wouldn't buy or sell this whiskey because it's made by a Missouri proslavery outfit."

Are you saying that Aggie's friends are proslavery?"

"Aggie doesn't give a hoot what they are as long as they're Irish. In the several months I've been here I have put away quite a nice nest egg from our arrangement."

"Adda, our family has always been against the evils of alcohol. Father was a prohibitionist. I'm a little surprised you'd be involved in this kind of business."

"Well, Augusta, over the months that I've been back here, I've heard politics talked over a glass or two of whiskey. I think Father took a social drink now and then, but in moderation. I have on several occasions talked to legislators who knew Father and they have mentioned to me that they would sometimes talk politics over a glass or two of whiskey. Mr. Gates and Father were close friends while they were Lecompton and he makes no bones about the fact that he misses Father and an opportunity to discuss politics with him over a glass of whiskey.

I asked, "How did you get into this business?"

"When I worked at the Cincinnati house, Aggie asked me once or twice to inquire in the dining room of mates or engineers who worked the river boats who were taking a meal with us to see if they had some pint or quart whiskey bottles. Once or twice I went down to the boats with one of them to fetch empty bottles for Aggie. Whenever I did, she would pay me something. After a while this became a routine and I continued collecting bottles for her when I moved to the Whitney House, because of the trade we get from the crews off the riverboats."

The cat was out of the bag when one of our infrequent boarders asked me, since he knew I had worked at the Cincinnati House and knew Aggie, if I could get him a pint of Irish whiskey and he gave me fifty cents. Well I knew I could buy a whole gallon of corn whiskey for fifty cents, so I figured it was whiskey that Aggie was putting in those empty bottles and it must be pretty special to fetch fifty cents a pint. That day soon as I could I went over to see Aggie with my fifty cents and suggested a partnership. My territory is the Whitney House.

We had just about finished with our hair, which we had been preparing for our session at Dagarian's, and I sensed we'd finished this discussion, too. Putting aside my disapproval, it crossed my mind to wonder just how much Adda had been able to save. A glance around her bedroom didn't reveal any signs of extravagance or recent prosperity, no matter how ill gotten.

We had put the finishing touches on each other's hair, knowing that the way our hair looked today would be on record for a long time.

When we came downstairs, we were a little early for our "appointment" at Dagarian's. The proprietor was seated at the same table where we had such a pleasant discussion on Tuesday. We told him we were going to Dagarian's shop and would be back well before supper.

The Bowles brothers, he told us, used to own and run the shop, that's now Dagarian"s, but one of the brothers, William, had died in Lecompton. The brothers were abolitionists from Missouri. "William Bowles served under Colonel Harvey. Like your father, he joined up in the summer of 1856, when the proslavery violence was at its peak, but was captured up at Hickory Point and was imprisoned, where he died of starvation.

The prisoners weren't given enough food and were there through the winter with nothing but canvas tents for protection. When they became ill, the U.S. Army wouldn't provide them with any medicine or allow any doctors from Lawrence to go treat them. Richard Hinton visited the camp and reported that 107 abolitionists were imprisoned there. But only 88 prisoners were charged and stood trial. We wanted him to go into the camp again to find out what happened to those nineteen missing men, but his first article had given the camp such notoriety in the States that Sheriff Jones and Governor Reeder were severely criticized by the proslavery authorities. I think it contributed to Governor Reeder's being dismissed and charged with treason two years ago. In fact, most of the pressure came from Washington. So you can be sure that put a stop to any more visits to the war camp by newspaper reporters."

"I knew that Mr. Hinton's article in the *Boston Traveler*, September/October of '56, which carefully listed 107 names including Father's. That article included a recitation of the meager rations that those prisoners had to survive on." I knew his published article and personal correspondence provoked a spate of Northern editorials and sermons, which resulted in all of the Lecompton prisoners being eventually pardoned by President Pierce. The last of them were out by early spring of '57. "When our father was released from Lecompton," I said, "he told us that about a dozen of those nineteen men had escaped, and the rest had died."

Adda and I put on our wraps and left for Dagarian's. On the way, Adda told me that, the proprietor of the Whitney

House was as 'thick as flies' with John Bowels, William's brother. "He thinks John Bowles also served under Colonel Harvey and he's told me that Mr. Bowles helped John Brown organize the Underground Railroad here in Lawrence. There's a rumor that over 300 darkies have already passed through here and gotten north. Last December, just before Christmas, John Brown led a raiding party into Missouri and personally brought eleven Negroes out and hid 'em for a while in this neighborhood. Afterwards he took them over to Tabor and used the same route east we used when we came here, only they went in the opposite direction. He spirited them up to Chicago, through Detroit, and then into Canada. He got help and open encouragement all the way. It was Mr. Brown's way of thumbing his nose at the new Fugitive Slave Law. Even with a big reward on his head and plenty of opportunities to capture him, even though it was a long road north, nobody ever turned him in."

"How did you learn all these things?"

"Working at the Whitney House is better than working at a newspaper."

"Well, I hope your curiosity doesn't get you involved in any of these shenanigans."

Adda gave me one of her confident, enigmatic half-smiles. "Don't let that hat disturb how we have arranged your hair, 'Ducky,' we're on our way to Dagarian's!"

LAURA AUGUSTA STEWART
Likeness made in lawrence in October 1859 during one my visits to Adda shortly after Chase's death

44

WE SETTLE A SCORE
November, 1859

We left the Whitney house early afternoon on foot and in high spirits anticipating having our likenesses taken with the new modern process. Although there was a wooden sidewalk in front of the Whitney house, it soon discontinued and we walked slightly uphill on the side of 7th Street toward New Hampshire Street. The river was at our back as was the chilly November wind. It was a bright day, but cold and we were walking directly into the sun.

Turning left on New Hampshire Street, Adda suggested we go west a block or two to get to Dagarian's. Patches of dirty snow remained here and there from the storm a few days earlier.

Looking ahead of us twenty-five or thirty feet, we couldn't believe what we were seeing, parked on the corner of 9th and New Hampshire close to the building facing east was a horse and a rather dilapidated two wheel buggy. The horse was facing us. A well-dressed man carefully stepped off the high end of the wooden sidewalk down onto the dirt street. As he turned left it afforded us a good look at him. It was none other than Mr. Randolph H. Diggle, the bank embezzler! Adda and I shook our heads in disbelief, but there was no doubt, it was indeed the person we thought it was. My first reaction was, I thought the rascal was in jail. That's what the bank believed. Well, obviously he's out.

Adda yelled, "Mr. Diggle, we'd like a word with you," and we increased our up hill gait. He looked directly at us, waved in such a way as to imply that he saw us but didn't recognize us as the embezzled Stewart sisters from Eldorado from whom he had stolen one hundred dollars cash and in the bargain deceived us out of two meals and a night's lodging. Maybe he couldn't distinguish us from all the others he'd embezzled.

We were now within a few feet of this portly, rather handsome scoundrel. Soon we were face to face with him but he seemed anxious to avoid us and began to get up into his rig.

"We knew you'd been arrested over in Missouri and brought back, Adda said. "Thanks to you, sir, the Riggs bank is showing us no mercy on our loan. Why aren't you in jail? How is it that after embezzling eight or ten of us, all abolitionists, and the bank you're walking around out here, free as a bird?"

"Ah, ladies, there is, even in these remote territories, a legal presumption of innocence. I am currently at liberty pending trial. If you'll excuse me..."

"Trial, what trial?" questioned Adda.

"I'm at large on bail pending trial in Judge Lecompte's court."

"Bail! Who would go your bail in this town? What kind of a judge would allow bail?" Adda asked.

"I just told you. Judge Lecompte."

Adda, more to me than Diggle, "Yes, I know that judge. He's a Pierce or Buchanan appointee, a proslavery holdover."

Diggle, "Yes, ladies, us Sons of the South must stick together and I've instructed my lawyer, who's from South Carolina to file with his court a Summary Judgment to dismiss."

"On what grounds?" demanded Adda.

"Insufficient evidence."

"You are not only a crook, you're crazy. There are eight families that my sister and I know of that can bring to court a bushel basket of evidence of your embezzlements and what about the bank's evidence?" Adda stated loudly.

Mr. Diggle then made two serious mistakes. He dismissively turned his back on my sister in the middle of this conversation, and he began to climb up into his buggy putting his body between it and the end of the wooden sidewalk, which was, maybe, two feet above the dirt road. Grabbing his right coat sleeve, Adda demanded, "Just a minute, Mr. Diggle, you owe us $92.00. You want to clear this up now or should we file with the Court to seize these assets?" and she pointed to his horse and buggy. "We have some good connections in this town. Our father was president of Eldorado and was in the Territorial Legislature."

Mr. Diggle ignored my sister and continued the process of getting up on his rig.

As he placed one foot on the little bent-iron step-up, his free left hand began to lift the butt of his buggy whip from its holder. Whether he intended to larrup his horse or give Adda a sharp blow with the butt of it was difficult to say, but Adda wasn't standing still to find out.

Just as Mr. Diggle had both feet off the ground, and was swinging his body up onto the buggy seat in this bent forward position, the back of his coat separated enough to expose a bright tan belt. My little sister, always ready to let her feelings match the opportunity, grabbed the belt with both hands ... and pulled. For what seemed like a life time Mr. Diggle's body seemed to defy gravity and remained suspended in mid-air, in a perfect sitting position between his wagon and the road.

When Mr. Diggle's ample behind landed on the frozen and sloping-downward frozen dirt road, the fall itself was more insulting than injurious. However, as his behind and legs landed, his upper torso, still moving, pivoted backward at the hip, which brought his back to a sharp violent halt against the plank ends of the wooden sidewalk. His fall backward against the sidewalk was so audible I was sure what I heard was a rib or two breaking against the protruding sidewalk planks.

His head had snapped back pointing his round red face almost skyward. His two eyes were both suddenly as open and dilated, as I'm sure, they had ever been; likewise his mouth, which seemed to be in a paroxysm between catching his breath and choking on a swallowed wad of chewing tobacco. The fall dislodged an upper set of false teeth that grotesquely protruded and stopped about half way out of his mouth. His hat came off and was immediately wind-scudded up hill.

I said, "My god, Adda, that fall against the sidewalk has killed him!"

"He doesn't look dead to me ... but if he is dead, poor soul, it's plain to see he must have been drunk, fell out of his buggy stupidly parked on a sloping frozen dirt road along side this wooden sidewalk.

"However, Doctor Stewart, before we report this scoundrel's demise and save the court the cost of his trial, let me test your diagnosis," whereupon she delivered a fierce swift kick just below the knee of his right leg. I half expected to see his kneecap come popping off to catch up with his hat.

Adda's kick caused the leg below the knee to jerk upward four or five inches. "Ever see a dead man move his leg like that? I learned from Doctor Weibley how to test for reaction; of course, his method was more professional than mine."

In the meantime, Mr. Diggle had, to my observation, not taken a single breath, though his mouth seemed to be working in that direction. Some tobacco stained spit was slowly dripping off his protruding uppers staining his gray vest.

Standing with one foot on either side of his left leg Adda bent over and in one deft motion relieved Mr. Diggle of his heavy gold watch chain, the same one that so impressed us when he relieved us of our Sorghum money: one hundred dollars of it making prairie chumps of us in the process.

The chain did not come easily into my sister's possession before it popped two buttons off his vest and in the leaving of his body I noticed, swinging in the afternoon sun, on one end of it was a fat little gold watch ... probably stolen.

Mr. Diggle still had not inhaled. Both eyes were open staring heavenward, but I was sure he was seeing nothing. He remained spread-legged on the frozen dirt road with his back angled against the protruding planks of the wood sidewalk. Adda plopped her loot in her little knit bag, walked forward between the wagon and building, thrust a hand under the seat and retrieved the canvas feed bag half full of grain. Approaching the horse she gave it an affectionate rub from his withers up along his crest and hung the grain bag under his nose as she was so curtly instructed to do by Mr. Diggle at our place last January.

She grabbed my right elbow and avoiding Mr. Diggle, in unison we stepped up on the sidewalk, our heels click-clacking on the wooden, tobacco-stained sidewalk, headed west up 9th Street towards "down town."

In less than two minutes, we were in a jewelry shop. The owner, she told me, was originally from Massachusetts, a staunch abolitionist, and a friend of the Robinsons, the Governor, his wife, Sara, and his brother. From the greeting it was obvious that Adda knew the gentleman, who in '58, like Chase, couldn't resist the siren call of the gold fields and like countless others, returned empty-handed to his old business, jewelry and buying gold. He frequently took his noon meal down at the Whitney house, was friendly and generous with the girls and occasionally joined his cronies for a two-hour after-dinner card game.

Adda quickly introduced me as her sister, Augusta from Eldorado, but didn't use my last name and in the same breath asked the jeweler if he would like to buy one of Father's gold chains. As she stretched it on his counter, I noticed she had disconnected the watch. In the middle of the chain hung a large off-white elk tooth held in a thick gold bezel.

Gathering the chain in his right hand, the jeweler hefted it and said, Adda, do you mind if I give it a little test to see if it's real gold?"

"Of course not." Whereupon he put maybe a half-drop of a clear liquid on one or two of the thick links, gave Adda a long one-eyed wink and emitted a little uh huh, signifying it had passed his acid test.

"You know, Adda, I can't buy this as a piece of jewelry but I will pay you the going rate for gold, which is for this quality thirty dollars per ounce. Will that be satisfactory?"

"Well that depends on what amount you finally arrive at. My sister and I are on our way to Dagarian's studio to have our likenesses taken with his new process; think the two of us are apt to break his apparatus?"

The jeweler disconnected the elk tooth, weighed the chain on his balance and on a little slip of paper made a calculation. "Adda, it's a nice chain. It's worth about seventy dollars."

"Seventy dollars!" Adda exclaimed. "Come on, that chain's worth twice that much. What about the elk tooth fit in this neat little gold sleeve?"

"I can't buy the elk tooth. See these initials ... B.P.O.E.?"

"Yes?" said Adda.

"That's the sacred emblem of the Benevolent and Protective Order of the Elks. I'm an Elk. Our code of ethics prevents trading in lodge recognition jewelry. Here, you keep it!"

"You fellows must shoot a lot of elk to provide all these teeth. What does your code of ethics say about that?"

"Gimme eighty-five dollars and the chain's yours," she said to the jeweler, having looked to me for some direction, some advice and getting none. "And here, you can give this elk tooth to your son to save you the bother of shooting another one, when you initiate him into your sacred order."

The Jeweler counted out $85 in miscellaneous gold coins and we were on our way, finally, to Dagarian's.

As Adda slid the coins into her purse, she smiled at the jeweler, reached over and patted his hand and said, "Next time you take your noon meal with us, I'll slip you an extra dessert no charge." She gave him a sly wink, grabbed my elbow and opened the door. It was a relief to smell the fresh air.

Outside I said, "Do you suppose he's still sitting back there on that frozen road?" Adda emitted a laugh so loud I thought it might make us conspicuous. She said, "Well, if he is, and I suppose he is, his fat old ass is pretty well frozen to that dirt street by now, eh? Don't worry about it. In this town, who's going to believe a cock and bull story coming from an indicted proslavery embezzler out on bail, about two girls, young enough to be his daughters, pulling him out of his wagon?"

"Yes and relieving him of his gold watch and chain!" I added

Adda was going to get the last word, "Well, he did have a four-legged witness but he ain't talkin'."

As we left the jewelers, knowing that my gleeful sister had eighty-five dollars in her pocket, I thought to myself, "I'm having a glorious afternoon, thanks to my little sister and I haven't once thought about my own despair." I was going to ask Adda if she thought I could get out of town before the two of us would be charged with assault, battery and theft, but I thought better of it.

In a few minutes, we were in Dagarian's. His overly warm shop was full of people ahead of us. I was a little surprised by the mixture of strange chemical odors and tobacco smoke, but as we glanced into a large mirror I was pleased to see that our episode with Mr. Diggle had not disturbed our "hair-do."

In the process of removing and hanging-up our wraps, a middle aged woman working in the gallery came over and briefly engaged Adda in a voice so soft I didn't catch any of it and had the feeling I wasn't supposed to. Adda said that in late summer of '58 father and some of the other state legislators had been in this studio celebrating and had their likenesses taken, as a group and individually. The package was picked up, she said by one of them later in the fall and taken to Leavenworth.

Adda said the woman was a widow. Her husband, who had been in General Lane's Army, knew Father. He was killed by proslavers in the summer of '58 and she's had odd jobs around town since then, too proud to go home.

Adda said she'd asked the woman to help locate those likenesses but she's had no luck so far. That's what all the secrecy was all about. So, there must be a likeness of Father someplace, maybe in Leavenworth taken before his death.

When our turn came, we went into a little closet-shaped room. Adda and the gentleman in charge exchanged a greeting that implied he too was a frequent patron of the Whitney house and she introduced me as her sister, Augusta. He asked us both to have a seat on a crude bench against a wall and we did. While he was fiddling with his apparatus, Adda asked him if he remembered making a likeness of Father some months earlier and the gentleman said, "Yes." He'd processed one-by-one a group of territorial legislators here for a meeting to work on the draft of the Free State Constitution.

While he was talking and we were listening, he casually lit a long match, held it to a little copper dish attached to his equipment and a flash went off before we realized what happened. He repeated that process by "doing" each of us one at a time. He gave Adda a little slip of paper and we left.

(Added later: these were the likenesses that Mister Woodward and Mr. Enos carried out from Lawrence on March 10, 1860, almost ninety days after Adda and I were in the Dagarian Studio.)

LAURA AUGUSTA STEWART

This likeness was made in November of 1859, while i was visting Adda in Lawrence. It was made in the afternoon a few minutes after we had settled our score with Mr. Diggle, who had earleir swindled $100 out of us.

I was 20 years old and a widow.

JOHN BROWN
1850s

JohnBrown

1800 - 1859

With permission from the Kansas State Historical Society.

Shortly after the Stewart family arrived in the Kansas Territory in the summer of 1856 most of the Free Soil/ Abolitionists' settlements were constantly threatened or under attack, mostly by nearby proslavery Missourians. John Brown was in the Plymouth vicinity helping to defend it. Augusta and Adda served him meals and came to know "the old captain", who gave them both a "Bowie Knife" for their "defense".

He was a frequent patron of the Whitney House in Lawrence, a small inn favoring abolitionists, where Adda worked on and off from 1857 until 1860.

Brown's frequent visits and speeches in New England helped to bring Kansas into the states free of slavery.

In the summer of 1859 Brown and several followers (some from Lawrence) laid plans to foment a Southern Slave uprising. To get the needed arms, he and his followers raided a government armory at Harpers Ferry on October 1859. He was captured; several followers were killed. John Brown was hung in December 1859.

45

NEWS OF JOHN BROWN'S RAID AT HARPERS FERRY
November, 1859

Adda came out early this morning and joined Mrs. Gates and me for breakfast. We had a grand visit. Word had already gotten out to the Gates' place about the fellow with broken ribs, who upon inquiry was discovered to be a proslavery felon out on a no-cash bail bond. We decided to include Mrs. Gates in yesterday's larcenous adventure. She hadn't known the gentleman but pronounced prairie justice to have been delivered. Adda left about eleven in the morning. She took the horses and said she needed to get back to set-up the tables for the noon meal and the Friday afternoon card game in the same room.

When Mrs. Gates invited her to come back for supper, she said she'd have to work supper at the Whitney House, so Mrs. Gates said, "Well, maybe I can intervene with my old competitor." She wrote a short note and asked Adda to give it to him. As she handed Adda the note, she said, "I've got to hear how you two came to be associated with an embezzler in the first place! We'll wait supper 'til you get here."

About 5 PM she returned, saying she had been "excused from supper chores" to visit her big sister, thanks to the note from Mrs. Gates.

As the three of us busied ourselves setting the table, I inquired if the Gates still had the contract to feed the Stubbs company and she said, "Yes, but the group we now feed in town at the Cincinnati house is smaller and there have been many changes since you and Adda worked for us before you all moved to Eldorado."

While Mrs. Gates and I reminisced, Adda seemed unusually quiet and so introspective I made a sisterly inquiry. She said she'd just come from a very disturbing discussion that took place after the noon meal; so disturbing they didn't have the usual Friday afternoon card game. She said it had left her shaken and upset. I thought to myself that must have been some "row" to upset Adda.

Mrs. Gates heard this and said, "What's this all about, would you mind telling us what happened this afternoon at the Whitney House, Adda?"

Adda, "Well, you won't believe this, but … John Brown, 'Osawatomie Brown' is, right now, tonight in an Eastern federal prison. About two weeks ago he and a company of abolitionists raided a federal gun factory somewhere in Virginia. Federal troops were brought in. Ten of Brown's men were killed. I'm sure we knew some of those poor fellows. Seven more were captured, and they think five or six escaped, including John Brown, Jr. who the reporters think might come back to Kansas. All this just happened, October 16th or 17th."

"Adda, what reporters? asked Mrs. Gates. "How do you know this?"

"Two eastern journalists showed up from St. Louis for the noon meal at the Whitney House and we served them like any other guests. One of them is from the *Boston Atlas*. After the meal they began questioning the proprietor in a way so direct it became acrimonious. The controversy soon attracted others, mostly our 'regulars' who had also eaten dinner. They soon clotted around the proprietor and the reporters. The reporters seemed to imply that plans and preparations for Brown's raid were not only laid out here in Lawrence, but right here, that the Whitney House was Brown's Kansas headquarters. The proprietor said, 'Well, I'm not so sure about that.' He asked them, 'What makes you think you know so much about John Brown's activity in Lawrence?' One of them said, 'Mister, we know plenty.' They knew that most of his financial backing is from all over back east, but they suspect that Mr. Brown still has staunch supporters here in Lawrence. The reporters were instructed by telegraph over in St. Louis to get out here and get the story."

"Well, of course, he has supporters here," Mrs. Gates said. "He's as big a hero here as in the States. For heavens sakes, we've all followed John Brown's activities out here. On every occasion he has fought for the cause of abolition, for the freedom of the slave, why most of us know about every raid he's made into Missouri to bring out a few Negroes and get them started on his railroad north. When he goes east to speak, we follow his travels in the newspapers. What do the reporters find so strange about that?"

"The reporters think the Whitney House proprietor knows more than he's willing to tell," said Adda. "His name has been linked to an interview published by William Phillips several months ago. It was an interview of Mr. Brown done, the writer claimed, in great secrecy, right there in one of the rooms of the Whitney House. The interview appeared in the *Boston Atlas* and one of these reporters is from the *Boston Atlas*.

"When some of the locals came to the proprietor's defense, I got the impression that each of them knew something about this arsenal fiasco but none of them seemed to have all the details, and they weren't going to let a couple of smart aleck out-of-towners push them around, but at the same time we were trying to get more details from them."

"Never mind all that, dear, what else can you tell us about Mr. Brown?" asked Mrs. Gates.

"Well the reporters showed us clippings from five or six eastern newspapers with headlines about Mr. Brown's raid, the size of his party, his capture. It seems he and his party broke into a small Federal arsenal in Virginia west of the Capitol and were able to get their hands on a huge supply of arms, powder, etc., which he intended to distribute to local slaves to foment an uprising, and the reporters say he's made no bones to his captors about his plans to continue distributing guns throughout the South for more slave insurrections. "Now here's the strange part. Instead of escaping, which apparently he could have done before daybreak, Mr. Brown and some of his party seemed to be resting or waiting for somebody or waiting for something to happen. They waited around in an old shed or warehouse for reasons nobody seems to understand. In the middle of the night while the raid was still going on a train came through the little town and stopped for water, or something. The conductor was secretly told by a local witness what had already happened. The train was allowed to pass on. At the nearest telegraph the conductor notified the authorities. Early the next day Federal troops swept in and captured the old Captain and seven of his friends. Ten or so of Mr. Brown's party were killed defending what they'd captured.

"One of the reporters said that around the arsenal there were dead bodies all over the place. It appears that Mr. Brown's party killed a few guards. There was a state of panic in the arsenal town, which is called Harper's Ferry. It's on the Potomac River and just a few miles west of the Army Camp at Frederick, Maryland. The reporters say there is deep concern in the South that Brown may have set off some slave uprisings. There is concern that several of Brown's party who escaped are Free Negroes. It is feared and speculated that they have headed south to carry out Mr. Brown's plans.

"John Kagi, who was with father in the Lecompton prison for four or five months, came back to Lawrence after he was pardoned and was often seen with Mr. Brown. The reporters said he was one of those killed in the raid, killed the second day of the raid, by U.S. Militia as he was trying to escape. When asked, the proprietor confirmed that Kagi was always with Mr. Brown when he stayed or had meetings at the Whitney House. One of the journalists said that Jim Redpath, the English reporter, was with Mr. Brown when he was killed. The other reporter disagreed on that."

Adda looked at us and said, "Did either of you know Aaron Stevens? He used to go by the name of Captain Ed Whipple. * He was one of General Lane's captains, was captured with Father in September '56 along with Mr. Kerr, Jerry Jordan" and nodding to Mrs. Gates said, "Your husband, Frank Swift and Aaron Stevens who was also veteran of the Mexican War, they were all put into the Lecompton."

"I'm surprised that with all the people we met in Tabor or a few months later in Plymouth," I remarked to Adda, "that one of them wasn't Mr. Stevens. I don't recall Father ever mentioning his name."

"He was involved escorting abolitionists into the territory over from Tabor and down from Nebraska City both summers of '55 and '56," answered Adda. "He was a close friend of John Kagi. Well, he was in the raiding party and they got him too.

"The journalists said they'd already had the trial, about a week ago, in Virginia. But I just don't believe that. I just don't think the courts can act that fast, but the reporters said, it's true. Brown and all those captured have been found guilty, but sentence has not been handed down yet."

Mrs. Gates, somberly, "Well, those Virginia proslavers will certainly hang them all, that is, if local hooligans don't break down the jail and get to them first. They hate John Brown with a passion, though I think he is more feared in the Deep South, where there are larger concentrations of slaves."

"The *Boston Atlas* reporter claims he knows both James Redpath and Richard Hinton," said Adda. "He said the two of them are out now in the States giving speeches trying to raise money and a big company of armed volunteer abolitionists to go down there and free them in the same fashion that John Brown

---

*In the Lecompton prison Aaron Stevens gave his name as Ed Whipple.

organized a company out here and obtained the release of his oldest son, John Jr., when he was in the prisoner-of-war camp in the fall of 1856. The *Boston Atlas* reporter claims that the federal government fears that they might be able to persuade a company of abolitionists from around Lawrence to join others in a plan to free the Old Captain. Virginia has already raised 4,000-armed men to prevent that. What they are really intent on preventing is a slave rebellion or an insurrection, which they fear Brown has started. The reporters speculated that if the government hangs Mr. Brown, his being martyred would spark a series of slave rebellions.

"Part of the reporter's excitement and curiosity is that when they captured him, papers in Mr. Brown's possession, implicated many of his supporters, financial backers and sympathizers including some here in Lawrence. For instance, one of the reporters stationed in St. Louis also writes for a Richmond, Virginia paper, said a letter to Richard Hinton * was found among John Brown's papers inviting him to meet the Brown party en route and to accompany the raiding party. That reporter said Hinton had been captured in Virginia a day or two after the raid and was summarily hung there. The reporters said it won't be long before the federals will be out here asking the same question they were asking today.

"They say that Ralph W. Emerson, in Boston, has written an editorial that is getting wide publicity defending Brown and Henry Ward Beecher, the preacher who caused the Sharps rifle to be called Beecher's Bibles is lecturing all over the North claiming Brown to be a national hero.

"Well, what's going to happen next?" I asked.

---

*A newspaper account said Richard Hinton was hanged in Virginia (Ref. Kansas Historical Collection Vol. 7, pg. 491.) Hinton was a reporter at the Constitutional Convention in Leavenworth in 1858. The report of his death was a case of mistaken identity. Hinton went on to organize a regiment of black soldiers for the Union Army. After the war he mustered out as a Colonel (in good health.) He later wrote several biographies of men of that period including a definitive biography of John Brown, published in 1894.

Adda, who seems to have recovered from her "preoccupation" before supper, paused, allowed a small smile and said, "Well, I certainly don't know."

But the way she said it, emphasizing I, caused me to ask, "You're not involved in any of this, are you?"

My little sister, who's obviously not so little anymore, looked at me over the flickering candle light and said, "If I were, you really wouldn't want to know, now would you?"

"Adda, this is different than hiding our notes that described the goings-on up in Plymouth."

"Oh, how is it different?"

"Well," I said, "I don't exactly know, but it's different."

Mrs. Gates came to my rescue, "Well, girls, let's clean up the table. It will be a lot easier than it was when we were feeding all those boys here two years ago," adding with a throaty chuckle, "but it won't be nearly as much fun," and she gave me a long wink and little knowing poke in the ribs.

After our sober supper, Adda went up to bed. Mrs. Gates and I had a short talk before bedtime. She invited me to stay with her the rest of the winter and to consider accepting my old job at the Cincinnati house, which she said she could arrange. The offer is both flattering and tempting but I'm so unsettled and restless I'm afraid I'd not be much of an employee. Being in Lawrence would be a good antidote to the depression of lonesomeness that comes over me at home. In Eldorado, I've become rather independent. I'm jealous of my freedom to come and go as I please. I know I gad about considerably and I'd miss that up here in Lawrence. And I've got my hands full in Eldorado. I'm ambitious enough to see if I can make a "go" of running the sawmill. The problem is, there is simply not enough building going on and what little there is, there's no cash to pay for the lumber and we have no banks to extend credit. I suppose the closest bank is here in Lawrence.

As much as I'd like to be back in Lawrence with Adda, she has her own life and I'm not sure I want to be just an employee again. I know a change of scenery and the socializing would be good medicine. But Father was always so independent and I want to see if I can work the farm.

46

PAUL, THE DISCIPLE, HAS A DISTURBING MESSAGE
November and December 1859

"I have a surprise for you," said Adda. "Reverend Perkins, the preacher who married you and Chase, is now in Lawrence, has a congregation and a church. He replaced a preacher whose wife couldn't stand the primitive conditions out here and their family returned to the States. Let's all get dressed-up tomorrow and attend his services. Mrs. Gates said she'd like to join us. I have friends you'll enjoy meeting who will be there."

The next morning, I recognized Reverend Perkins immediately. He was standing in front of the church, not a whit changed since our wedding ten or eleven months ago, handsomely greeting his arriving people on a chilly blustery overcast winter day.

By the time we got off the wagon and up to the door, those preceding us had all gone in.

As he returned my smile, it was obvious he couldn't place me or remember my name. He cleverly solved that problem by grasping my right (gloved) hand with both of his, looked past me and exchanged greetings with Mrs. Gates, noting it was a lovely day.

"You don't remember us," and pointing to me Adda said, "You married my sister, Mrs. Chase, last January out in Eldorado. You were good enough to come down from Chelsea after your

Sunday service and marry them. It was the first wedding in Eldorado. I'm Adda Stewart. I work here in town at the Whitney House. I've been attending your services, well, off and on since last summer," adding with a twinkle in her eye, "I might even join your congregation."

We filed in behind Adda, who I swear had a wave or a greeting for half the people in the congregation. She seemed to think we needed to be up close to the pulpit and walked the length of the church to be almost in front. I asked her in a soft voice if she was having trouble with her ears. Her response was to give me a little poke. I appreciated the sisterly affection, but where she poked me-and in front of all those people-was totally inappropriate. I would rather have stayed toward the back of the church.

Soon one of the deacons closed the front door and a lady organist began playing a familiar hymn on one of those little vertical, foot-pumped organs that were becoming popular in churches back in the States when we left three years ago.

The reverend rose, stood behind a short rostrum, which provided the assembly with an almost unobstructed view of him.

The church was austere in its decoration. No stained glass windows, rough ceiling beams all exposed, a one-step-up wood floor platform in front of the congregation. A framed slate mounted on a post to the right of the rostrum indicated the number in attendance last Sunday as thirty-five and that the hymns to be sung today would be numbers 27 and 65. Clearly visible from where we sat, I could read from the same slate board that today's message would be taken from Epistles of Paul. A cast-iron stove to the left in front of us had an orderly pile of wood behind it. The church seemed warm to me, though I had removed my coat. I really didn't need to be so close to the heat.

We sang another old favorite and I could hear Reverend Perkins' strong voice soar out over his congregation. After the hymn, he offered a benediction…mostly 'churchy' clichés and familiar nostrums.

He remained standing nervously, I thought, cleared his throat and said, "Friends, this morning I want to explore the concept of oppression with you and look to Paul for some guidance on handling it. And I want to read you a passage from Corinthians on the subject of charity, which some modern translators are using synonymously and I think occasionally inappropriately with the word love, love as used in the poetic sense, in the romantic sense.

"The history of oppression runs in cycles. Because of our convictions, our sympathy for the slave, the actions we have taken, we've been oppressed." He paused and looked out over his small and well-scrubbed congregation. "Every blessed soul with us today, especially those of you who came out here in '54 through '57, has been oppressed to one degree or the other by the evil forces of slavery. We were oppressed by a proslavery element that to the great surprise of many of us was to discover the oppressor was already here and that they had strong allies in the territorial courts, their friends from Missouri, the so-called Army of the West with their preferential treatment and neglect, particularly of this town, this oasis of freedom in a desert of oppression.

"And, of course, the proslavery sentiment stretched to 'high places,' the U.S. Senate and the President of the United States. And doesn't the Dred Scott Decision remind us all to include our Supreme Court in this National shame? But on a larger scale that oppression is puny and quite tolerable, compared to the oppression still imposed on a class of people we have been championing, which we intend ultimately to liberate by the strength of our convictions.

"However in the recent two years, my friends, the tide has turned and although the slave is still the slave, those of us who came out here for the cause of freedom, freedom from slavery in this territory, we've turned the tide, yes, thank God. With great sacrifices we've turned the tide. Only a handful of men, great and small, related or known to all of us, have by bravery, perseverance, the force of arms and sacrifice, put a stop to that oppression. And the balance of us has done our duty by being here, by supporting them, and by voting. Oh, how many times have our votes been counted? And finally a year or so ago all those votes for freedom were piled on one pan of the great democratic scales of justice. The proslavery votes were piled on the other pan and what happened my friends? Well let me tell you again what happened," and his voice took on a shaking thunder "freedom won. There will be no slavery in this territory and when we become a state, there will be no slavery in the new State of Kansas." I could hardly control my emotions knowing that my father helped bring that about and is not with us to enjoy his effort.

A murmur of amen welled up from the congregation coupled with, "Praise God" on my right side, half of the congregation stood. Just because others were standing, I saw no need to."

Reverend Perkins stretched both arms out over his flock and motioned them to be seated. "Now we will be faced with a new problem while finding ways to cope with the old problem that brought us all across the prairies. The new problem I want you to think about is charity-love. We must find it in our hearts to forgive and then treat with love those who oppressed us."

He looked out over his small flock. "Ah, ha, I see consternation. I see a frown here and there. Forgive them! Many of you, who have suffered and lost, loved ones, say 'never!' I understand that emotion. It's human. But we must rise above it and find it in our hearts first to forgive, then to offer charity, to extend a hand of Christian fellowship."

Adda poked me. She reached over and pulled my head toward hers and whispered, "If he thinks I'll ever forgive Hildebrand, he's wasting his breath."

The preacher seemed to look directly at Adda and me and said, "As hard as it's been on us, dear friends, we've broken no new historical ground here in Kansas. We've uncovered no new form of treachery. Not even a new form of oppression have we discovered. All those who have gone on before us have, over the centuries, covered this ground," and he dropped his voice.

He opened the big Bible before him and in a soft voice said, "Let us see what Paul, Paul the wisest of the disciples…let us see how in Corinthians Paul would advise treating this problem.

"Citing Leviticus Paul speaks directly to us that faith, not law, is the basis of life, every last abolitionist of us resent that slavery is condoned by law, the Constitution, and indeed is upheld by our elected President. Paul would find a metaphor linking Israel's condition during his time when Roman Centurions were backed by Roman law emanating from the Roman Senate and Caesar Augustus. Their Empire included Israel at the time of Christ and continued fifty years later during Paul's time. Comes now our Roman Centurion, our equivalent to Pontius Pilate, seated in Leavenworth with orders not from Rome but Washington, orders that in the execution amounted to oppression. In Paul's day it was no different except it was carried out on a much grander scale, for all of the known world, except Asia, was under Roman Rule; and thousands of people in their empire were slaves.

"Well, I tell you in the spirit of Paul, our Supreme Court's ruling and its social and economic policy is wrong and it shall be struck down by our faith-our presence," and he allowed himself a little smile of forbearance and added, "by the exercise of our brand of Popular Sovereignty." As he paused to refer to his notes another chorus of audible "Amen" welled up from his congregation. Someone directly behind me said, "Yes, yes, thank the Lord." Although I agreed with them, I wasn't sure that it was necessary to affirm it verbally, audibly…not in church. It disturbs the solemnity, frays the dignity and is mildly irritating. I've never appreciated or approved of these spontaneous oral confirmations from the congregation. It smacks of Southern Baptists, reminds me of hot summer evenings in tents and sanctimonious Midwest revivalists. By pausing, I thought Reverend Perkins seemed to encourage them. It seemed to please his vanity.

He continued, "Almost 1,500 years before the birth of Christ there was another cycle of oppression to be confronted and that story is a keystone in our culture.

"Moses, born a Jew but raised in the opulence of the pharaoh's palace, ultimately gathered up his people and fled Egypt and its oppression.

"The oppressor, history shows, almost always has the law on his side.

"Moses was not long beyond the Red Sea before he realized he needed a new set of laws to improve the behavior and change the culture of his followers who had spent all those years in Egypt.

"When Moses came down off the mountain, he had a new set of laws, so profound in their simplicity that they continue to serve us 3,500 years later.

"Moses taught us that in fleeing oppression we must look for and obey a higher law than those imposed by the oppressor. That lesson applies to us and to our noble experiment here in Kansas."

Reverend Perkins used a long pause to refer to his notes and resumed, "The second message of Paul is more difficult. Though we are succeeding politically in this territorial contest and that success has come about painfully because we decided to follow a higher law. In finding our way, the new way, we should look to Scriptures for guidance.

"We must deal with our hard-won fragile success charitably-with love for one another, particularly for those with whom we have such profound difference, otherwise as Paul tells us, we've accomplished nothing.

"Oh, my friends, these are difficult times, just as were the early days of what we now call the Christian era.

"As a Jew, Jesus was very concerned with what he saw as corruption in the old established church and believed, as did his disciples, it was time for change-for reform. After all, some 1,500 years had lapsed since Moses came down off the mountain with what was then a set of new laws calling for behavior entirely different from the practices they learned and followed all those years they were in Egypt.

"In addition to reform, Jesus and his followers had another, probably more pressing problem at the time and that was the Roman occupation of their land, the Roman subjugation and oppression of his people and how to cope personally with this Roman oppression.

"And finally, dear friends, I want to examine with you one of Paul's central themes, a theme that distinguishes Jesus and his disciples of the New Testament from Moses and the Old Testament: the concept of charity, the lesson that Christ tries to teach us in the Sermon on the Mount, to love one another."

It was the Reverend Perkins' opinion that Paul more than any of the other Apostles argued for and explained Christ's teachings on love, for which various translators and some Christian denominations occasionally substitute the word Charity and vice versa. "In our time the Mormons," he said, "define charity as the highest, noblest, strongest kind of love. Heaven knows they have not been dealt with charitably in this country. Their concept of charity does not denote mere alms giving; it does not denote a mere act or deed-nor benevolence. He said it was too bad that translation from the Greek to the English resulted in such limited vocabulary that it makes the word love cover so many aspects of human behavior including in this case charity." His remark quickly called to my mind Mrs. Weibley's similar observation as she offered comfort and solace after Chase died in distinguishing between the love I had for Father and the love between Chase and me. I seemed to have a momentary spasm of anguish as I realized that the physical love that Chase and I knew was gone, yet in his absence I seem to love him all the more. I was aware that a tear rolled down my cheek.

After that lapse, I resumed following Reverend Perkins' thought and was soon taken up with his excellent dissertation, particularly since I wasn't all that informed on Paul, but had remembered a smattering of Corinthians. He was obviously an excellent public speaker and we were up close, and the church was warmer than it needed to be whether I liked it or not.

He continued, "We are fortunate that Paul was so well-educated that the Christian literature has been forever enhanced by Paul's ability to write so well, that if we look we can find instruction from Paul in every aspect of our daily lives, physical and spiritual." Pausing occasionally, he said, "Our current noble experiment" (I suppose he meant the abolitionists coming to Kansas), "sacrifice has been experienced by all, suffered by many and some of us have learned to cope with death and its consequences…yet Paul speaks of hope and admonishes us not to indulge excessively in grief for when our loved ones die, they will see Christ." That idea was so applicable to me that it was a distraction again and in the contemplation of resurrection of seeing Father and Chase, I missed his next few sentences and dwelled on a sentence of my own that I thought he should have used, but didn't.

"Blessed are they that mourn for theirs is the Kingdom of Heaven."

I thought, since Chase's death, losing him, then losing the baby, there have been moments when I've considered the Kingdom of Heaven to what life on earth will be without him. I felt the preacher's words were aimed directly at me and in my grief over Chase I saw no hope, no redemption in my despair except eventual resurrection.

I recommended paying attention just as the pastor was saying that Paul assures us that out of grief comes hope, but it was difficult for me to concentrate.

"Paul now instructs us with unusual eloquence in some of God's most basic blessings and he does it by making comparisons with blessings we have with those we might not have. In First Corinthians chapter 13 Paul says,

Though I speak with Tongues of Angels and have not Love, my expression is as insignificant as a tinkling bell.

Though I have the gift of Faith to understand Mystery … a Faith to move mountains.

If I have not love, I am nothing."

For me, those two lines ended his sermon. That's all I heard. "If I have not love, I am nothing." The words, like hammers hitting a huge bell reverberated like an echo in the canyons of my mind. The way I heard Paul's words explained my predicament in a nutshell. I have lost my true love: I am nothing, a spiritually reprehensible nothing. Worthless.

Of course, I interpreted that phrase in a self-centered self-serving way and it stunned me. As Chase's dying gasps and moans stabbed my heart, Reverend Perkins' words were hurled like a Corinthian spear from his rostrum stabbing into my brain.

I had the sensation of suffocating. My ears were ringing; my throat went so dry I thought I'd choke. Suddenly I became very thirsty. The Church was warmer than it needed to be and I was not comfortable being up front.

My only reaction was to flee, to gather up my skirts and leave. Though there was a center aisle, I was closer to the left side and I stumbled past Mrs. Gates, Adda and another couple. In leaving, I was quick and indifferent to any disturbance I might be causing.

Outside I was able to catch my breath and I walked away briskly, didn't care which direction, just walked away, with his words, with Paul's condemnation delivered by Reverend Perkins ringing in my ears.

"Though I speak with Tongues of men…and have not love, I am nothing.

Though I have faith…can move mountains… and have not love, I am nothing."

I have no idea how long I walked around the neighborhood chewing on Paul's condemnation of me, before I came to my senses and asked someone for directions.

When I got back to the church, Adda, Sammy and Mrs. Gates were in the wagon, waiting. The overcast weather had not changed. It was chilly and windy. It was not a "lovely day."

I signaled an excuse and walked into the empty church. Reverend Perkins was alone in the wooden pews busily folding up hymnals and putting them away. My walking in was audible and he looked up.

As I approached him intending to apologize for the disturbance, I sensed that he knew some part of his sermon had been the cause for my temporary loss of control, that I had no alternative but to leave, in suffocating panic to flee; but as I stood there facing him, I knew I couldn't articulate that, nor should I expect any help from him in the comprehension of my behavior, so I stood there a few seconds, gathering my senses and said, "I'm afraid I took your message too personally. You see, my husband died just a few weeks ago. You had no way of knowing that. I'm bothered that it might not have been his disease that killed him. I'm beginning to think it was wrong medication: bad, inept doctoring. But he's gone and occasionally I slip into a terrible state of despair…I'm not at all sure I'm strong enough to bear this burden. I just can't seem to get over it…and I paused to decide the limits of what else I cared to reveal but was conscious that I didn't want to impose on the poor soul twice in one morning, but I did want to try to explain what it was that caused me to leave before it was time.

The preacher came to my rescue. We were now almost face-to-face with the back of a pew between us. He said, "Yes, I recall I was closing my message with Paul's remarks about charity and love, when you left. I wanted to dwell on Paul's admonishment about the importance of love."

I thought, I don't need to hear this again, so I nervously interrupted, "I see Paul's appraisal here as an intolerable condemnation of those of us who mourn, who are grieving. For you to tell me that though I have faith but have not love, I am nothing …that is such a condemnation, is so intolerable it only adds to this burden of grief that can occasionally overwhelm me…as it did in your church this morning."

There was a long silent pause, as tears welled in my eyes, but I had found the strength to say it. I could see he was trying to help me but he was also trying to find a buffered way to explain Paul that was not so disturbing to me.

He said, "First, Mrs. Chase, I can't tell you how sorry I am about your loss. After your wedding in Eldorado, I was so pleased to read a few days later in Chelsea that I had performed the first wedding ceremony in Eldorado and prayed to God for guidance about locating a church there or in Chelsea.

"Now let me give you some comfort. You've interpreted Paul's message too narrowly, maybe even mistakenly, and I can understand why. Paul didn't mean if we were personally denied love that denial rendered us insignificant. He meant as a people if we possessed all these other virtues and abilities and talents, but can't show charity, if we can't love one another including our defeated adversaries, then our other accomplishments and talents amount to nothing. You need to think about this more broadly, philosophically. I'm afraid you took my message too personally, but I must say I'm flattered that you were paying such close attention."

Lately I thought I was getting over Chase's death. Little measurements of my attitude and social behavior confirmed it. I was enjoying company a little more. I wasn't so panicky about the prospect of my own company if I didn't have a boarder or visitor for the evening or better yet, an overnight stay. I was laughing a little more. I refound humor in small things again and so I thought the wound was healing. But this morning in church, the solemn music, the preacher's words, well chosen and intentionally, designed to evoke strong emotion, worked to make me aware that I was still vulnerable. And the preacher, if he'd used a knife, couldn't have opened that wound more painfully than he did this morning by using those condemning words of Paul, "That without love, you, Augusta Stewart, you are nothing! You have been spiritually ostracized and that's from an authority no less than the Apostle Paul."

Even now I'm not sure I heard everything he said, I attempted a smile and said, "I noticed, sir, that you referred to notes, that you turned a few pages during your sermon. I'm wondering if I could borrow them. I'm writing a Journal and I'd like permission to use your notes. I'm spending a few days in Lawrence with my sister and the Gates Family. I'll return them before I go back to Eldorado."

He said, "Certainly." He turned, walked up the center aisle to his rostrum, gathered three or four pages of notes, returned and handed them to me and said, "Mrs. Chase, I want to give you a little assignment. I want you to read the first and second Corinthians, before returning my notes and I want to spend twenty minutes with you reviewing this assignment. We will both learn something from it. Paul's metaphors are the most profound in the New Testament. And maybe we should discuss some parts of the Book of Job. Are you familiar with that old testament story, Mrs. Chase?" I thought, why is it that every Christian, whom I meet, who learns of my loss, seems to need to instruct me that if I can comprehend Job, I can suddenly find an answer to my dilemma?

I made a mental note to study both Corinthians and the Book of Job, whether I could do it before returning, I wasn't sure.

The apology and the discussion calmed me down but left me very introspective. I'm afraid I was not much company on the ride back to the Gateses' place.

I left Lawrence early enough on November 22nd to get to Lecompton during daylight hours, where I arrived a little after noon on a nasty cold snowy day. In the old stone Territorial Capital Building, I inquired where Judge Lecompte had his office. He was still the chief territorial judge, though Judge Cato, who tried and convicted the prisoners-of-war in '56, had resigned.

Locating the room, I spoke with an officer of the court who was familiar with the Diggle Bank fraud case. I told him I was from the Stewart family who first settled up in Plymouth and later founded Eldorado, where I currently live, run a farm and a sawmill. I was surprised to learn that the case was identified as a territorial criminal case and might be tried by Judge Elmore, who usually presides over at Leavenworth. Judge Lecompte, who is the chief judge of this court and for that matter remains the chief judge of the whole territory, is rabidly proslavery and had been appointed by Franklin Pierce.

I asked the gentleman, whom the plaintiff was in the Diggle case, attempting to see if the bank had a legal interest or not. With some impatience he informed me that in criminal cases the plaintiff isn't named. I asked if Mr. Diggle was named defendant. He said, "I suppose so, and that's not his real name."

I asked the gentleman if the nine or ten of us who had been embezzled were named plaintiffs or would we be subpoenaed as witnesses. With some contrived impatience he said, "No! I jes' tole you, in a criminal case nobody gets named plaintiff."

I decided not to pursue my second question. Then I inquired about what steps I needed to take to appear in Court as either plaintiff or as witness for the prosecution, if it's a criminal case. It took me a while to figure out that this gentleman with a strong Southern accent had no intention to be cooperative or informative. After I had been in his presence a full ten minutes, he seemed to pause and carefully scrutinize me. He asked me if I was related to the territorial legislator out in Eldorado, named Stewart, Sam Stewart? I quietly said, "He was my father."

Then I asked him how he knew Father and he said, "Your father was a real trouble maker when we had him as a prisoner in the fall of '56 over there in the 'Yard'," and he pointed east, down hill toward the old camp site.

The gentleman said that he was Sheriff Jones' commissary officer, when the sheriff was warden. He said, "I was the one who gave your father permission to take a team of government horses and the prison wagon up to Lawrence and other abolitionists pest holes to look for donations of food, clothing and supplies for the prisoners. It was my act of Christian charity that probably kept your Father and a good many other…stinking abolitionists… alive that winter. You know we lost a few of your father's friends that winter… not enough of 'em to suit me. You know what I got for my generosity? Nothing! Not a single thank you, not even from your father!"

"Well, for heaven's sake, he went out like that looking for supplies because the supplies the Army and the territorial agency responsible for running the camp, did supply were inadequate. I read Richard Hinton's article on conditions in that camp," I replied.

I knew there was no point in pursuing either topic. I said, "Sir, I will file a formal request with the judge to be named plaintiff or as witness in the upcoming trial of the gentleman who embezzled bank funds and I'll send a copy of my letter to Governor Medory."

"You do that," and he aimed a wad of tobacco juice at a spittoon I couldn't see and rubbed the remaining juice in his mustache on his sleeve. He continued, "He really didn't defraud the bank, you know, just a bunch of dumb abolitionists, mostly west of here. I don't think the bank intends to press charges."

"What makes you think that?" I questioned. "'Cause the bank gets lots of business from the territorial government and it would be kinda dumb of the bank to aggravate the 'establishment.'"

Well, of course, he meant the in-place proslavery establishment. It was turning dark in more ways than one as I left

Lecompton late that afternoon, heading home, with plans on making three or four stops on the way.

47

Eldorado's First School "Marm"
December to Christmas Eve, 1859

It was November 27th before I got back from Lawrence. It seemed to take forever to get the house warmed up. Cleaning up was so depressing that I couldn't bear the idea of spending the night here alone, so I decided late in the day to go up and visit the Cordises. They invited me for supper and I stayed the night with them.

Tom's blacksmithing business is very slow. He thinks he's too far west. The business he does get is mostly from the wagon trains going north and west through here.

About midmorning, I rode up the river to the Martins' place, got there in time for supper and stayed the night.

Mr. Martin has accumulated quite an inventory of logs. Some are stored at our place and some at his. We talked about starting up the mill to saw his lumber. I told him the biggest problem is simply feeding the boilers' fire box enough wood while waiting hours for all the boiler water to get ready to "go to work" and the colder it is, the longer it takes. Well, Mr. Martin knows all that. I told him that when I go back home, I'll get Pete Gillespie to commence a fire in the boiler but he should wait a full day before coming down. He said he'd use that time to sled logs down. I told him I'd be happy to keep steam-up on the boiler full time if there was enough building business in Eldorado to justify it but there isn't, and that's been a disappointment. What I didn't tell him was that more than half the wood, we do saw, is sawed on credit, long credit. I'm still waiting for payments on the Watt's job and those were delivered months ago.

During supper, Mr. and Mrs. Martin graciously suggested I stay with them the balance of the winter. It's an attractive offer since the three of us think alike about the importance of manners and behavior out here on the frontier but I think I like my personal privacy too much to be comfortable in that arrangement.

After I helped Mrs. Martin clear the table, we had a nice tea with her elegant English "service;" it was over tea that Mr. Martin brought up a rather sobering suggestion. He's English and very formal, addressing me always as Mrs. Chase. He asked if I'd ever consider selling our share of the sawmill. Father told me on more than one occasion that "we" own the "lion's share" of the sawmill. I suppose one of Mr. Martin's motives in the discussion was to remind me that he owns a share in it and I quickly wondered if I could find a record of what he paid for it…and indeed if he has paid it.

I said his question had never entered my head. He explained that he could simply buy out the Stewart share and wouldn't disturb the ownership of the remaining shareholders.

I made him this promise: that if I did decide to move, perhaps back to Lawrence to be with Adda, he would be the first to know. I also told him I had to consider some loyalty to Jerry Jordan who, in my husband's absence, has been the major saw operator.

He said, "Mrs. Chase, don't confuse providing ordinary income to a loyal worker with partial ownership of the enterprise."

He must know something I don't know. I don't see any confusion here at all. I'll have to look through Father's papers to see if I can find what share of the sawmill Mr. Martin owns and also what the size was of the total investment. I don't think I want to ask him those questions and reveal I don't know.

I left their place the next day mid morning and stopped at the Schaeffer's for dinner, where Mrs. McKinney was also visiting. The McKinney's came into Eldorado early enough to vote for Father and the Minneola Constitution and they knew Chase. The Schaeffers and McKinneys both have school-age children.

Mrs. McKinney told me that a committee of Congregationalists from Ohio had tried without success to get Reverend Perkins, the preacher who married Chase and me, to choose our area over Chelsea. I explained I'd just come back from Lawrence and discovered that Reverend Perkins had settled the matter by deciding that we are all too remote.

She went on to tell me that a committee of local parents had held a recent meeting and decided now that Eldorado and vicinity has an adult population of almost one hundred, it's time that we begin to think about a school for the children.

The Committee asked Mrs. McKinney to contact me towards starting a school and that they would rely on her opinion to determine if I was qualified for the job. It seems that Mrs. McKinney had already commenced her inquiry. She knew that most of my formal education had been in private schools back in the States. She was aware that I kept the books for Father's various ventures, that occasionally I did the arithmetic in Father's "Form Book," the book he used to enter in his surveyor's raw field data. She also knew that I had the Town ledger that showed the original cost and balance, many of them delinquent, owed on each land claim. From Dr. Weibley she discovered I have a smattering of Latin, which I presume is more than most of Eldorado's citizens. Well, in the "land of the blind, the one-eyed is king!"

I was flattered; of course, that the Committee was considering me and that she'd already begun her inquiries. She said that Elizabeth Cordis had given her an inventory of the books in my personal library, which with raised eyebrows she labeled, impressive. In looking over the list she said, "Just who is Stendhal?"

This, of course, told me more about her than vice versa. I wondered what she would report to the Committee if she knew that Howland had given me, before he left, a copy of Daniel DeFoe's *Moll Flanders*. My edition, imported through Philadelphia, had been published in England. When publishers attempted to print it in the states, Boston banned it. Well, I've read it, indeed, some of the spicier chapters twice. An interesting tale but really quite unbelievable, whereas, the three different translations of *Minon Lescaut* by Abbé Prévost were equally spicy and also previously condemned by the Church, but it is really more believable, though tragic.

Oh, yes, someone had incorrectly reported that I won the lyceum debate two years ago. That was Adda, of course. But Mrs. McKinney was enjoying her authority and speaking so fast I decided the correction could wait.

In discussing where to locate the school, Mrs. McKinney preferred I do the teaching up her way or more precisely that we locate the school up-valley. I wasn't opposed to that. In fact, we both acknowledged that her location might attract some scholars from the outskirts of Chelsea. I told her I'd prefer to do it at my place, at least for a year or so. We have by far the largest house in Eldorado and there are other practical considerations in locating the school elsewhere, like heating the schoolroom in the winter. Who starts the fire? Who provides the wood? In the winter my house will be warm. I'm not keen on riding a horse or a buggy some distance in the early morning winter snow and wind to another location, then putting up with the bother of building a fire and getting the place halfway livable before the scholars arrive. I'd probably have to carry my own wood. And I insist on a floor in the schoolroom, and I don't mean a dirt floor. I'm not going to run Eldorado's first school in a cabin with a dirt floor, constantly on guard for snakes.

We have an uncivilized domestic problem here on the prairie, so embarrassing we rarely talk about it; namely, snakes. Snakes, big ones and several varieties including two varieties of Rattlers insist on sharing our quarters, particularly if the cabin has a dirt floor. They come and go as though they own the place.

I was in the Cordis house after Tom put a floor down in the kitchen. His flooring, which we sawed, contained knots. In time, as the wood dried, the knots loosened and fell out leaving a few knotholes. I can recall sitting in their parlor last summer and watching a snake stick his shiny head and two or three inches of his body up into the kitchen to survey its prospects. I quietly mentioned it to Elizabeth. She said, "Oh, that pest is back again, is he?" and she located Tom's long barreled pistol, took careful aim, fired and missed. Of course, the snake disappeared. On close scrutiny I made two observations: three bullet holes in the wall near the floor meant she'd either killed snakes previously... or missed. I noticed Tom had nailed little tin can lids over other holes in her floor.

I said, "Elizabeth, why hasn't Tom covered up this hole?" She laughed, and came close to me and said softly, so's Tom couldn't hear, "Augusta, shooting that old pest, you just saw... is my second favorite indoor sport," and she gave me a little affectionate poke in the ribs. She still had a big grin on her face and continued to hold Tom's long pistol.

Several days later, as I recalled that event, it dawned on me that Elizabeth Cordis' remark was her attempt at humor between two young married women...except I'm now a widow.

But returning to the class of dwelling we should choose for Eldorado's first school, I said I don't intend to have an arithmetic lesson interrupted by a visiting prairie snake, and I'm certainly not going to carry a side arm into a classroom of scholars to exterminate them.

Returning to our interview, I asked who'd provide my pay, reciting the offer I had, to remain in Tabor and teach for $100 per year, though the Iowa school year was only seven and a half months. She said, "We haven't decided whether to pay by the season or by the scholar."

My response was, "I preferred a mutual commitment, a commitment by me to teach for a term and a commitment by Eldorado to pay me for a term."

Mrs. McKinney, "You mean you should get $100 per year whether there are four or fourteen?" "Yes."

I learned later, neither plan was very good. We have no taxes to support anything: schools, a sheriff, town streets, etc., so we'll need the beginnings of a city or county government to do this and, of course, we lack these. In the meantime, the parents will have to pay the bills and cash is in short supply out here.

So, absent a local government, if individual families want their children educated, we should meet again and decide what it's worth to each family...and what it's worth to me. Once I open my house to the town's offspring, my cost and bother is pretty much all the same whether I have four scholars or fourteen.

This issue was not resolved but Mrs. McKinney said she'd discuss it with the school committee.

I said, "Well, you're now informed about teacher rates in Western Iowa. Trying to be both humorous and to control this part of the interview I said, "Rates this far west might be a little higher." I had made up my mind to accept their offer to teach but I wouldn't do it for less than $100 per year.

Mr. Schaeffer invited me to stay over and I accepted. I left their place the next day delighted that my mind was distracted from my sorrows by an entirely new stimulating idea-teaching. The prospects, would in time, I hoped banish the persistent twin despairs, that have plagued me since the deaths of Father and Chase. Absent schoolbooks, I will spend the time until they arrive by doing a lot of classroom exercises. I will emphasize arithmetic and spelling. When the books come we'll include reading.

I gave some thought, or really fantasies, to a suitable curriculum. We will read from the classics including the Old and New Testaments. We'll examine in great detail the Ten Commandments and various psalms. We'll try to understand the Beatitudes. There are a dozen stories in the Old Testament whose lessons we'll explore and some that we won't explore: such as God's strange intervention in brotherly love, as revealed in the Cain and Abel story. The daughters of Laban, Leah and Rachel, and the differences in their romance with one of our first polygamists…well at least a bigamist, Jacob. Adam and Eve have too much unexplainable mystery for me to present; likewise Samson and Delilah or King David's dalliance with Bathsheba. (I always wondered what she was doing out there on her open-air verandah bathing in her "all together" in sight of what she had to know was the King's palace. And I've never forgiven David for his arrogant handling of that affair, even though it produced Solomon.

We will discuss Jacob's love for Rachel and their son, Joseph in Egypt and, of course, Moses and his leadership of all those Jews to their Promised Land. I will proudly point out to my scholars that Moses is the first abolitionist in our culture. I will point out to my scholars that as modern day abolitionists, what we all have in common with Moses out here in the Kansas Territory.

Moses, of course, after his rescue from the "bull rushes," was raised as a prince in the pharaohs court and had a position of authority, but he seemed always to be nagged by the knowledge that "his people," all 600,000 of them, were slaves, so it was some sacrifice for Moses to sever his high-placed connections, gather-up a huge population of Jews and lead them to Zion.

It was his position of leadership under the pharaoh that gave him the confidence that he could indeed inspire the Jews to leave and could lead them back to Israel, though I doubt he could have done it without that lecture on leadership that his father-in-law, Jethro, gave him.

The modern analogy is, many abolitionists, particularly those who uprooted their businesses and careers and families and came to fight slavery and to fight against it were really modern day Moses…and I wondered if we were now in the equivalent of the biblical wilderness shaking off the old established customs and finding new ways.

On the way home I was so mentally stimulated about my new prospects I stopped by Conner's Store to inquire if he had any slates. He did and with some assumed authority I ordered twelve. He had four in stock and I like their shape (eight by ten inches), dark green Vermont slate held in a wood frame. Fractions converted to decimals have been printed on part of one side of the frame. The ABCs in upper and lower case occupy all four sections of the frame on the other side. We'll use soapstone or chalk for writing; whichever is available. Conner has both. That will be nice for the younger ones. I suggested he send the bill for all twelve and a box of chalk to the Eldorado Education Committee.

When I told Mr. Conner about the interview and my plans, he smiled and said he knew something about it. Mrs. McKinney had approached him, he said, and he heartily recommended me!

As I prepared to leave, I mentioned to Mr. Conner, "I do believe this will be the western-most school in North America."

"What about Texas and California?" he replied. "Don't you suppose those people who were in Texas before the War with Mexico and those Gold Seekers who went through here ten years ago have schools by now?"

I conceded and made another attempt at uniqueness by saying, "Well, then we'll be the western-most school in the Kansas Territory."

Mr. Conner smiled, "I'll give you that, Mrs. Chase, unless the Army has a school at Fort Riley."

Even though Chase has been dead almost three months, I still derive some deep personal satisfaction by being addressed as Mrs. Chase.

It was getting late in the day and I invited Mr. Conner to come by for supper. He closed-up his shop and we drove to our claim in his wagon. I'm afraid it wasn't much of a supper. In addition, the cabin was cold when we walked in and that was a nuisance.

The next day a flurry of snow and its constant companion, the Kansas prairie wind, blew Mr. Weinbury all the way down from Chelsea, where they boast a new post office. He brought a package of mail, which included a couple Eastern newspapers.

One letter was addressed to Chase from Jerry Jordan who's in Chelsea, an unpleasant reminder of just how long it's been since he left our place running the sawmill and moved to Chelsea to run the grist mill up there and a letter from Adda.

Snow blew in all over everything. Mr. Weinbury knew Chase and knew Chase had died. Pointing to it hanging on the wall, he wanted to know if I would sell him the guitar? First, I had to get over being offended, and then I realized it was a reasonable question. While I was pondering his question, he said that Mr. William Woodruff (also from Chelsea) had died and asked if I knew him.

"No," I said.

"Well, he was an abolitionist and a politician your father knew."

Returning to his question about the guitar, I said that was Chase's guitar.

"I know that, but I don't suppose you play it and I think I can learn. With Chase dead it seemed practical to me to make an offer to buy his guitar and that's why I brought your mail down." He paused, looked at me and said, "My offer to buy the guitar has hurt your feelings. You're upset about giving it up. I'm really sorry about Chase." And in his embarrassment he turned away from me and became overly concerned fumbling with buttoning his coat, which he hadn't taken off, wrapping his scarf more tightly around his neck and while all this conspicuous dressing up was going on he simply turned on his heel, opened the door and left.

He had been here for such a short time; little clumps of unmelted snow fell off his clothing on his way out. I followed him to the door but couldn't find anything to say-nor he to me. I don't know why I didn't bring myself to shout a "thank you" for the mail and the newspapers but I didn't, I guess, because I found his motive to bring the mail down offensive, even though he had gone out of his way to bring it down, and in such miserable weather.

The proslavery territorial establishment is still intent on denying us these basic services, like the post, though I guess I should find a little gratitude that we have a new post office this far west, even if it's in Chelsea. It's there only because the post office in Archer had closed. I don't know who the politician was that obtained the post office for Chelsea but you can bet your bottom dollar if my father were alive, that post office would be here in Eldorado, probably in our house (*added later* "In '61 or '62 Eldorado did get a post office. It was located in Mr. Conner's store.)

I heard that Archer had been laid out on land that included an Indian reservation, mislocated by faulty surveying, hence the reason for abandoning the settlement. In Plymouth it was common knowledge, though never, ever spoken, that Archer was a north bound "stop" on the Underground Railroad and John Brown also used that route north. So, maybe the proslavery establishment used the faulty surveys as a way to eliminate Archer as a stop on the Underground Railroad. Little do they know?

Adda and I, when we were living that winter with the Strongs, often quietly speculated that the mister was involved in this project, but one simply didn't ask those questions. It was too dangerous. Captain Henry, when he visited us in Plymouth from the Pony Creek Army Camp, made it crystal clear that aiding fugitive slaves was a serious offense and could, if prosecuted, lead to a death penalty. I can't imagine their killing a white man for that offense, but it was a threat we all took very seriously, especially since the people enforcing that law were all proslavery and knowing our proclivities on the subject would have been delighted to "catch us in the act." Of course, the trail to Archer was a north-south section of Lane's Trail. That was no secret.

As I watched Mr. Weinbury ride off on his horse in little whirlwinds of snow, I knew I couldn't stand in the doorway bareheaded with the snow blowing in like it was, so I closed the door and turned to the pleasant prospects of the mail, particularly, Adda's letter.

Lawrence, KS Terr. Dec. 13, 1859.
Dear Augusta,

In the middle of a raging blizzard yesterday something neat happened and I want to tell you about it.

Do you remember last August when that Russell, Majors and Waddell Freight outfit, bound for Santa Fe came and waited several days for repairs in Eldorado? Father was gone; he was back here politicking. Remember how well dressed they were with their red and white plaid cotton shirts and yellow bandannas. I remember 'cause it was your 19th birthday, August 8th a year and a half ago. They had ten loaded wagons and sixty mules, bound for Fort Riley and other forts down on the Santa Fe. Some of their mules needed shoeing and two or three of their wagons needed some blacksmithing. While Tom Cordis made the repairs, the wagon boss asked about buying a claim in town. He was worried that, when the railroads link-up Chicago and St. Louis with all the western forts, their freighting days with mules would be numbered. He was looking for a place to settle down and was considering Eldorado.

I went over there nearly every day often taking them some milk and eggs, and I'll confess I enjoyed a little devilish delight when I discovered that my visits made Frank jealous. You'll recall on one of those visits I came home with one of their heavy plaid shirts, which I still have.

The first day I got to know one of the "skinners," nicknamed Davenport by riding with him up to Tom Cordis' to inquire about the repairs, they needed. They called him Davenport because he had a girl friend in Davenport, Iowa. You'll recall he was a little older than me. I arranged to be over there when I knew he had to harness-up the mules and I'd offer to help him. I learned to cuss the way muleskinners cuss. I picked up some pretty salty language from Ol' Davenport, which, of course, is old news to you.

He and the wagon boss were in town yesterday.

They were on their way up to Leavenworth to pick-up another westbound load. Remember, they had a two-year contract. The boss gets his mail at the Whitney house and they took their noon meal with us. It was really nice to see them again. They weren't looking forward to this next job because the weather is <u>so</u> bad. The boss gave Davenport yesterday afternoon and evening off. The blizzard kept-up all night so they didn't leave to catch-up with their outfit 'til this morning and it was snowing when they left.

Yesterday afternoon I walked with him down to Dagarian's where he had his likeness taken: first time. We had a nice visit. He's really a very interesting fellow.

Last night after supper I got off early and we went up to a "Hop" at the Eldridge House. We came back about 10 PM. Dancing is so popular in Lawrence now, they had two "Hops" going on last night, the other one was at Turner's hall. Both places were full and a regular Kansas blizzard going on outside. Can you beat that?

He and the boss stayed here last night. He's really funny: I had sore ribs from laughing so much and you'll be relieved to know that when he's away from the mules, he doesn't swear at all.

Well, his Iowa romance has cooled way off. It seems while he was away on freight jobs, this girl friend was carrying on with another skinner, actually a friend of his. Early this fall, she got married but not to "Davenport."

He wants to see me again; probably when he comes by to pick up his likeness from Dagarian's. He thinks I'm a little older than I really am. So if they come through Eldorado in the next few weeks, and the subject comes up, you needn't be too specific about my age or yours for that matter. He thinks we're both three or four years older than we really are! Oh, yes! He said to send warm regards to my big sister out on the Walnut. They're enclosed.

Adda

P.S: By the way, he's from Pennsylvania. His real name is McNair (Scotch) and first name is Marion: cute, eh?

The New Hampshire paper, *Independent Democrat*, that I notice costs one cent, carried a notice of Albert Chase, son of Albert M. and Sarah Chase, age 18 years and 10 months, dying of typhus. (So Chase's younger brother is dead but this article leads me to believe his mother has survived, in spite of the hurry-home-your-mother is dying letter last July 29th, that propelled Chase east, though, thank heavens, he didn't get any farther than Lawrence. Several pages of the paper are missing. No doubt that section interested some post office or letter carrier between New Hampshire and Eldorado.

It started out to be a lonely Christmas Day, although the weather was rather pleasant. About 10 AM, a girl so young and small I wondered how she got up on a horse, came in and inquired if I was Mrs. Stewart and handed me a note, unsigned except it began at the top with the word "urgent" and ended with "urgent." It was written by (or for) our old neighbor to the south, Mary Rackliffe. She was concerned that she might "deliver" today and hoped I'd would come down and help. The Rackliffes came out here in '57 when we did and we've been friends ever since. Since she attended my wedding, I did wonder why the letter was addressed to Mrs. Stewart.

I told the girl to ride back down and tell them I'd be there directly. Actually I wanted to see if Elizabeth Cordis would go with me. She's had two babies and is much more informed on these matters than I.

As I put on my winter coat in preparation for going out, I was momentarily gripped with a spasm of pure joy, a wave of elation…that someone had asked for my help, that someone needed me, that being asked to help Mary Rackliffe with delivering her baby meant I wasn't on an isolated island. It was of course, more complicated than that. I've been afraid that in my widowhood and without Father as an anchor, I would become a social pariah. Widows and orphans don't fit in. Society knows it and the widow knows it.

In riding Old Kate up to Cordis', the day suddenly looked brighter, I became radiantly happy that I wouldn't be alone on Christmas Day but I soon realized it wasn't just that. The real happiness came from knowing that a neighbor out here on this isolated frontier had asked for my help and I was more than willing to provide it.

When I arrived at the Cordis place, Elizabeth was cutting Tom's hair, which my entrance interrupted. The big blacksmith stood up and said, "Well, look who's here." He had a large white sheet loosely draped over his shoulders. She said, yes, of course she'd go and began making preparations. Tom said, "What about this barbering job?"

Elizabeth retorted, "It will just have to wait."

I left Kate at the Cordises. Elizabeth and I came down with their wagon. She brought two large enamelware dishpans and some cotton toweling. Though the down-valley breeze was with us as usual, it was warm, sunny and quite mild for December with no snow.

We arrived at the Rackliffe's midafternoon and exchanged Christmas greetings. Mary almost shouted, "If you'd brought Mrs. Weibley, we could have a reunion of the Eldorado Ladies Undertakers Guild (a reference to our laying out Mr. Curl several months ago,)

The house had the pleasant "oven" aroma of sage and I was curious to know what she had been baking, but didn't ask.

Mary Rackliffe was in unusually good spirits, very big, was up walking around. To my "experienced" eye she looked like she was a long way from delivering a baby. She's my age, give or take a few months. Elizabeth and I agreed to stay the night and it's a good thing we did. Their stovetop was hot and unoccupied. Elizabeth said, "Just in case, I'm going to begin warming up some water," and she filled one of her big dish pans and arranged it on the stove, so that heat from two stove lids would in time do the trick. She stuffed the firebox with more wood.

As soon as we came in, I noticed that the Rackliffes had acquired a new stove and I was a little envious. The cast iron firebox door had a little isinglass window allowing one to assess the quality of the fire inside without opening the door, as I must say, very elegant. The firewood can be put in from either the top through one of four cast-iron lids or through a hinged door in the front, the one with the little window. I wanted to say something about the stove but I didn't want my envy to show, so I directed a comment on the elegance of the stove with such a large oven, etc. to Mr. Rackliffe.

He laughed and said Mary had been pestering him ever since they came out to Eldorado for a bigger stove, one with an oven, and finally got one through the catalogue. He reported he had harvested an excellent 100 acre corn crop in September/October; kept about half of it for feed and sold the balance to the quartermaster over at Fort Riley adding that, "I also sold them five young beef. The officers over there must like veal. That, Mrs. Chase is how we bought the stove."

Before we arrived, Mary had baked some prairie chickens and Irish potatoes in their "jackets" in her new oven and we sat around their large table enjoying the supper together and discussing local and national politics. Mr. Rackliffe often discussed with Father getting into local politics. I've known since we came out in '56 that they are both strong abolitionists with strong Free Soil sentiments. Mr. Rackliffe claims to be a Whig and when he speaks of the party, has serious criticisms of it, as did Father and for that matter, my political mentor up in Emporia, Mr. Plumb, but I won't go into that now.

As the other two ladies began clearing the table and cleaning up around the stove, Mr. Rackliffe and I remained at the table. He asked with a bit of sympathy in his voice how I was getting along. The reference, of course, was to my new domestic situation brought on by the death of Father and my husband. I tried to respond by saying the teaching job, though a pleasant distraction was inadequate.

Mr. Rackliffe, as young as he is, maybe two or three years older than myself, said something to the effect that these recent twin calamities must have left me pretty unsettled.

I wasn't sure that I wanted to discuss my personal problems with a neighbor, but Mr. Rackliffe's next question led the conversation away from me, anyway. He said, "With your father gone, and all that, who, Augusta, do you think we should run for the Territorial Legislative seat your father vacated?"

I said I'd never given it much thought except, I said, "If Chase were alive, he might have run at election time. He was starting to get very interested in politics. On one or two of his trips to Lawrence he went out of his way to meet and talk with office holders in both Lawrence and Topeka. Why do you ask?"

"Well, I'm thinking seriously of trying to represent this district in the Legislature." Warming up to the idea I said, "Well then, why don't you?"

Mr. Rackliffe is inclined, as are a good many of us, to look to religious scriptures for solutions for our problems. He asked me how familiar I was with Job of the Old Testament. I told him as a youngster I'd heard several sermons on Job but if there was a lesson in Job for me, I really didn't understand it. He said, Well, suffering is a profound subject, so profound that in my opinion the New Testament, using the lessons of the Old, has made suffering a major theme in the Christian philosophy, that only through suffering can we find redemption and salvation. The message of Christ is much more concerned with suffering than love or charity, he explained. Job's suffering was meant to be a test of his faith in God. Jesus was a Jew and probably one well versed in Old Testament lessons. He surely knew that in the end Job persevered, rejected his wife's advice to "curse this God" that's brought us to such calamity, taken our family, our house, the wealth we worked so hard for. "Curse him and die," she said.

"I always thought that the lesson of Job was that suffering was God's punishment for wrong doing. Why else did Job ask for mercy," I said. "We ask for mercy when we admit to doing wrong and expect God…or society…to give us mercy, a form of preferential treatment. Our literature is full of examples of God's mercy. Shakespeare advises us not to examine the quality of it."

Mr. Rackliffe said, "No, Augusta, you've got it all wrong. The lesson of Job is, in my opinion, that all this suffering and loss imposed on Job was a test of him and his faith in God, not punishment. Punishment for evil is certainly a strong theme in the Old Testament, but that's not the theme here. The lesson here is through Faith we achieve salvation and restoration, faith, not wisdom. One of Job's friends tell him that man cannot acquire enough wisdom to comprehend his fate; to comprehend what's happening to him. Yes, Job questions why he was born and wishes he were dead, two things he doesn't comprehend but he never loses faith in God.

"Then several centuries later the Christians continue this theme of salvation through suffering. Jesus certainly knew the Story of Job and in my opinion expected God not to forsake him on the cross, but we know that in three days he was taken up to Heaven. Resurrection was the reward for faith. We know in the end Job's health was restored, so much health in fact that he and his wife had ten more children, three of them girls of outstanding beauty and grace, which is the note on which the Book of Job ends: beauty."

This discussion lasted well after 9:30 PM. Mary was resting in bed and Elizabeth had taken a chair over by the stove and was reading by a coal oil lamp. Mr. Rackliffe said, if I didn't mind, he would turn in and as he began to look for his nightclothes… suddenly I heard a gasp. Mary said, "Oh, my god, I think I'm ready" and she sat up in bed.

"How do you know?" I said.

"That was a real spasm in my lower belly. Oh, Oh!" and she finished that with another gasp.

Elizabeth put her book down and became very alert. She asked Mr. Rackliffe if he had a watch or a clock. She said she wanted to begin timing the pains. I had brought my Gunn's "Book of Medicine" with me and began to look up "Pains-Childbirth" when Mary sat up, swung her legs over the edge of the bed and began rubbing her swollen belly.

"Mr. Rackliffe, give me a hand getting this bedding off the tick. There's no point in messing up these flannel sheets and the quilt," demanded Elizabeth. "Do you have an old tarp we can lay on the tick? We can clean that tomorrow. I have a large piece of flannel, we'll slide under your wife."

Fifteen minutes, maybe a half hour passed, I don't remember, I simply lost track of time, but Mary Rackliffe was now back in bed. Though the cabin was warm, she was sweating heavily. Except for gasps and an occasional grunt she seemed rather quiet but restless in her labor.

About 10:30 PM, maybe it was eleven; the pains were coming frequently and regularly. Elizabeth was timing them. Mary had bent her knees and pulled her legs up close to her body. She said, "Oh, shoot, I'm going to move my bowels," but she didn't.

Elizabeth, who was standing over her, suddenly said, "Mary, bare down. You're ready. Grunt, Mary, push, I can see top of your baby's head." In a few more minutes the little head was out and I was concerned that Elizabeth might be moving and pulling the baby too much.

In another few minutes she delivered a beautiful little baby girl. I said to Elizabeth, "What do you think she weighs?"

"We don't have time for that now."

Earlier Elizabeth had put two or three Turkish towels on the table. She put her elbow into the dishpan of water on the stove to test the temperature, added a quart or so of cold water and began briskly washing the baby. She began barking orders like a drill sergeant in the army. She told me to take the string (which she'd laid out) and tie off the umbilical cord, pointing to the spot. I did. Then she said, "All right, now cut the cord right here," pointing again, and I did. She muttered something about the tag end falling off the baby in two weeks.

Then she ordered me to rub and press down on Mary's lower belly. While I was doing that I asked Mary, who is my age, give or take a few months, how she was. She had stopped sweating and tried to smile, her lips were dry.

"Mr. Rackliffe, give your brave wife a little drink of water." And he did.

In ten minutes Elizabeth had washed off the baby, totally immersing her once or twice in the big dish pan and had wrapped her up like a mummy in a piece of flannel she'd brought for that purpose, and in one smooth motion rested the baby on Mary's (now deflated) belly. I couldn't believe it. That little tyke began to nurse. Talk about miracles! Before Midnight of Christmas it was all over. The baby had nursed at both breasts and had a runny black bowel movement.

We both had taken turns pushing and rubbing her belly. Mary said she thought she could feel things pulling back into their old "location."

"Yes, and being able to nurse will be a big help in that direction but it will take several weeks,' advised Elizabeth.

After the baby was asleep, Elizabeth cleaned Mary up as best she could with warm washrags.

I was exhausted. Mr. Rackliffe had made a place for me by the stove. As soon as I lay down, I was asleep and I slept like a log until dawn, when I heard the baby cry, I looked up; Mary had rolled the youngster over for her first, day-after-Christmas breakfast.

These mysteries of life, if examined, seem to be beyond all comprehension.

48

MY STRANGE SOCIAL STATUS
December 1859 to July 1860

It's the day after Christmas and Elizabeth and I decided our two patients were getting along well enough they could do without us and we prepared to leave the Rackliffe place. As we were getting up into the Cordis' wagon Mrs. Carey arrived, intending to help. Elizabeth dropped me off on her way home. I almost pleaded for her to come in for a cup of tea. In a sudden spasm of reluctant foreboding, I knew I'd be racked with a depressive loneliness the minute I set foot inside. But she was anxious to get home, laughed and said, "I've got to finish Tom's haircut!"

When I came in, there were two letters and two more New Hampshire *Democrats* newspapers for me on the table. I immediately wondered if Mr. Weinbury had played postman again and shot a concerned glance at the wall to see if the guitar was still there. On the *Democrats* front page they were still lamenting the death of poor John Brown, this time going into many details of his unsuccessful raid, but more bothersome to this Yankee editor was that the uprisings that Mr. Brown hoped to spark, have failed miserably to commence. And as this paper went to print, weeks ago they had passed sentence on more of Mr. Brown's disciples.

I received a letter from Adda this morning dated January 8, 1860 with lots of news. She says that Lewis Tappan has returned from the gold fields. I wonder if that is the same Tappan (who, as I recall, was called "Sam"), the staunch abolitionist who with Preston Plumb and Alfred Pierce brought that huge shipment of rifles and other arms, barrels of gunpowder, and other supplies down to Plymouth from Nebraska City, in October of 1856, and transferred all that cargo to James Redpath, who had thirty wagons and 300 people waiting, mostly men anxious to get to Topeka. Thank heavens the Army hadn't established their camp near us on Pony Creek that afternoon.

Anyway, Adda reported that this Mr. Tappan, who she referred to as "such a nice old man", was going to Leavenworth, so she asked him to please inquire about or try to locate over there the likenesses taken of the Free State legislators last November 10, 1859 in Dagarian's including, of course, Father's. When he returned, she said he reported also searching other galleries in Leavenworth. He said that there'd been a suspicious fire that destroyed some Free State records. "Perhaps those likenesses were consumed by the fire," Adda speculated.

I immediately answered Adda's letter, took it over to Mrs. Frances to leave for Mr. Conner to take out. He is planning to visit his claim in Olathe this week.

I wonder who's going to take care of his store: I wonder what's happened to that other Irishman who came out west with Mr. Conner. Maybe he's starting to farm the Olathe claim. I don't seem to recall his name and I haven't seen him around lately.

January 23, 1860: One year ago today Chase and I were married. I've managed to keep the furniture arranged more or less as it was on our wedding day and I can envision it all as though it was yesterday.

What a gay party it was. Yet it was serious when it was supposed to be serious.

It's remained sunny and bright all day. I fixed a little snack at noon for myself but didn't eat much. I was distracted by my plans to visit Chase's grave. In my loneliness, my greatest consolation, and I escape into it frequently, is the knowledge and certainty that Chase truly loved me. In our tender moments he said he idolized me. He would lay his cheek next to mine and whisper that I was beautiful, that everything about me was beautiful. I had waited so long for his affection. I take great comfort in knowing that some joyous thing happened between Chase and me that is beyond my ability to describe. As I remember our ecstasies, they are all gossamer stuff, emotions, music, but not something that I can't describe in words. Nobody can. That's why good poetry and prose for that matter on love is so rare and invariably inadequate for those of us that have known such joys. All poetry can do is stimulate our memories of the inexpressible pleasures that, if we've been so blessed to have had them, the memories are there, indelible. The common thinking and writing today among Christians is that in the hereafter we are all united with our loved one. I hope that is so. I want to believe it. In that way I could spend eternity with my beloved husband.

Since I didn't much feel like eating, as I put things away I gave some thought to whether I should go to the grave alone. I had already decided to go; the question was whether I should go alone. In the past, I'd always asked for company and got it. I couldn't very well ask Mrs. Rackliffe in her current condition. Mrs. Carey was helping with the baby, so she was out and Tom wouldn't take kindly to my coming back today, seeking his wife's company again, never mind the purpose. So that didn't give me much choice.

Slightly after noon I took Kate and the wagon and went over to the gravesite and stood there, leaning against the wagon. From the knoll I could look down on our little settlement and see a few changes; i.e., a cabin now where, a year ago was open prairie. I saw a wagon or two off on errands of their own; off in the distance I could hear a dog bark, otherwise except for the wind it was eerily quite. No smoke was coming from the sawmill and that was a disappointing omen.

It's strange. My father is dead; my husband is dead, my only close relative, my sister, Adda, is in Lawrence. Yes, I know dozens of people here in town and surrounding areas and I share their friendship to varying degrees but I really have no loved ones close by.

Although I had bundled-up, it was really quite cold up there. On the way home, with the sun on my back, I could feel the wind coming down the valley, I had this strange notion that now I really only had two friends: myself and my journal, and there are times when I'm alone that the pangs of being alone with my own company is almost more than I can bear. My escape is to visit somebody, or go to Lawrence and visit Adda and Mrs. Gates.

I have a clipping from the December 1859 issue of the St. Louis newspaper that just got here about Abraham Lincoln debating someone in Leavenworth…and here I am 160 miles away. Oh, what I wouldn't give to have been able to hear that speech. I wonder if Adda got up there? In my next letter I'll ask her, though she's not as concerned about politics as I have always been. I'll ask Adda if she can get from the Leavenworth *Territorial Register* a copy of his speech. I've sent to a Chicago publisher fifty cents for a bound copy of the debates with Mr. Lincoln and that rascal Senator Douglass, though I should be more charitable with him, since we turned his invention of Popular Sovereignty on its head. I haven't received the package yet.

It is now February 4, 1860, and I went over to Mr. Conner's Store for some shopping and inquired if he'd replaced his inventory that the Indians took in the August 8th raid. I'm still looking for spoons and knives. Mrs. Rackliffe and Mrs. Frame were there engaged with Mr. Conner over a science article in the *Herald of Freedom*, the Lawrence newspaper that was quickly resurrected after being burned out in May 1856 by proslavery hooligans.

The article claimed that there would be a full eclipse of the moon on February 6th and if the sky is reasonably cloudless, the newspaper says the phenomenon will best be visible on the "North American Prairie!" Well, we planned a big "Eclipse" Supper Party at my place, February 6th; that's in two days. When I extended the invitation to Mr. Conner, he laughed heartily and recited an Irish limerick about a young lady named Muldoon, who believed babies came from the moon. It was funny and had a nice rhyme but was not very nice.

In terrible February weather Mr. Ashmore of Fall River brought in a bundle of mail and stayed until he could get warmed-up: three letters from Adda, a new cloth bound ledger I'd ordered from Brooklyn and two *Leslie* magazines, one for December, one for January. I'm so glad to get the *Leslies*. The first thing I did was to check the table of contents to see if installments of a serialized Charles Dickens story I've been following, were there. They were. I've missed November, but I'm sure it will catch up with me.

Toward the end of Adda's first letter she said, "Count your blessings that you aren't here, although I could sure use your company. Things have changed at the Whitney House. Now I'm being treated 'like a dog'," and she signed it your loving sister. Now who would treat Adda "like a dog," old Mr. Stone? Adda's new beau, the gunsmith? She doesn't even give a hint and it's not like my sister to complain about how she's being treated. It's more like her to trumpet how she settled a particular score, recalling her aggressive plans for Hildebrand, her athletic treatment a few weeks ago of Mr. Diggle, never mind what happened to his gold watch and chain. The other letter was more cheerful, but it wasn't dated so I couldn't tell which letter had been written last or first. Maybe I'd better get up to Lawrence and see what I can do to help Adda.

Adda's third letter was actually a large envelope containing several clippings of eastern newspapers, all dealing with the death of John Brown and the terrible status of members of his raiding party. She had obviously been saving these. One dated December 15th of last year carried news that a Judge Parker had sentenced John Brown to be hung on the gallows in Charleston, Virginia on December 2nd of last year and he was. The article says that the trial had ended on October 31st. The jury took less than one hour to declare Mr. Brown guilty as charged. Apparently he was sentenced later but the article doesn't say when. (Where was I on that date or on December 2nd?)

When I was visiting with Mrs. Gates in Lawrence from November 6th to the 22nd, Adda came out the evening of November 11th to relate an afternoon ruckus in the Whitney House by two newspaper reporters from St. Louis making rude and insinuating inquiries about old John Brown and his Lawrence backers. They said that the trial of John Brown had already taken place. We couldn't believe it. According to these articles it was true. In November he was in prison, not yet executed, but in prison.

One article dated Jan. 21st describes the trial of Albert Hazlett (who also called himself William H. Harrison), who together with John E. Cook, escaped Harper's Ferry but was captured in Pennsylvania. Mr. Hazlett was not tried with the October/November group. Cook's trial was on November 9th. The Jury found him and the others guilty. They were sentenced to death by the same judge. John Cook was executed December 16th. (The second article says that Albert Hazlett wasn't hung at all, but is still alive!)

The first article described the great detail used by Mr. Brown's attorney in trying to get him declared insane. Had that plan succeeded, the Governor could have put him in an institute for the insane, but the lawyer's tactic failed.

An article from a Baltimore paper dealt with details of Mr. Brown's hanging in Virginia on December 2nd. The Government was worried about some sort of uprising, possibly a northern retaliation, etc. so over 1,500 soldiers were ordered to be at the site. This Baltimore, Maryland editor, who obviously attended the hanging (a southern state but not deep south) spoke of his admiration for old Mr. Brown's courage while quietly and patiently waiting on the gallows platform as the administrators worked out certain last minute technicalities, including certain local officials being allowed to come up on the scaffold platform. Then before the actual hanging they were escorted off.

After the hanging, his body was placed in a well-made coffin of polished black walnut and sent north with Mrs. Brown for burial, though she was not able to retrieve the bodies of her two sons Oliver and Watson. *I don't know why the editor thought these personal details were necessary.*

A different editor (Philadelphia) made a lengthy comment on Brown's sanity or insanity, saying in effect that if slavery is now and has always been a mark of civilized sanity, then surely Mr. Brown's seizure of the Government arsenal, his killing the guards there was an act of insanity and should be, as it was dealt with as the law provides. But if the concept of slavery, as some civil authorities, both here and abroad, claim as Mr. John Brown certainly claimed that slavery is a form of insanity; if it's not simply unjust, but a form of social insanity condoned for economic reasons, then Mr. Brown's behavior was simply a very courageous act, for surely the editor says, if soldiers kill the enemy in a justifiable war, as in the French and Indian war or the war for independence, are those men insane? Clearly no! Gallant and courageous? Yes, but insane, no.

This editor quotes William Lloyd Garrison, who he says has been promoting and instigating abolition of slavery since at least 1831, when he first published his magazine on the subject, the *Liberator*, (of which I am both a critic and a subscriber.) The gist of this editor's article is that Garrison, after thirty years of struggling with the concept of non violent disobedience, seems to be considering a conversion to Mr. Brown's religion. He knew Brown. He had argued with him and other radicals more than once, that slavery could in time be abolished by reason, debate. Brown always disagreed. In an editorial written by Garrison since John Brown's death and given great circulation in the north, he claims now to believe that John Brown was correct all along, it will take violence and bloodshed to destroy slavery in the United States. This Philadelphia editor questions what will happen to the National Anti Slavery Society and its loyal followers, an organization started and kept informed by Mr. Garrison. This society stands for gaining freedom of the slave without violence. If Garrison joins radicals who he has denounced over the years and begins promoting violent abolition, what will happen to this group he's worked so hard over the years to persuade to the contrary.

A late night entry February 6th: The invited Eldorado neighbors gathered at our house for a pre-eclipse supper and during it the topic of conversation was, "What is an Eclipse" and I was disappointed in our level of knowledge.

The supper was enjoyed by all. Elizabeth Cordis brought a chocolate cake, and after supper we had a pre-eclipse tea.

About nine o'clock, Mr. Conner and Mr. Rackliffe, our two local lunar experts, went outside to estimate visibility. They returned to report that it was a reasonably clear night, that the moon was full and well above the horizon, but there was nothing to suggest an eclipse. We all speculated about the "lunacy" of the Lawrence editor who wrote the article.

In a half hour or so, someone looked outdoors again and said, "Well, it does seem to be getting darker and the moon isn't full anymore."

We hurriedly put on our coats, went outside and what a sight! There was only a crescent of moon showing, except at the tips of the crescent the light continued in a thin circular luminous rind, quite spectacular in itself. The crescent was getting smaller by the minute and soon the full illuminated moon was gone leaving a thin ring of light, which formed a lunar halo. Otherwise this was a total eclipse.

In a few minutes the crescent appeared on the other side (south side) and in about forty-five minutes the full moon was restored to its normal luminosity.

With oohs and aahs we filed back into a warm house. Luckily there was enough hot water for another pot of tea and we "eclipsed" Elizabeth Cordis' chocolate cake.

As the new Eldorado school marm, I asked my guests what the phenomenon was, that we'd just witnessed? What obscured the moon's light? It wasn't the sun getting between the earth and the moon? We know that the earth is between the sun and the moon but how does that make an eclipse? I wondered how often we get a total eclipse? I asked if we get light and heat from the sun, why doesn't the moon provide heat as well? Elizabeth Cordis ventured that moonlight is really reflected sunlight. Mr. Conner said, "Nonsense. The moon is so far away it's like any other star. We see the light but don't feel heat." And what do editors know that they can predict such an event? Much to our surprise, we received no enlightenment from a rereading of the Herald's article.

I was amazed that in this day and age none of us could provide a plausible explanation for what we had just witnessed up there in the heavens. To change the subject Mr. Conner recited his limerick about the "Lady named Muldoon." This time the men enjoyed his Irish poetry so much they encouraged him to recite another: about an Old Maid from Cape Cod: I was afraid his poetry was going to get out of control, but the ladies got up and began looking for their coats and gloves. It was now almost eleven o'clock.

Oh, yes. I had three scholars in my class today, and the classes will be held here at my house for the foreseeable future.

I taught nine scholars today, this February 13th, and I note that the girls are better about their assignments than the boys.

I'm glad I've kept old magazines and newspapers. Until the books I've ordered through Conner's arrive, their reading assignments will come from those sources.

Two of my younger scholars, however, can't read at all. They have only recently mastered their ABCs, so I don't need books for them. In fact, one of the older girls, acting as my assistant takes those two into the kitchen area and writes on her slate those familiar two and three letter words that have been used for thousands of years in the learning-to-read process.

Though I'm enjoying the teaching and the responsibility, being the first Eldorado school marm has posed three problems: nobody from the committee has approached me to reach a salary agreement. Knowing I'll have scholars to teach has greatly reduced the time I have to visit with my neighbors and I've been teaching only a few days and I realize I must either feed my students at noon or they must bring some food with them from home. As soon as the scholars discovered I would share my own noontime meal with some of them, nobody brought a lunch to school. So far, I've simply warmed something up, but if I feed ten or twelve hungry youngsters every day, it won't take long to deplete my larder.

As though she was reading my mind, Mrs. Schaefer paid me "in advance" today with seventy-five pounds of unground wheat or barley. That's the only payment I've had so far. I know Mr. and Mrs. Rackliffe plan to go up to Chelsea to get some corn ground at Hayworth's. I'll ask them to take my grist up with them. I'll send along a note to Jerry Jordon who's running the grist mill up there, because there wasn't enough business down here to keep him. He was running our sawmill and I miss him.

I had twelve scholars today and dismissed them about 3 o'clock in the afternoon. I sent notes home with most of them saying that I'd appreciate it if I could receive some pay for my teaching. I also said I wanted a few days to myself in March, as I intend to go up to Lawrence.

I'll be anxious to see if any of the scholars or their parents shows up here in the next few days with even a token payment. Though I could use the cash, it's not just the money; many of these same people had also taken advantage of Father. Some have failed to make their land payments, or failed to pay him or Chase or Frank Robinson for that matter for the surveying and filing of claims. Of course, there are exceptions: Tom Cordis owes us nothing; likewise, the Martins, the Careys, the Rackliffes and Dr. and Mrs. Weibley.

After trying for two years Mrs. Carey has a healthy baby boy, this Tuesday, March 6, 1860. So, she must have been rather "far along" when she volunteered the day after Christmas to help Mary Rackliffe just as Elizabeth Cordis and I were leaving. The

Carey's baby was a few days old when I visited. We tried to recall when we saw each other last. I said I would have been more than happy to come down and help with the delivery but she said she'd heard such glowing reports about the school at my house she didn't want to disturb my teaching schedule. She didn't say and I didn't ask who helped but I did ask if they'd called Doctor Weibley and she laughed and said, "Let me tell you something about our famous doctor. Sometime last October, I know it was after the prairie fire, probably mid October when I was maybe four month's along but hadn't quite started to show, Doctor Weibley happened to come by. I was pretty sure I was "with child," but it would be my first one, so I had no prior experience. I did not disclose this to the doctor. It was well before my time but I asked him to examine me anyway. My lower legs and ankles had started to swell-up a little and I was concerned about it. That doctor said I had dropsy and prescribed an herbal remedy to reduce body fluids. Can you believe that? Well, I wasn't going to say to him, "Doctor, I think I'm getting ready to have a baby." He said, yes I had <u>dropsy</u>! Well, when I told that to Mr. Carey, we agreed we'd not use his medical services again. I'm about to post a note to him telling him not to send a bill for those services." I asked her if she took the "dropsy" medicine and she said she did. She leaned forward and with in a soft voice, but a big smile said, the swelling did go down but "I peed a lot."

    I was cleaning house this morning. It's March 10th. I had decided temporarily at least, to discontinue teaching. I like teaching and I really enjoy the children and the activity takes my mind off my strange social predicament but I certainly don't like being taken advantage of. Other than seventy-five pounds of barley grain from the Schaefers, I've not received a penny from the other families. Indeed, I've regularly fed my scholars a noontime meal from my own larder, which means I need to plan for that, bake bread, make sure I have some meat I can slice, etc. That certainly wasn't in the original arrangement. I've mentioned to the older ones that their parents might see fit to send down a ham or a side of bacon, ten pounds of flour, some bread, but nothing has materialized. I know many of them are poor, etc.

Late in the day while I was cleaning-up and rearranging the furniture, Mr. Philip Woodward, an old friend from Lawrence and a traveling companion, Mr. Enos dropped in. I invited them to supper and to stay over. Mr. Woodward brought a most welcome package from Adda, which contained a sweet note and finally the two likenesses of us taken last November 10th at Dagarian's. I was so pleasantly relieved to see that the strenuous side-street "dust-up," we'd had with Mr. Diggle that afternoon, had not disturbed our hairdos. Of course, Adda had been more strenuous than me but her likeness is just beautiful and a very good representation of my sister. I am so happy to have these likenesses I can barely contain myself. I like Adda's better than mine. I seem a little stiff and not as jolly as I really was that afternoon, but it was so pleasant to get them and as though that wasn't enough, the package included a letter from Uncle Charles (Father's brother) with Ambrotypes of himself, Lauretta and Bella, our cousins.

Adda reports she is still working at the Whitney house but says it is not as pleasant or exciting as it was last year before the Harper's Ferry raid and the demise of John Brown and his friends. She says a gentleman named, Nathan Stone, is now running the place. He is old and cranky, not nearly as nice, she says, as the previous proprietor who has left Lawrence following some awful accusations and recriminations. At least one Government committee from Washington, D.C. came out and made serious inquiry about John Brown's local associates, trying to decide which Lawrence citizens were involved in financing his activities. This wasn't the first time that Washington had sent investigators to Lawrence to inquire about John Brown's activity. (She was referring to official inquiries following the so-called Osawatamie Massacre.)

Adda says that Mr. Stone is stingy, given to rumor and is hard on the kitchen help. She says Aggie Rourke was for a short time running the kitchen, but is back working for the Gates over at the Cincinnati house. She says that Mr. Stone dislikes the Irish, he continually complained about Aggie's cooking and spread rumors about the "quality" of her social life. Adda notes that Mr. Stone suspects that Aggie Rourke was quietly selling Missouri moonshine to select Whitney house patrons. She says in the letter that occasionally a wagon from Missouri would pull up by the back porch, which was customary for deliveries. Aggie would invite the driver in but the girls never actually saw any whiskey come into the kitchen. They simply had opinions. Well, that widow you met last November when we had our likenesses taken at Dagarian's is the new cook. She's a nice lady but can't hold a candle to Aggie. Nobody has ever tumbled to the little lucrative partnership that Aggie and I have. In fact, our business has picked up so nicely we've raised our prices. I've found a regular source of flat, one-pint bottles (for our trade) through a mate off one of the riverboats that docks at the bottom of the hill. When their boat is in port, he always spends a night or two at the Whitney house. He brings me the bottles from the boat's saloon. He thinks I fill them with local herbal medicine, which, of course, is partly true!

    Mr. Stone had previously worked for the Gates but had strong differences of opinions about running small hotels and they parted company. Adda's letter says that Mrs. Gates has warned her and the other girls not to allow Mr. Stone to be "presumptuous" in his personal relationship, and not to allow him to be tardy nor short on the pay at pay day, a practice he's used in his previous positions.

    During supper Mr. Woodward said after they make a delivery west of here at White Water they would return to Lawrence. I asked if they could arrange for me to go with them to Lawrence. They stayed for supper and spent the night with me before going on to White Water, and we had a most pleasant visit. During supper Mr. Woodward said he would not only be delighted with my company, he would be relieved. At the time I didn't quite understand this comment. But a few days later, as I will report, I did.

Well, things didn't quite work out as planned. Mr. Woodward decided to go on to White Water alone this morning. Mr. Enos and I will go to Lawrence without him. We'll use our team and wagon. Mr. Woodward has taken his team and wagon. The gentlemen seem to have worked this out before breakfast. Mr. Woodward said he'd try to catch-up with us en route. Well, that way I'll have my own team in Lawrence.

Before we could get away, Mrs. Frame came up to see me off, asking me to deliver a package on our way to Mrs. Barrett this side of Chelsea. I couldn't just excuse myself, so we had a pot of tea together, which delayed our departure an hour or so and aggravated Mr. Enos a bit.

We are traveling in our wagon with our team. Mr. Enos is a big talker. It wouldn't be so bad if what he had to say were the least bit interesting. It's just small talk. I don't know whether he thinks he's obliged to entertain me or whether I'm his captive audience. Knowing we were going to be on the road together four or five days, and knowing I didn't want to offend this obliging soul, I told him that my recent personal arrangements had not worked out as planned and that I had set aside these four or five days to think about what has happened to me in the recent year or so and I had hoped for some solitude to try to figure out what I wanted to do with my life as a result of all this.

Before we left the house, Mr. Enos helped me toss my traveling trunk up on the wagon. I had packed enough for several lunches for the two of us and put it in a wicker basket just under the seat. Mr. Enos was curious about three or four books I brought along, strapped with the leather belt and fancy patent buckle Erastus Howland had given me before he left for the Cherokee Nation. The books were between Mr. Enos and myself. We'd hardly left our place and he mentioned, "You intend to read all that stuff between here and Lawrence?"

"Well, no, one of the books is really a bound journal and I try to make an entry every day though I seldom am that faithful."

He wanted to know what in the world I could find interesting enough out here to ever write about. That was when I made a big mistake. My response was intended to be in humor.

"Well," I replied, "we're going to be on the road together four or five days and you seem to be rather talkative. I wouldn't be surprised if I wrote a line or two about you, I'm trying to learn to be a writer."

Well, it took us an hour or so to get to the Barretts, their place was a little off the road toward Chelsea (which is also off the main trail to Emporia), but during that time I got an earful from Mr. Enos.

Mrs. Barrett was happy to see me and I her. After they left Eldorado and had given us some furniture, they went on to the Kansas Gold Fields. Things didn't work out and they returned to this area. I inquired about the doctor. "He's just fine," she said, "but he isn't home, though I'm expecting him."

Mrs. Young, from Eldorado, was also in their Parlor with her twins (who looked to be eight to ten months old). She said she wanted Doctor Barrett to look at the children. She certainly knows Doctor Weibley, but now seems willing to come all this way for medical services. I didn't press the inquiry knowing that my talkative driver was anxious to make it to Indian Creek by supper. And we did. It was twelve miles; about three hours and Mr. Enos hardly paused for breath. I declare I think he expects me to write his biography and it looks like that's what I'm doing.

Towards sundown we got to Indian Creek and spent the night at the White's place. It had a huge buffalo skin stretched out and nailed onto the outside south wall. They call this a boarding house. Humph! It wouldn't pass for a stable in Detroit or Chicago: a dirt floor, one big open room, with a big stone chimney in the middle, not a picture on the walls. We ate a fair supper of some kind of game stew that lacked salt, needed more vegetables and fewer bones, was served on a long table facing the wall. No chairs; we all sat on stumps. I had asked Mr. Enos to kindly bring in my trunk and I'm glad I did. Before supper was over I had to put on a wool sweater and wished I'd brought some wool socks for my cold feet. There was a ten-mile an hour draft across the floor.

Mr. Enos asked Mr. White, "Why don't you chink up those holes? Some of them are big enough for a bird to fly through without folding his wings."

"I chink them all the time, but every time it rains, it washes out the filler," Mr. White said.

Mr. Enos told him he needed plaster, not mud. Chase would call this "Yankee" house in that several houses he built for Yankees put the fireplace more or less in the middle of the room rather than on one of the walls. Midwesterners like their fireplaces in the wall. A large square limestone fireplace had been built in the middle of this room extending to the ceiling. Four main roof beams rested on a stone shelf at the top of the limestone masonry. Those beams extend out to the four corners of the cabin. The roof beams were at ninety-degree angles to each other, which supported four slanting roof sections. The cooking was done out of one side of the fireplace. Mrs. White did not own or use a stove. Opposite was a smaller opening, which I suppose, was intended to warm the other side of the cabin. Wood could be fed into the fire from either side of the fire and it was. Thank heavens Mr. White seemed to have plenty of firewood and he was very generous with its use. However the house had so many gaps between the logs and around the windows that if I stood or sat more than two feet from the fire, my backsides were cold.

I was assigned a raised wood pallet on the dirt floor for a bed. No mattress, but a lumpy tick full of prairie feathers (grass) served as one. Chase called such fillings, "a donkey's breakfast." No blankets, but two heavy Quaker quilts just barely kept me above freezing. During the night two small goats tried to join me in my boudoir.

At dawn Mr. Enos was up making a fire and would occasionally attempt a friendly remark to me even though I was still in bed. He said the goats woke him up. I was awake and had been for hours.

We had a hot porridge breakfast that lacked salt. No bacon but some cold hard-boiled eggs and teakettle tea. The Whites don't believe in real tea or coffee. But I suspect that tea selling for $15 a pound or $5 for a little 4 oz tins and a man working for someone else making a dollar a day is the real reason. We were on the road by seven and I do believe it was warmer outdoors on the wagon than inside the White's boarding house. The Whites must be Eskimos to stand that house. Mr. Enos, said to me, with great humor as we waved good-bye, "It will be a cold day in h___ before we stay there again, Mrs. Chase," and I agreed with him. This is March. Can you imagine what a January night in that place with our Kansas wind and snow must be like?

By seven in the morning no sooner did we get rolling and Mr. Enos commenced regaling me. Finally I said, "Mr. Enos, I'd like a little quiet for myself if you don't mind. I've had some terrible things happen to me and I want to try to think them through. In fact, if the road isn't too bumpy, I might try to read a little." Mr. Enos was not going to be easily stifled.

"Awright, but I'm curious what it is that you need to ponder, if I may ask?"

"The previous winter," I replied, "that's the winter of 1858 and 1859 my father, whom you didn't know, was killed by a horse thief down in Neutral Country. There was an accomplice, a Mr. William Hildebrand who has a claim over near Mr. Conner's store. He's alive: my father's dead. I have reason to believe my father's killer is alive."

"My father came out here to serve the cause of abolition."

Mr. Enos interrupted, "So did I. I came out from Oberlin, Ohio. There are more abolitionists in Oberlin than any place else in the country. Did you know that John Brown came from near there?"

"Yes, yes, Mr. Enos, I know. You asked me to explain; let me explain. My father so firmly believed that there should be no slavery in this territory when it becomes a State, that within a few weeks of our getting here, he joined the abolitionist militia, fought a few battles and by mid September in 1856 was captured by the U. S. Army and interred in a war camp until New Years Day of 1857. President Pierce pardoned him and about eighty more by March of that year.

"My father with a small group of friends founded Eldorado that summer. My sister and I came out in November. Father was killed a year later but in the meantime he had been elected to the territorial legislature representing Butler County, and he worked on the Committee drafting the Free State Constitution.

"Last January I married Jacob Chase. I don't believe you knew him. Nine months later my husband died, so, you see, I'm a widow.

"We own the sawmill on the Walnut, but it hasn't cut a stick of lumber for three or four months. There is just no business, I think we are simply too far west for commerce; that and a few other things are what I need to think about."

Mr. Enos was simply not going to be quiet. "Mrs. Chase, what will you do in Lawrence?"

Just then we began a jolting decent down into a dip in the prairie. "Now hold on," he said, "we're going to ford Duck Creek. It's not deep but it will be bumpy. Then in a few hours we'll be in Emporia."

"Mr. Enos, Duck Creek is at least twenty, maybe twenty-five miles from here. The Phillips have a claim at Duck Creek right on the trail; we're old friends. It comes before Cottonwood Creek to the southwest of Emporia, pshaw, you're nowhere near Duck Creek. We won't see Duck Creek until noon tomorrow. I think you're on the old east-west Osage Trail and have been since we left the White's this morning. I thought you knew where you were going. We need to be going northeast to hit Emporia. This time of day the sun should be on our right side, not in front of us. That trail's ruts up there are twice as deep as these ruts. From Eldorado to Topeka is the Old Santa Fe Trail, though there are some freighter cut-offs."

As the horses approached the downward slope I hesitated to ask but I did. "Have you ever used the east bound trail from Eldorado to Emporia?"

There was a long pause as the wagon rattled down into the draw and began crossing the creek. A hundred yards upstream a white-tailed doe and her youngster were taking a drink. Our noise and violent motion caught their attention but they ignored us.

The horses began to carefully pick their way through the rocky stream, occasionally one would hesitate while the other moved on, which would slightly shift our direction and progress through this shallow crick. The real problem came with four steel wagon wheels, each in its own way trying to accommodate the randomly placed and irregularly shaped boulders. These streambed stones had been made round by centuries of slow grinding ice-enclosed glacial travel when this land was according to Father one vast glacial ice field.

These stones weren't large, but they were big enough to lift one wheel completely out of the water while the opposite corner was tilted down having just rolled over or slipped off to one side of its boulder.

This side-to-side, front-to-back jostling demanded all our attention lest we be pitched out forward or down and off to one side or the other.

We were never in any danger and except for the inconvenience; I think the horses enjoyed the cool water. It was already getting to be warm but they hadn't worked up a sweat.

With the crick's slope behind us the wheels soon found a smooth, yielding prairie surface. The wagon leveled off and resumed its comfortable normal horizontal motion. Although a few scattered fleecy clouds temporarily obscured the sun, it was obvious that the trail Mr. Enos was on headed almost due east. Back up on the prairie, Mr. Enos was (unusually) quiet.

"I take your silence to be 'no' in answer to my question." More silence.

"Mr. Enos, I'd suggest you turn now and head due north from here 'til we pick up the Emporia road. It will travel generally northeast. We've got to go diagonally through all of Chase County before we're even close to Duck Creek, then Emporia. I've taken the road to and from Lawrence so many times I know all the landmarks and you're way off the trail."

Mr. Enos remained quiet, but he did turn so that the sun was exactly on our right side. I took out my pocket compass and was conspicuous about using it. I couldn't tell whether he was chagrined or was pouting, because I knew the trail better than he did, but I didn't care. It looked like I was going to have a little peace and quiet.

It took a solid two hours steering due north on the open undulating prairie before we slid into those deep familiar ruts of the Santa Fe Trail and began seeing the occasional cast-off piece of surplus furniture, rusted farm implements, etc. all scattered along the trail. There was a schooner heading southwest away from us a mile or so and up ahead was a small freighters' outfit. A little north of the trail was a stand of hardwoods along a creek bed. Pointing to them I suggested we water the horses and take a little lunch. I took out some baked smoked turkey, a half loaf of chewy, hard crusted bread and a crock of spiced applesauce I'd put up last September or October, oh yes, and some unclabbered milk.

While Mr. Enos watered the horses, I spread our little picnic on the wagon seat and shooed the dust flies away. Later I found a little draw, sat down on its bank and with journal number two more than half full, began an entry that was intended to be a summing up of my situation. I always think better if I write down what it is I'm thinking about. The sun was out and the prairie was buzzing with spring bugs and insects, though thank heavens it's too early for Musquitoes. I must have written without interruption for an hour.

When I walked over to the wagon, Mr. Enos was under it, asleep. He had tied the braces to the front wheel. Well, we had five or so hours before looking for a night's lodging. I knew just the place and it was not going to be on the open prairie.

49

MEDITATIONS ON THE ROAD TO LAWRENCE
March 12 to March 15, 1860

Well, I'm looking forward to getting to Emporia, though we won't be there for a couple of days. I would so like a lively evening of politics with Preston Plumb, barefoot or not.

On the road up here I had this little whimsy, but I'm not sure I could pull it off—Adda could: to find an old pair of men's shoes, wrap them up with a bow and present them to Preston Plumb with a little note reminding him of his visit with us in Plymouth in September of '56 when he, Sam Tappan and Mr. Pierce brought in all those supplies for Mr. Redpath. He came into our cabin and spent the evening giving us a political education. I still remember how fired up he was about the new Republican Party, that John Fremont would be the next president, etc. All the while he was barefoot!

Mr. Enos' silence on the way to Duck Creek gave me some blessed relief. I used the quiet time to think over my situations and the choices I would soon have to make.

The changes in my family life, my marriage, even the expectations of my future compared to a year or so ago are almost beyond my comprehension. In the span of less than a year I've lost my father, then my husband.

To accommodate our privacy, following our wedding, my sister moved out and went back to Lawrence. She seems happy enough there now not to want to return to Eldorado. I can't say as I blame her. In that short span of time I've gone from knowing exactly who I was and what I wanted to be, the daughter of the town's founding president and member of the (Free) State Legislature, an owner and operator of probably the western most sawmill in North America to being fatherless and a widow. With the two men in my life both alive they and Adda were central to my being. I was who I was from my relationship to them. They were objects of my care, attention, sociability and affection. With my husband it certainly went beyond that, as he would be the father of our children. With his demise and my father's, my neat, conventional, domestic arrangement lay in shatters: destroyed. Living alone, I'm not even sure I could defend myself against someone intent on doing me or my property harm, white man or Indian. Though protecting myself from danger is a concern, it's not the one that's upper most in my mind. My major concern is loneliness, which, as I see it, is different than simply being alone. I did not choose or want this solitude. What I wanted, what I had, was just the opposite. My loneliness is now so absolute it's created almost a palpable form of uncertainty; that is, I'm a less certain person now than a year ago and I expected it to be just the opposite. When I visit neighbors or they visit me, I enjoy their company but even in their presence I know now I'm different than they are. When I leave them, they have each other and their children, while I am childless and a widow. I have been profoundly set back. Being without a husband has somehow made me socially deficient. When I was still unmarried, though already nearing my twenties, I wasn't very happy with those circumstances because they made me feel as if I weren't like the other young women my age. Father wanted me happy and he wanted me married. Those two conditions were not only equated in his mind, they were the social equation of the day. I knew it was normal to be married, if not married, to plan for it, to look forward to it, and how I longed to achieve that social distinction.

Though Father's murder orphaned us, I had been marriageable well before he died. The fact, that I wasn't married, that I hadn't married, seemed to be a favorite subject for some of our (humorous) neighbors to speculate about and they would plague me about my unmarried status with hints that I was surely headed toward spinsterhood and, just as often, I had some concerns along that line myself. In reality I had entertained more than my share of proposals of marriage, none of them solicited or encouraged by me, except for Chase. I'm sure one or two of those proposals came about because the men here on the frontier outnumber the women. That fact certainly increases our offers, if not our eligibility!

And then with unbounded joy and anticipation I finally married, married the man I loved. Yes, it was an odd courtship, but in our own shy and clumsy ways we persevered and were rewarded with incomparable bliss. Again, I knew who I was: I regained some of the domestic security I'd had I had before Father's death. I looked forward to spending my life with Chase. Once we had agreed on a date, there was no question about my single minded devotion to him and I presumed, no, I knew he would return that love and loyalty in kind. I wanted to have a family like Grandfather Charles and Grandma Hannah Gates Stewart had. Maybe not quite twelve children like them, but certainly a family. I wondered if in time, and after I earned it by living soberly and well, I'd have some gift like hers, not that I particularly wanted to speak directly to God, as everybody said she could and I'm sure she did, but some particular gift or talent that everyone in my family would say, "Oh, yes, it's her gift," (whatever it is.)

Although living so far west isn't easy, Chase and I had enough to live on comfortably. He had plenty of carpentry work. Cash payment was a problem, but a tolerable problem, one we could manage, although I believe that if we had a bank (that could provide mortgages) and was closer than Lawrence, even the cash problem would have been alleviated. Chase and I also had an income from the sawmill. It could produce all the timbers he needed for his jobs, with some excess mill time available to saw up timbers for others either from our inventory or their own logs. Chase and I seemed to be on our way to having a good life, with enough money for our needs, and the prospect of a nice normal family.

Sometime during our blissful prairie honeymoon I conceived, as I fully expected to, and I looked forward to the joys of motherhood. While I was awaiting our child, my thoughts often went back to a memory I had of Father, when we were crossing Iowa and he had told me how much he had loved my mother, and that I had been the product of that love. I hoped I would be able to share the same kind of moment with my own child. I often thought, while Chase was still alive—and even after he died—that someday somewhere, perhaps in the umbrella of an afternoon rainbow, I would explain to our child how he or she was the product of the love shared by Chase and me. Well, now even that won't happen. It just won't happen, because eight months after our wedding, my loving husband died, and so has the child of our tender union.

It will take me a long time to adapt to my new social status, not just to its solitariness but also to the feelings I have of being abnormal and dispossessed.

Before Chase died, I had my life all figured out. The way I had arranged my future like one of those sets of drawings Father always had tucked away that provided instructions to build a sawmill showing all the integral parts to make it work: the boiler, the piping, the big saw blade, the drive belts, "the works." My plan was just as exact and would allow me to be who I wanted to be: married to Chase, the mother of his children, settled in a community that could offer us an abundant social life and secure financial prospects, and it looked like Eldorado would do just fine for those hopes. We would visit with Adda and her family.

Father would continue in politics, run the sawmill, which would grow and prosper. Our children, Chase's and mine, would grow-up knowing their grandfather, Aunt Adda and their cousins. We had "the works" for a family, but it's all gone now. When things don't turn out the way you hoped, what do you do? Shakespeare said, "There's a divinity that shapes our ends." Well, that's an interesting observation, but at twenty, what do I do with his idea? I have yet to see any divine intervention unless what's happened to me in the past four years, since we left Detroit, is because of divine intention. If it is, I will resist with all my might because circumstances are so far from the ideal life I had looked forward to and planned for.

I am trying to sort things out. Do I want to be a farmer? Do I know enough to survive as a farmer? Other than a vegetable garden in Michigan, I had never farmed until last spring when Chase, Adda and I planted the corn. The twenty-five or so acres of field corn was enough to feed the cow, two horses all winter and have plenty left in the corncrib that the chickens and night animals seem to get into.

If I'm to farm, the only two animals that could break and plow this rich but hard prairie soil, as Chase, Adda and I discovered last spring, were our two reliable old friends who pulled us across Iowa. But both Tempus and Fugit are dead now, dead from some mysterious disease carried on the wind or the river water, I didn't know what it was, nor do any of my neighbors who also lost cattle. I lost one milk cow but have one remaining and she produces. The cows were both from Missouri. I probably should have gotten Iowa cows, but on the other hand, that might not have made any difference. Old Tempus and Fugit were from Iowa and they didn't make it.

Well, I still have eight laying hens and a rooster, though night animals continually try to take them.

Of course, there are also wild prairie chickens and turkeys out here. Game is plentiful, but thanks to the generosity of my neighbors I've yet to shoot a bird.

I think I could manage running the sawmill, if there were enough customers with cash to keep it operating, even if sporadically. The last time we had a fire in the boiler was when tom Cordis and Henry Martin sawed up some of their own logs. That was nearly three months ago, just before Christmas. I remember, because I spent the night of the twentieth with the Martins, the occasion when Mr. Martin broached the subject of my selling the family's share of the sawmill to him. I have an inventory of timbers cut to size for building projects, left over from carpentry jobs Chase had been planning to do, and I have a yard full of logs, both hardwood and softwood, but not a single standing order nor, for that matter, any prospects. Some people aren't building their homes out of wood but out of prairie sod. This type of home construction isn't widespread but I do see some of it, and it looks unhealthy to me. If we get snakes in a log cabin, what sort of vermin do you suppose they must put up with in a house with sod walls?

I realize now, in hindsight, I should not have gotten rid of the syrup mill. Mr. Eastridge made his offer when it was not operating and not producing cash. But I have come to see that the cash we used to run the house after Father died came mainly from the sale of our syrup, either when we sold it directly or from money we collected from the grocers who sold it though we occasionally didn't see that money.

Besides local customers, we would often sell a quart now and then to outfits passing through. Due to our location, there was hardly a day but what a group of gold seekers or an Oregon- or-California bound train didn't cross the Walnut.

Freighters, though, had become our best but irregular customers, especially the eastbound outfits who had made their deliveries and were anxious to get back to Lawrence or Leavenworth for another load.

The McWhorters skipped town in March a year ago owing us forty dollars for syrup I'm sure they sold. The last time I tried to dun them for the money they owed us, he only coughed up ten dollars. I didn't know then that they would be leaving in the next day or two. Had I not sold the mill to Mr. Eastridge last spring, we could have milled up gallons of syrup in the fall and I'd have that cash now. I shouldn't have sold the mill.

The other mistake I made was in how I handled the sale itself. Instead of taking back the share of the sawmill, I ought to have asked Mr. Eastwood to pay me cash. I didn't make a hard-headed enough business decision because I let my feelings get in the way. Of course, things were different then, Chase was alive and we earned income from his carpentry jobs and from the sawmill, which was operating more regularly then.

I sometimes make a bit of money from travelers who pass through by asking twenty-five cents per meal when people eat here with us plus twenty-five cents a night if they stay over.

The well, which we wouldn't have gotten dug without the good-humored help of that fine Irish lad, Mr. Dempsey, yields water with too much iron and other minerals in it for me. As I boil it, in no time at all, a hard layer of sediment builds up on the inside bottom of the kettle. I suppose it's better there than in my body. Yes, I could carry water from the spring by the river, and on special occasions I do, but it's bothersome in winter.

I had been hoping that my new occupation as a schoolteacher would provide a salary, but I don't think I can even count on that. I enjoy teaching and I think I'm good at it. But the parents who send their children to me don't seem to want to pay me for my services. It is not just that I resent not being paid. I find this neglect of their agreed-upon obligation offensive. Their reluctance to come forward with some payment takes away some of the dignity that should be associated with the job. I'm put out that my neighbors might be taking advantage of me, knowing that I'm a widow and don't have either Chase or Father around to remind them of their obligation. By teaching, my time is not my own anymore. I work hard at teaching. Being with my scholars all day denies me the opportunity to visit with my friends and neighbors, which has been my habit. I'm sure the parents don't think of it that way, but that is the case.

I don't intend to run the school as a labor of love. I need to pay for my groceries, like everybody else.

There are mission schools in the eastern part of the territory but they are supported by contributions from like-minded congregations in the States. We don't have that kind of thing out here. I've given some thought though, to contacting one of the eastern abolitionists committees and suggesting that now that we have enough Free State settlers in the Territory to guarantee the vote that they divert some of their financial resources to education. I know Lawrence has already set aside land for schools and a college.

But does anybody back in the States care about us out here in the Territory? Now that popular sovereignty is dead and buried, but not, in its intended grave, ha, ha, the debate seems to have shifted from our local fight to make the Territory a Free State to the national problem of slavery. I've received nary a single scrap of anything from any eastern abolitionist group, even though Father was an antislavery Legislator. Oh yes, I read old copies of Reverend Garrison's editorials in *The Liberator*, the magazine he publishes, in which he celebrates our "victory" in the game of popular sovereignty. I'm sure he continues to print the magazine, but Howland and Father were the ones to subscribe to it and other Northern journals, so I'm now at the mercy of my relatives in the States to keep me posted. I do get occasional copies of Mr. Douglass' newspaper, the *North Star*. In my opinion Frederick Douglas is a little too strident in asserting that there should be "immediate freedom for the slave." The obligation to "do our part" always seems to go from them to us out here in the Territory. He wanted us to defeat the proslavers by being more aggressive. Like John Brown, he thinks the only way abolition will win is through bloodshed. But now that we've got the vote and will surely prevail, what do we do now?

But I have to worry about my own concerns first. I realize now that I need credentials and skills way beyond just being a schoolteacher or a willing Free State immigrant, with a sawmill and some land, to stay alive out here. As a schoolteacher I thought I'd have at least $100 a year, though I didn't expect to live on just that. Well, so much for those expectations.

It's easy to say, "Well, I'll just stick it out. If I can't live as Father thought we could from the proceeds of the sawmill, until Eldorado grows more prosperous I might be able to eke out a living off the farm," but even that is proving difficult. All of these losses and changes remind me of my conversation at Christmas with Mr. Rackliffe about the book of Job. Job expected to live out his days in comfort and respectability but then God put him to the test, which included the loss of his children and his worldly possessions. I'm not supposing or suggesting that God has singled me out and is putting me to a test but the loss of Father, Chase and the baby is certainly an unplanned for personal catastrophe. I'll admit that what

Mr. Rackliffe told me about the meaning of Job was an

interesting distraction, but for me, not a usable explanation. It certainly hasn't helped me understand my own situation any better.

While I had been contemplating my prospects, Mr. Enos had concentrated on driving us to Indian Creek, speaking very little during the several hours it took us to get there.

Mr. Enos and I spent that night with a Quaker family at Indian Creek, which included a warm hearty supper. The family was affiliated with the Quakers at Emporia.

I knew one of Judge Lambdin's sons who had a claim between Indian Creek and Emporia. I thought I'd take my chances in stopping there to inquire of the Judge's whereabouts. Father had surveyed Judge J.C. Lambdin's claim in Chelsea the summer Eldorado was founded and I had met one of his sons there the following spring. As luck would have it Judge Lambdin was returning from a Territorial Council meeting and was visiting this son.

We took our noon meal with him and explained my current situation and asked him to do some legal work for Adda and me, helping us get Father's claim and sawmill ownership transferred to us. He said he'd be glad to do it. I didn't go into great detail about our plans, as I wasn't sure about them myself, but I left it at letting him know that by midsummer Adda and I wanted to have the opportunity of selling out our Eldorado claims, if we so choose. The old lawyer said that would give him plenty of time.

The Judge, Mr. Enos and I talked a little politics. Judge Lambden seemed pleased to tell me that last November (the election on the 8th) he was elected to the Territorial council, representing several western counties including our district where they continue to "polish" the Free State constitution. "We miss your father on that council," he said. His remark put a lump in my throat and my eyes grew misty.

After lunch and the discussion, Mr. Enos and I left for Emporia. In the afternoon, we crossed the real Duck Creek and I went out of my way to point out the local landmarks to my traveling companion.

Late that day we rolled into Emporia and sought lodging and food at the Storrs' place. Who should be there but Mrs. Woodruff, the widow who Mr. Weinbury mentioned when he brought me some mail from the new Chelsea post office a day or so before Christmas. The same day he made an offer to buy Chase's guitar. I gave some thought to expressing condolences to Mrs. Woodruff but decided against it, simply due to the hustle of arranging our lodging, and I really didn't know her, though Father knew her husband. Miss Minnie Post and Mrs. Barrett were also staying at the Storrs' place. Seeing Mrs. Barrett was a surprise, since we had visited at the beginning of this trip.

Last summer, Miss Post wanted to establish the first Sunday school in Eldorado and asked some advice from me as to where we should meet. Her question contained a strong hint to have it at our house since I was already teaching school there. But Maggie Vaught, who wanted to locate the Sunday school in Chelsea, prevailed. (She later was among those who wanted my school to be up in Chelsea rather than at my house.) (I never attended the Sunday school in Chelsea, though I held Miss Posts intentions in the highest regard.)

Mrs. Storrs assigned me a room with Mrs. Woodruff and Miss Post. Miss Post is about my age and was very curious about my books. While I was seeing to Mr. Enos about bringing in my trunk, Miss Post began reading in my journal and was at it when we brought the trunk in. At first I mildly resented her nosiness but she made a rather flattering remark about some of my recent entries and said she too had lately suffered the loss of loved ones and wondered if there might be some mutual gain by sharing our experiences. We did have a discussion before supper but I sensed that she was simply inquisitive about our family, my marriage to Chase, and my widowhood, asking me how I was handling it. "Are you experiencing a change in your social position?"

"No," I said, "why should I?"

"With your father who had been President of Eldorado and in the Legislature, now dead and with poor Chase gone, and nobody to run the sawmill, I would assume that things would have changed for you, socially."

I was offended by her assumptions about my social and economic situation. Actually, I guess my offense stemmed from the obvious truth in her remarks, but I certainly wasn't going to admit that to her since there seemed to be a morbid side to her curiosity and it was none of her business. I think I felt as though she was saying, "Augusta Stewart was getting her comeuppance." Detecting a mean spiritedness in her remarks, I suggested that we go to supper. Walking downstairs I asked how it was that she was so well informed on current events in Eldorado. She said she was a friend of Mr. and Mrs. Buchanan (that's the same Mr. Buchanan who made the mistake of challenging Adda to the

Lyceum debate.) When Mrs. Buchanan came out and joined her husband, they filed a claim in Chelsea, where they remain according to Miss Post.

When I was through here last November I made note of a foundation going in for what looked to me like an unusually large building for "these parts." Well, Emporia now boasts a four-room hotel with all the bedrooms on the second story and rather spacious rooms on the main floor. I am consumed with curiosity to know if Preston Plumb built this hotel; 'wouldn't surprise me.

The following night we stayed in Versailles, which is southwest of Lecompton but on the Santa Fe Trail. We arrived in the outskirts of Lawrence late the next day on Thursday, March 15th. Mr. Enos invited me to stay with his family, though I'm not very far from the Whitney House, where Adda is. We got here about sundown and as though Mrs. Enos knew we were due in, she had prepared a very nice supper. They have two daughters, Emma and Helen, both about Adda's age, maybe younger. They helped with the meal and their enthusiasm and curiosity in greeting their father reminded me of the way Adda and I used to miss our father when he was gone and the good times we had when he returned. What a cozy little family. During the meal I couldn't help but feel a little envious of the warm affection these people show each other. Mr. Enos, in their presence, is an entirely different man than the loquacious driver who was so sure of himself leaving Eldorado, but soon got us lost on the prairie.

As much as I loved Chase and our family, before and after our marriage, I realized tonight in the presence of the Enos Family I never fully appreciated at the time the happiness we had together.

50

LAWRENCE
D. H. MONTAGUE TO THE RESCUE
March 16 to June 1860

On Friday, March 16th, Mr. Enos brought me over to the Whitney House in a buggy. Adda already knew I was in-town. Mr. Woodward, Mrs. Enos' traveling companion who had gone on to White Water from our place, also arrived last night in Lawrence, is staying at the Whitney House and spoke to Adda about our travel arrangements. Mr. Woodward and his two friends, John Crocker and Amos Cutter all got drunk last night at the Whitney House, apparently celebrating some sort of a reunion.

I stayed with Adda Friday night. She and Mrs. Crocker (who's upset with her husband's behavior) had tickets to attend a combination musical and lecture by a Mr. Phillips, who is from a speaker's agency out of Chicago. Although I was invited along, I grew weary of listening to Mrs. Crocker cluck her tongue about her husband's behavior with Mr. Woodward and Amos Cuter. I wanted to say to her, "Instead of complaining, count your blessings. You have a husband." I enjoyed the music (before and after the speech) much better than the lecture. But it's nice to be back where these cultural benefits are available even to the working classes. I added that observation because it looks like my current situation has reduced me to the "working classes." In less than a year I've slipped from being an employer to an employee.

I asked the new proprietor at the Whitney House for a job and was hired. So, both Adda and I are now to be working for old Mr. Stone. Adda said they aren't as busy now as they were prior to John Brown's death.

Elections were to be held in Lawrence March 21st and that's today. Liquor always gets poured far too freely whenever we have a Territorial election. Father used to say it seemed to be a necessary lubricant. There's so much liquor available to those eligible to vote, since Illinois "corn" whiskey is now only thirty cents a gallon, I don't expect to see many sober voters. It was two years ago this month that Father was elected a delegate to the Minneola Convention to work on the Free State Constitution.

After the polls closed, a fellow, a little under the Election Day influence, came in and inquired politely if he was too late for supper. We had already cleaned the dining room. I took him into the kitchen to see if the cook would serve him. But the new cook, who is afraid of Mr. Stone, was hesitant to feed him after hours. I should add the cook is the widow who had been working part-time at Dagarian's. Her husband was killed by proslavers two years ago. She's really a very nice lady, but doesn't want to jeopardize her job. I don't know why she's so concerned. She hasn't been paid for weeks.

If Aggie Rourke were still here, she'd gladly have rustled-up something for him, even if he was just a little drunk. Aggie herself enjoyed a "nip" now and then—said it eased her lumbago.

While the cook was deciding whether to offer the stranger a meal, he was standing very straight against the big kitchen table with both hands grasping its edges. I was struck by his fine posture, even if he was a little tipsy. He seemed to be someone I'd met, but I couldn't place him. He was a tall, rawboned man, dark hair and open face, clean-shaven, about Father's age. He had a very engaging smile. He seemed sober enough to focus on me and began scrutinizing me to such an extent it embarrassed me in front of the other girls, who were scurrying about cleaning-up.

After a minute or so he said, "Say, I know you. You're Sam Stewart's daughter from Plymouth. Don't ya rekanize me for hevvins sakes? I'm D.H. Montague from Plymouth. I served with your father in the old Town Company." We were in Lecompton together. After your dad got out, I took sick and lost about forty pounds down there. They kept me in, hopin' I'd die. I fooled 'em and was finally paroled out." He said he had been released three years ago this month.

"Before I got out, I was assigned commissary duty, that is, I was allowed to go out and find food and other supplies." He laughed and said, "I inherited your father's old prison job.

With a serious look, he added, "The provisions your father and Mr. Kerr brought into the prison helped over a hundred of us get through that miserable winter."

Then he paused. "Last I heard of your Father, he had gotten into politics and had founded a settlement out on the Walnut River, so what are you doing in Lawrence?"

Then he got even more personal and said, "What's a daughter of Sam Stewart doing working in a place like this?"

Adda, who by now had joined the kitchen audience, which had grown to five or six girls, said, "We're earning a living, Mr. Montague, that's what we're doing. Father was killed in November of '58 and there's not enough business out in Eldorado to keep our sawmill busy."

Adda's comment was so startling; her words seemed to have a sobering effect on Mr. Montague.

He diverted his scrutiny from me to Adda. "Sam Stewart dead-I don't believe it!"

"Well, it's true and that's that."

"Ah ha, then you're the other daughter. We heard a lot about you two and your beautiful mother when your father and I were in Lecompton together. You must be the left-handed one who could take off a Turkey's head at 200 yards with a Sharps," Mr. Montague gave Adda an approving look.

Adda looked at the other girls who, of course, were looking at her. She beamed. Suddenly her already solid reputation as an independent working girl acquired a new and enviable facet, enhanced by this handsome stranger's revelation.

I don't think the Whitney House is a good place anymore for young ladies like you," said Mr. Montague. "With the demise of John Brown and some of his followers, the departure of the previous proprietor who was a staunch abolitionist and those Eastern Journalists, the clientele of this establishment has in my opinion dropped several notches. Since Nathan Stone took over, this hotel has gotten a questionable reputation." Then addressing all of us in the kitchen he said, "Just let anybody harm or offend in any way these two ladies from Plymouth and they'll have me to answer to."

"Mr. Montague," Adda, her voice softening,

"We aren't from Plymouth anymore. We left there more than three years ago. The only people we know who might still living be living in Plymouth are the Van Curens."

Mr. Montague acknowledged her comment with a nod. Then addressing his rapt audience, he said with a flourish, "There are a lot of us that owe Sam Stewart, the father of these two ladies, more than we can repay, so for his sake, I'm going to keep an eye on them, and there'll be hell to pay around this town if any of one mistreats them. Just spread that word around."

The cook, who seems to be about his age, appeared caught up in this rather boozy but affectionately articulated chivalry said, "Mr. Montague," you just sit down. We've got some chicken stew and a couple dumplings left over from supper. We'll fix you up."

One of the girls put a plate and a large spoon in front of him. The cook ladled out some stew. Mr. Montague seated himself and commenced eating. Adda and the girls drifted back to their duties. One-by-one they left the kitchen and resumed cleaning up in the dining room and setting the tables for tomorrow's breakfast. On one of the occasions, when Adda and I were both in the kitchen, Mr. Montague asked me if I'd seen any of the "veterans" of the Lecompton.

"Yes, I've seen Captain Cracklin, Frank Swift and several others."

Adda added, "Before we moved out to Eldorado I worked for Governor Robinson's brother's family and often saw Sara Robinson, the Governor's wife. Was she in Lecompton while you were there?" Mr. Montague looked up from his plate, smiled but didn't answer.

"And Augusta worked for Mr. and Mrs. Gates, both at their place out of town and later at the Cincinnati House. Mr. Gates was paroled a few months after Father. Most of these men and more are all around town, so you'll be seeing them."

He put his spoon down and smiled. I think the stew and a mug of hot coffee the cook had served him had sobered him up.

"Because your father and I were older than most of the men at Lecompton, we were often given special responsibilities, like the commissary duty. And we would often assume other responsibilities. In my case I had served in the Mexican War, went in with the Massachusetts Volunteers. I often acted as drill sergeant for the prisoners. For exercise and to show the proslavers that they couldn't break our spirits, I'd muster our boys from the Plymouth and Lexington companies in the prison compound and we would perform some very smart close order drill."

"Close Order Drill?"

"Yes, close order drill is the ABCs of military training. It's the first training step toward creating a basic military unit out of twenty to forty individuals who one week before, down over the years, had been on a Roman farm or had been French, or German peasants or New England farmers. By close order drill, they are taught to behave or perform a task as a military group. First they simply learn to march and maneuver as a squad on the parade ground. They learn to listen and obey commands of experienced leaders. These commands might require precise movements executed together and immediately. But in later formations they are expected to follow commands from the company commander who is following orders from the head of the battalion and so on up the chain of command.

"It is the age-old system of military training and discipline that's evolved over the centuries to take farm boys and in sixty to ninety days get them organized enough to obey military orders, to do as they are told by their experienced leaders, to accomplish a military goal so that they can fight as a squad, win and stay alive for the next battle.

"But I'm afraid that in our society, because we're all supposed to be born equal, the concept of leadership is baffling. A leader by definition is an elite person but in our new society elitism is shunned because it is in contrast to equality. Of course, that's all political humbug. Oh, you can take a history course and learn how kings or other potentates behaved as leaders or how great generals George Washington, Napoleon or Caesar led their armies, but you don't learn how to lead from reading history.

"You can read Caesar's commentaries from cover to cover but I defy you to tell me what the ten ingredients were that made him a leader. Can't do it.

"That's why leadership is so important, yet there's not a school or college that specifically teaches you how to become a leader. In the military, men are trained to be leaders but only up to the sergeant's level. From then on if a leader emerges, it's a random event. Thomas Jefferson, who was a perennial student, pestered Congress to establish a school for Army officers back east on the Hudson but he knew all that such a school could do was to simply increase the odds of producing better military commanders. West Point was founded nearly sixty years ago, but in the first major combat that had West Point graduates in the field, the British burned down the Capitol because our military leadership wasn't able to stop them. When the British tried to repeat that in Baltimore, ten thousand Maryland volunteers using their own guns fought off the British and saved the harbor. They were obviously better organized and had better leadership.

Officers from a military school don't automatically guarantee success. And that was also true forty years later, when we fought the Mexicans and we beat them, little thanks to a cadre of junior grade officers from West Point. Our best leaders in the Mexican War were politicians in uniform, and most of them were Democrats—Southern proslavery Democrats, it pains me to add.

"In Lecompton we were so good at close order drills that those Southern guards including those who had also served in the Mexican War, like me, and had enough military experience to appreciate sharply performed drills, respected our discipline even if they had to pretend otherwise."

I don't know why Mr. Montague went into all of this while he was finishing his super. He seemed to want to talk to somebody and what he had to say was certainly interesting.

Before we went to bed I asked Adda if she remembered him from Plymouth and she said she did. Neither of us, though, could recall seeing him at Lecompton, when we visited the camp with Father in January three years ago.

I don't now where Mr. Montague spent the night, but it wasn't at the Whitney House.

The next morning the cook said to me, "Augusta, it looks like you've found an old friend. How long did you two talk after I turned in? It was just a rhetorical question.

I bumped into Tom Cordis and Mr. Stein today (April 15th.) Tom and I had a nice visit. He says things are so slow in Eldorado that he's seriously thinking of leaving, going to the gold fields, not to seek gold but to find customers for his blacksmithing. He says it's been such a dry spring that the farmers in our area are very worried about how they'll make it through the winter, if they have a poor harvest.

Mr. Stein has some very bad news. Mrs. Carey has died. My first thought was her baby. He is just six months old. I asked Mr. Stein what would happen to the baby, but he didn't know. Well, there are three people out there that will know, Mary Rackliffe, Elizabeth Cordis and Mrs. Martin. I'll write them all today. Someone's got to take care of that little boy.

More bad news Deputy Marshal Arms, who was a friend of A.D. Searle helped Governor Reeder escape from the Territory in May of '56, was shot and killed in Topeka last Thursday by another upstanding local, John Ritchie. It seems that there was some kind of fracas that warranted Mr. Arms arresting Mr. Ritchie. Deputy Marshall Arms is a brother-in-law of Mr. Eldridge, the owner of the Eldridge House, where they brought him and laid him out in a little room off the big lobby. Many of his friends have stopped by to pay their last respects. I didn't know either gentleman personally. The dead man's widow and three children were sent for from Wyandott.

It's rather peaceful around here at the Whitney House now. Mr. Stone has gone to visit relatives in Detroit. He left without paying, Adda, the cook, two other employees and me what he owed us. That's a month's salary for me. He owes others even more. We are managing to run the place just fine without him. After all, the boarders, who are declining in number, don't care one way or the other whether he's here. Unlike the previous proprietor he is not interested in Territorial politics and has nothing in common with any of them, especially our "old regulars."

It is now Sunday, April 22nd. Though Adda's been quiet about her beau, the gunsmith, I've discovered his name is John Graton. He has recently moved from a small shop at #45 New Hampshire Street to larger facilities on the east side of Massachusetts Avenue between 7th and 8th street (later to be named Henry and Winthrop streets.) He makes guns to order and repairs them and sells all sorts of ammunition. He squired Adda to a dance tonight but I've not had the pleasure of meeting him yet, though he used to eat here occasionally I understand he boards mostly at the Eldridge hotel where he's more apt to meet a higher-class customer. They say he's substantial enough to place advertisements in most of the territorial newspapers. John Graton is four years older than Adda. I wonder what it is about Adda that seems to attract older men, like Davenport, the teamster, Frank Robinson, Erastus Howland, and now this gunsmith. Each of these fellows is several years older than Adda.

A month has passed. It's already the third week of May. News and energy: both scarce. I haven't heard much about what is happening back in Eldorado, though I am aware of several departures. Tom Cordis has indeed left, but instead of the gold camps in the Rockies I heard he headed for California. The York family has also left Eldorado, and so has David Upham. Old Mr. Chapin is farming our claim and I wish him luck! I hear it hasn't rained once out there all spring.

I'm rather discouraged with my lot. I thought the social life in Lawrence would help pull me out of this chronic despondency and it has some. There are plenty of new faces, but I've lost so much of the independence that I thought I would have achieved by now. I've been working at this place (Whitney House) since my arrival March 21st and I've not been paid a penny. Mr. Stone's been back from Detroit for a month but I can't get a nickel out of the old skinflint. I nag him almost daily.

Mrs. Gates warned us about him. She sure knew what she was talking about. When I accost him about back pay, he says things like, "We're a little slow now," (which is not the case) or "I'll take care of it shortly."

If I press him, he says, "Now don't be impudent. I don't like impudent help." On more than one occasion he's called me a pest. Maybe I should quit. By quitting I could get my back pay, I think. I'd visit with Mrs. Gates about collecting from him but she's traveling back East. I just don't know what to do. It's so embarrassing socially not to have some spending money. Some social events call for clothes I didn't bring with me and it really bothers me that I don't have the money that I've earned to buy a few simple necessities. I need a pair of dress shoes and can't afford them. But what really annoys me is Mr. Stone's effrontery, his assumption that he can do as he pleases with regard to the female help and we have so little remedy.

With the prospects of a poor crop this summer and all the available surplus farmland around Eldorado, I don't see how, if I did sell the farm, I'd realize much, but I'll bide my time. Adda's in the same "fix" but she is such a blithe, buoyant spirit, that things that aggravate me, like not being paid for two months, Adda handles with aplomb. I like that word; I wish I had more use for it. I made up my mind today and told old Mr. Stone to find someone to take my place.

He said, "Well that won't be a problem-how soon you leaving?"

I responded that, when I left, I expected to be paid in full.

His response was, "Fine, the sooner the better." I presented him a little slip of paper with an accounting of what he owed me. He mumbled something like he had no idea that I'd accumulated such arrears!

"Me," I said, "I haven't asked you to accumulate anything. All I wanted was to be paid on time. You know you've failed to pay me ever since I set foot in this place."

"That's not entirely true. I've given you food and lodging. You've had a roof over your head and you've eaten the same food every day as the boarders."

At noon today, June 12th, I applied for a job at the Eldridge House and had no idea it had become as elegant as it has, inside. When I was here last, they were still making repairs from the damage done by Sheriff Jones and the Missourians in May of 1856.

Walking out of the lobby, whom should I run into but our old Plymouth friend, Mr. Montague? He had just taken his noon meal there and was in the outer lobby lighting up a "stogie." He was preparing himself for a spit-fest by nudging a big brass spittoon over to his chair with his foot.

We recognized each other simultaneously. He was sober, very well dressed. He politely inquired how we were, how things were going at the Whitney House, etc. I said I'd just quit my job there and was hoping to get a job here at the Eldridge House. He said, "Well, I'm not at all surprised you left old Stone." He said, "Ever since the death of Old John Brown and the departure of his compatriot, the previous proprietor, who was so well liked in town, the clientele at the Whitney House has dropped several social notches."

"Mr. Montague, we all have to make a living." He nodded in agreement. After a pause he said, "You know, that was a very nice gesture of your cook to feed me supper election night when I was in 'my cups' and you had already cleaned up. How is she?"

"The cook quit, too," I said.

"What about your sister?"

"He hasn't paid her either."

"Well, well, sounds like you two girls and the cook have a grievance or two with Mr. Stone, eh? Want to tell your old abolitionist friend about it? I told you before I'd be looking out for your interests."

I rather wished Adda had been along. She would know how to handle this. I was embarrassed to admit that I hadn't been paid a penny since accepting employment there, that's over two months now. I could use some help getting my pay but it was truly offensive that because I am a widow, Mr. Stone had been able to take terrible advantage of me. And there were other classes of abuse practiced by Mr. Stone on the female help so much more embarrassing than withholding pay that it will take someone other than me to describe. Were Father or my husband alive, this would not have happened-both of them would make fast work of this rascal.

But Mr. Montague's next remarks saved me the explanation that I had been ashamed to make. He said, "Well, I wasn't so drunk that night in your kitchen that I've forgotten what I said. Anybody, I mean anybody that takes advantage of either of you two Stewart girls has got me to deal with. That is the least I can do for my old comrade-in-arms."

By now he had his cigar on fire and had released one huge gob of brown tobacco juice, squarely hitting the spittoon as though he'd had considerable practice.

With a bit of male mischievousness playing on his face he said, "Miss Stewart, what degree of abolitionist do you suppose old Mr. Stone is?"

I was puzzled by his question and remarked, "I don't think he's an abolitionist at all." He's only been in the Territory a few months.

"Do you think he's made enough of a contribution to our cause out here that gives him a right to mistreat two young lady friends of mine?" He waved his cigar like a baton. "I suspect that he is a zero-degree abolitionist."

He saw I was puzzled by his comment.

"Well, your father and I figured out during a rare moment of levity, when we were prisoners that we had become 32nd degree abolitionists.

We both came out here voluntarily and that's worth five degrees. I'm from Springfield, Massachusetts and your father is from Michigan. We joined General Lane's Army voluntarily: that's five more degrees. We fought at least five battles on behalf of Free Soil. That's ten degrees. And we survived starvation and sickness in Lecompton— that's another twelve degrees. If you add all that up," he said, with a big grin, "you get thirty-two degrees.

We earned our right to be here peaceably. And now we're beating them at the polls in a voting contrivance of their own, so we don't have to put up with aggravation from the Missouri pukes or the proslavers passing through or the Johnny-come-latelies like Mr. Stone from North or South who can't possibly appreciate what some of us," and gallantly pointed his cigar at me, "have gone through to make this Territory more livable. You just let old

Sergeant Montague take care of Mr. Stone, yep, that was my rank in both the Mexican War and in the Lexington Company. He spit with such vigor it rocked the polished spittoon again. As I walked off the porch, he stood-up, gave me a salute and said with a smile, 'My regards to the cook.'"

This was Tuesday, June 12th.

The next afternoon I went over to the Whitney House to get "my stuff." I had almost forgotten about my interview with "Sir Galahad" Montague. I was really quite preoccupied with my economic condition and whether my plan of quitting would result in getting paid-up. And I was not at all sure that I would find employment at the Eldridge House.

In the kitchen I bumped into the cook. "Augusta, something strange has gotten into Mr. Stone," she said.

"How's that?"

"He paid me in-full this morning and said he'd write a letter of commendation if I needed it but wanted me to stay here!"

"Where is he?" I said sharply, remaining unimpressed and indignant. She pointed to the lobby.

In spite of the cook's good news, I was prepared to be quite snippy with Mr. Stone. He was seated in the lobby in the same chair that the previous proprietor sat in last November when I visited Adda and we had our likenesses made at Dagarian's that afternoon. I walked over and stood in front of him. He was puffing on a cigar. He greeted me so cordially, I wasn't sure it was Mr. Stone until he looked up at me.

"Ah, Miss Stewart, I'm now financially able to clear up the arrears the house owes you and your sister and I hope you both change your mind and stay with us," he said with such cordiality I couldn't believe my ears.

That was the first I'd heard that Adda had considered quitting. I asked if staying was a condition to getting paid. "No, of course not, I have your money in this envelope."

I counted it and it agreed with the invoice I'd given him plus pay through today, June 13th. (The old rascal obviously assumed I'd stay.) When I had the money in my purse, I said, "No, Mr. Stone, I'm still quitting. You are neither a polite or considerate employer. In Eldorado, we owned a sorghum mill that was operated by help. "We've had employees. I'm from a family of employers," I said. "My family never treated any employee the way you've treated Adda and me. You want others to hold you in high regard because you derive some personal dignity and respect from your position here. Why then do you deny respect and dignity to your employees? Your success depends on the hard work Adda and I and the other girls do. Why can't you treat us as you wish to be treated? But you know, Mr. Stone, more than anything else, I resent the way you act as if we are nobodies. For two months you didn't even know my name. I was "Hey there." I've worked hard all my life but I want my work to be appreciated and want to be acknowledged as a human being. A good way to show that is to be paid and paid on time, and not to have the pay put into question. I think you enjoyed putting me in the position of having to nag you for what I earned. That, sir, was unforgivable. You wouldn't dream of behaving like this to a man, so what gives you the right to treat women in such a shabby way."

As I started to leave, he said, "By the way, you and Adda seem to have a friend, a Mr. Montague. It appears he also knows the cook."

By now I had my hand on the front door knob. It was a warm, sunny day and the early afternoon sunlight through the bevel in the front door's glass spread a beautiful spectrum of colors on a white tablecloth near the door. As though I had acquired a spurt of confidence and articulation from the bright colors on the table, I turned around and said, "Yes, he and my father were comrades-in-arms under General Lane during the battles out here in 1856. That was all before you came out here—men like them made the Territory safe for business people like you."

"Just one minute please," he said, "I've heard of 32nd degrees in the Masonic Order. Before you leave, can you shed some light on what a thirty-second degree abolitionist is?" I presume you and Adda are abolitionists. Just what is a 32nd degree abolitionist?"

That's when I knew for sure that that Mr. Montague had been as good as his word.

Pulling the door open, I turned and said, "I'm afraid you'll have to discuss that with my attorney, Mr. Montague."

"Why, I didn't know he was an attorney," said Mr. Stone.

By now I was on the front porch, I had closed the door of the Whitney House behind me in more ways than one and was headed for the wooden sidewalk out front. I said to my self, "I didn't either but it sure got your attention." I could hardly wait to relate all this to Adda.

51

CONVERSATION WITH A PROSLAVERY LAWYER
June and July, 1860

Now that I have quit my job at the Whitney House, I have to find other lodging. I have decided to room with Sarah Goss, one of Adda's close friends. She's already invited me several times to come stay with her. Adda has decided to remain at the Whitney House now that she expects to get paid regularly, thanks to Mr. Montague. I'm hopeful I'll find work at the Eldridge House.

I've been visiting with Mrs. Fisk, a frail lady who is trying to run a small boarding house. She has asked me to help her if I don't get work at the Eldridge House. Lord knows she needs it, she is so sickly, has only four boarders, and can barely manage that.

I've been so busy I haven't had time to put down the details of a situation developing at home that requires some serious thought.

Last Friday, Mr. Rackcliffe came into town, located me and after the pleasantries said the crops in the entire Walnut River Valley are drying up for lack of rain. The grasshoppers eat the few shoots that do come up. He said everyone who can muster the means is leaving the county including himself, Mary and the baby (who they've finally named Ermie.)

His advice was if we want to salvage anything of our claim, including the house, we'd better go home. (Of course, one of my current quandaries is; where *is* home? In Eldorado or here in Lawrence where I'll be subject to the whims of employers, like old Mr. Stone?)

Adda was not a party to this discussion with Mr. Rackliffe, but I knew she needed to be aware of what was happening back home. I hoped I could get her to consider this matter. Adda doesn't seem to be having her mind on anything but romance. She is quite impressed and flattered by the attention, not to mention gifts that she's been receiving from her gunsmith friend.

Whether or not I'll get Adda's opinion on this matter, I've decided what I'm going to do. If the Rackliffes are moving, and the Barretts have already moved, if Tom and Elizabeth (Cordis) have left…and I don't know about the Martins or the Careys… if most of our friends have left or are leaving, there's very little reason for me to think of Eldorado as home anymore. I'd love to continue teaching but if the parents are so poor or indifferent as to pay me, there's precious little future for me as Eldorado's school marm. The one hundred dollars I'd been counting on from teaching, simply isn't going to come to pass.

So as soon as I can arrange it, I'll return. I'll sell old Kate and the milk cow. If the Martins are intending to remain, I will inquire if Mr. Martin is still interested in buying our share of the sawmill. On the way home I'll pass through Emporia and tell Judge Lambden what I'm up to and get instructions from him on how to proceed.

It is Sunday, June 24th, and Adda came by Mrs. Fisk's place for a visit, but only for a few hours. She's going to a church social with Mr. Graton and others this evening. I'm invited but my proper clothes are at "home" and not here.

I discussed with Adda my meeting with Mr. Rackliffe and what I'd decided to do. Adda's response was to say that we could discuss all this much better at the new ice-cream parlor that has opened down town. She said, announcing as proudly as if she were the place's proprietor, "The parlor serves a new style ice-cream." She added that she too had gotten her back pay from old Mr. Stone and would treat me to a dish.

On the way over I asked Adda if she knew about Mr. Montague's intervention on our behalf. Adda laughed that contagious laugh of hers and said, "Oh, yes, it's the main topic of conversation and will be the source of gossip at the Whitney House for weeks. Katie Jones heard the whole altercation."

She said it began with an exchange of heated words between them. She said Mr. Montague took Mr. Stone by the collar and threatened to march him down New Hampshire Street to the Kaw River to baptize him into the abolitionists' religion. Mr. Stone immediately assured Mr. Montague that this was all a misunderstanding with some excitable females, telling him that if there was any back pay coming, it was his bookkeeper's error, which he would correct this very day. Mr. Stone presented Mr. Montague with a glass of whiskey and a Caribbean cigar. They had a smoke and some congenial spitting together in the front parlor.

"After they finished their cigars, according to Katie, Mr. Montague got up, thanked Mr. Stone for his hospitality, looked him in the eye and told him that he shouldn't think that a cigar and a glass of corn whiskey would alter his opinion of him. Mr. Montague berated him, saying that he had badly mistreated you, me, the cook, all of us abolitionist friends of his who had to work, because their men folk are dead at the hands of proslavery rascals. Katie says he then told him, "I shall keep an eye on you to honor your obligation to them and to be speedy about it."

With that Mr. Montague left and old Mr. Stone began nervously putting all the back pay in little tan envelopes and passing them out. Adda said all the girls were so impressed with Mr. Montague that she's enjoying some new status, since they all know he's her protector. "Our old friend from Plymouth is much older than any of them, but they are all interested in him and they want to know more about him.

"Now here's the juicy part," she added. Mr. Montague and the widow cook are going to the church social tonight with us… ain't that swell?"

Adda said that right after the noon meal yesterday Mr. Stone came over and gave her an envelope with her back pay and did the same for the cook and Katie. It seems he owed Katie more than the rest of us Adda said, "That's not the half of it." Adda said. "You remember Katie was to get married. Well…it seems her sweetheart unintentionally intercepted a letter addressed to her from the East by paying the postage due. The letter revealed she wasn't really marriageable after all. She has four children in Illinois."

Going to the new ice cream parlor was a first rate idea. Adda and I laid our plans. We'll go back to Eldorado together, leaving no later than Thursday, June 28th. If we can find a buyer, we will sell the house, the sawmill and all three claims, then return to Lawrence. Before we discussed our travel plans, I explained to Adda my recent visit with Judge Lambdin and the assignment I'd given him to see if she found any fault with it. She agreed. We could take our wagon and team, which would be convenient to bring our household belongings back to Lawrence. I'm glad now that Mr. Enos and I brought them up here in March. I've kept the horses at Mr. Gate's place. Maybe it would be easier for us to take the stagecoach and ask Mr. Woodward and Mr. Enos to freight our stuff back. Hauling is what those gentlemen do for a living, but we didn't decide.

Later in the day, I explained to Mrs. Fisk what we were up to and she asked if she could come along with us. She's not at all well and thought she would visit relatives in Emporia and try to recover her health. I told her it might be a very hot trip, because of the unusual summer but she is certainly welcome to join us. I told her we plan on leaving Lawrence, early this coming Thursday morning. That will give her four boarders time to find other accommodations.

We've been on the road three days from Lawrence. We left as planned last Thursday but decided to go back with Mr. Rackliffe in his one-horse wagon. He had been in town buying and soliciting supplies, mostly food, to provide relief for the settlers around Eldorado, whose farms are failing. He has a full wagon being pulled by only one horse. Mrs. Fisk is with us too. Last night when we arrived here in Wakarusa, someone at the boarding house remarked that we'd never get up the hills west of town with our load being pulled by only one horse. He recommended a gentleman just west of town who had oxen for rent. Adda, Mr. Rackliffe and myself took an after-super stroll to see just how steep this hill was. We concluded, while still enjoying a nice twilight that the man's advice was right and we would need help.

It was going on 9:30 PM before we located the gentleman he had recommended. The owner of the oxen was a most interesting fellow. As is the custom, the oxen we rented had names, Thunder and Lightning, except he referred to them in German as Donder und Blitzen. He guaranteed that if we used his oxen, we'd get up all the hills at six miles per hour and nobody would pass us.

Before we parted company for the night, Mr. Rackliffe struck a bargain that we would hire him and the oxen to take us all the way through Clinton to Duck Creek where Mr. Rackliffe's horse would take over. By then we'd be over the serious hilly part of the trail. We agreed to get going directly after breakfast.

While we examined "Donder und Blitzen," now by moonlight, the owner told us that he had been a lawyer in Missouri, who got more harassment than business from the residents thereabouts, as they are mostly abolitionists. To make ends meet, he owns and rents three teams of oxen, helping over-loaded freight wagons navigate these local hills. Sensing immediately that we were abolitionists he quickly informed us that he didn't let his "Missouri" attitude interfere with economic opportunity.

The gentleman seemed to be about ten, maybe fifteen, years older than me and was a veteran of the Mexican War.

In 1845, he and another lawyer from northern Missouri had volunteered to join the army in response to circulars from President Polk's request for mounted cavalry. "After we volunteered," he said, "since most of the boys in the Missouri regiment didn't have horses, we couldn't qualify to be in the cavalry, so we were grouped together into a new unit called the Missouri Volunteer Regiment of Foot Soldiers. As we organized ourselves to become a regiment, the troops elected me Colonel. The one other officer was a Kentucky-born lawyer named Doniphan.

Our regiment had four hundred volunteers, all of us from Mason County over in western Missouri. We took a riverboat to Fort Leavenworth, where we trained and received our rifles and uniforms. Our regiment was part of the Army of the West, except we were one-year volunteers. At Fort Leavenworth our unit was put under the leadership of General Stephen Kearney, a regular Army officer, and we gained another three hundred soldiers, all Army regulars. At first there was some concern that our lack of training and untested stamina would slow the entire regiment down, but in time even the old regulars agreed we had what it took.

He said, "Before we left Fort Leavenworth we were fitted out with various freight wagons, a kitchen wagon, horse-drawn cannons, caissons, guns and other supplies, and were ordered to march to Santa Fe in Mexico and capture it."

Well, it was almost midnight and we decided we should wait 'til morning to hear the balance of his adventure in Mexico. We headed back to our lodgings in Wakarusa, intending to get on the trail as early as possible tomorrow so we could be on our way during the cool part of the day.

We got away as planned an hour or so after sun-up the next morning, July 1st. We drove Mr. Rackliffe's wagon out to the

Colonel's place, immediately put Donder und Blitzen into their yoke and, before 9:30 AM headed west.

For two or three hours we managed all the hills just fine. But just before Clinton it suddenly clouded-up and started to rain and the ruts got very slick. One of the oxen slipped and fell to his knees with two legs inside the rut and two legs out. In trying to recover the ox jostled the harness and sprung loose from the yoke. He was so strong and badly behaved he nearly upset Mr. Rackliffe's wagon and would have if the wagon had not been so heavily loaded. In hindsight Adda and I should have rented two livery horses and taken our big old reliable Studebaker back there in Lawrence, but we didn't. Anyway all we had was our trunk; the rest of the load was all Mr. Rackliffe's.

Mrs. Fisk, whose condition has not improved since leaving Lawrence, was on the wagon trying to stay dry. She was visibly upset and frightened by the animal's behavior. "I am feeling so poorly," she whispered to me. "If the Emporia Stage comes along, and if Adda and you don't mind, I'll try to take that." Just as quickly as the rainsquall came up, it quit, and the sun came out.

Mr. Rackliffe and the owner of the oxen struggled for a couple of hours to get Blitzen back in the yoke, without success. The stage to Emporia came through. We hailed it. It was full, but the driver stopped out of curiosity and addressed a few words to Mr. Rackliffe, who mentioned Mrs. Fisk's condition. A Mr. Adams, a passenger on the stage, heard the discussion and made a public declaration that he'd paid full fare all the way through to Fort Riley where he had important business and "by god" he was not getting off. Mr. Rackliffe, who was a little on edge from wrestling the ox in all that noonday heat, poked his head all the way inside and said to Mr. Adams, "Who asked you, anyway?" I was afraid there'd be a fight. Le Roy Rogers (Mrs. Fisk's cousin) happened to be in the hack going to Emporia. He recognized his cousin and gallantly got out, making room for Mrs. Fisk. And if that wasn't enough, Mr. Rogers was carrying a letter for me from Mary Quirk, an old school friend in Detroit.

The driver of the stagecoach maneuvered up out of the ruts to get around us.

Now with the addition of Mr. Rogers, we had one more man in our group. He tried to help Mr. Rackcliffe and the Colonel put the yoke on the ox but he was no more persuasive with the creature than they had been.

The mid-afternoon sun was blazing. There wasn't enough breeze to disturb a dandelion fuzz head, which was unusual for Kansas. Though we hadn't yet reached Clinton, the Colonel said we'd been over the most serious hills. Well, that was some relief!

While the Colonel was trying to persuade Blitzen back into the yoke, Adda asked, the Colonel if his regiment ever got all the way to Santa Fe on foot.

"Indeed, we did, and as soon as we got there, without so much as a day's rest, we attacked the town and conquered it." He laughed. "There wasn't a Mexican soldier to defend it!" He said he had joined up in the summer of '46, when he was a struggling young lawyer in St. Louis and had been eager for some excitement. "I went into the Army out of a sense of duty mixed with ambition. Of course, being a soldier also offered me an opportunity for responsibility way beyond my years and certainly my ability. I loved the Army and the authority it gave me. Everyone in my regiment joined out of patriotic fever. We wanted to protect Texas, its people. You see, even ten years after Texas had its own revolution and declared its independence, Mexico threatened to take it back. And of course we also wanted to help our nation pursue its God-given right to expand all the way out to California. In those days Mexico also claimed California."

The Colonel said that he believed that the idea of expanding the frontier out west had started with President Jefferson that we had a right, a duty, we called it destiny. "I'd have stayed in the Army if they'd kept me but one week after he war was over I and the volunteer soldiers were discharged."

The Colonel added that although he had agreed with the goal of expanding the size of the United States, he now realized that the Mexican War had also been driven by President Polk's political proclivities. "He ran the war with officers who were mostly Democrats and it didn't hurt their careers if they favored slavery since it was no secret that Texas was going to come in slave.

"I saw a roster after the war that showed we had about thirty generals in the field half regular Army and half volunteers." President Polk invited volunteer generals to bring in their mounted militias from their home states but only if they were Democrats. And that doesn't mean that the other sixteen or so generals of the regular Army were Whigs. I don't think I could name five Whig generals among the regular Army generals. Of course, the first one who comes to mind is Zachary Taylor. President Polk really had to stretch to replace him after his big successful battle at Buena Vista but replace him he did, even with another Whig, Winfield Scott. Of course, General Taylor and the Whigs evened-up the score and replaced one-term Polk at the next election. John Fremont was a good Whig general, not as good as General Taylor, but good. Well, I've named three Whig generals and I can't think of any others.

"There were at least two Irish-born. Both were volunteers, and both were Democrats. Probably a third of that army was foreigners, mostly from Ireland. So it was a very political army, and was suspicious of Whig elitism and suspicious of any form of military aristocracy, particularly West Pointers.

"A newspaper reporter from Atlanta, who was all fired up about seceding to form a separate nation of the South with slavery, traveled with us during our entire Mexican campaign. I don't care much one way or the 'tuther' 'bout slavery. My people in Missouri had two or three slaves. We could've gotten along just as well without them but it was the social thing to do if you could afford them."

The Colonel described other campaigns in Mexico, which ended in a long march to the East coast where they boarded ships bound for St. Louis via New Orleans.

"In New Orleans during an interview the Atlanta newspaper reporter was still with us and who had been keeping a detailed journal, wrote in a newspaper article that our marches from eastern Kansas to Santa Fe, then to Monterey, exceeded 3,000 miles and compared in valor and endurance to any marches in history including the long marches of Napoleon and Hannibal, and I was a party to all that."

By the way, General Persifer Smith, who is running the Army of the West now, headquartered over in fort Leavenworth, was a volunteer militiaman from Louisiana, I believe. He is a dyed-in-the-wool Democrat and, as you know, he has his position here because he favors slavery for the Territory.

"Those were the best years of my life. Nothing I've done since then holds a candle to my time during the Mexican War.

"Afterwards I went home to St. Louis where there were so many lawyers I had a hard time finding work. Nobody knew me in Mason County, and then I got some unwanted notoriety when I tried to defend a group of Mormons, who had been mistreated. I could have won that case if the Mormons had just kept their opinions about slavery to themselves. You know they are almost as rabid in their abolition of slavery as some of you Yankees. Well, they insisted on expressing their opinions to the judge and jury, who were all proslavery and we lost that case and here I am renting out poorly behaving oxen."

Adda laughed, went over to Blitzen, the troublemaker, and gave him a slap. Looking at the Colonel, she said, "He was pretty well-behaved until he found out he was pulling a load for some abolitionists."

While the Colonel, Mr. Rackliffe, Mr. Rogers, Adda and I were all cajoling and wrestling with Blitzen, trying to get the ox back into his yoke, I noticed an eastbound, three-wagon outfit approaching us on the trail.

Our wagon was facing west, its wheels in the ruts. One harnessed ox, Donder, was standing quietly in the middle rut, where he was supposed to be, occasionally flicking its tail against swarms of pesky green-headed flies that seem particularly attracted to an area just under its tail. His reluctant partner, Blitzen, though hobbled, was standing to one side of the trail ignoring our entreaties and our pushing and shoving, occasionally bending its head to graze on the yellow-greenish grass, but absolutely refusing to be yoked next to its companion. At least three hot midday hours had been used up by this nonsense.

Three approaching eastbound, ox-drawn wagons were in bad shape with all kinds of articles hanging and banging from their sides. Half of this outfit was on foot. That's not unusual, except their shoes and clothes were in terrible shape and these people were far more disheveled than normal for a group of travelers. They were now forty to fifty feet west of us. They started to yell at us to turn, around and go home. Someone shouted, "If you are bound for the gold fields, for God's sake, stop right here! We've just come from Pike's Peak and are heading back to the States. You don't know what you're in for."

In a few minutes they began maneuvering up out of the ruts to get around us on the trail, for by then those who were walking had surrounded Mr. Rackliffe's wagon. They didn't offer to help with Blitzen. They just began regaling us about the problems we could expect between here and Pike's Peak. We tried to tell them that we live in the Territory but couldn't get a word in edgewise. They simply assumed we were bound for the Kansas gold fields. They said they had spent the winter in the low mountains and had lost three members of their party, two men and a woman.

Two of the people spoke up. They were so dirty and dressed so disorderly that at first I didn't know they were women. In a rather matter-of-fact way they explained that the winter in the mountains had made them both widows and that they'd traveled west with their husbands on this very trail in a small train last year.

They both looked so young to be proclaiming widowhood. They were my age, give or take a year. My first reaction was pity. I felt so sorry for these two. It took several seconds for the obvious fact to sink in: I too was a widow.

The rear half of the canvas covers on their second wagon was gone, exposing a jumble of household stuff. Mr. Rackliffe asked, "What happened to your 'sail'?"

"We had to use it to make trousers and work shirts for the men. Mining was very hard on the men's clothes.

"There's no gold out there. It's all a hoax, a terrible hoax and the foreigners, you wouldn't believe the number of foreigners out there…don't know where they all come from. You can't understand half of them and they'll steal you blind.

"Why didn't you go on to Oregon or California?" asked Adda, but got no response as the widows and their traveling companions were busying themselves going around our wagon and the stubborn ox, who was still out of harness and indifferent to all the hub-bub.

Their wagons got past us and settled comfortably in the eastbound ruts. One of the widows, who was on foot, tarried a bit. "Don't use the Platte River Route," she said. "If the water don't kill you, the snakes will. That water ain't fit for a mule. It's half mud and you can't strain it. One night I strained a gallon seven times, seven times mind you, and the water was brown as a hazel nut."

As she walked by me, she came close to me and asked if we could spare a little food. I wasn't surprised by the request.

I pulled off the wagon the wicker basket that contained our food, opened it and began to offer her some of its contents. Rather than politely making some choices, she simply dumped the contents of my basket into a large pocket she'd quickly made with a fold in her flapping canvas apron. "God bless you, sister, and good luck," she said, and then hurried to catch up with her outfit. A small scruffy dog and a medium-sized pig followed her. As soon as they were beyond hearing range, Adda said, "Those people simply lack perseverance, probably city people, not very resourceful."

The Colonel spoke up and said, "Those kind need a lot more than just perseverance; they need endurance and leadership. During the Mexican War I learned that there is a big difference in people's level of endurance. I survived that war mostly because I didn't get shot. But all other things, the foul water, the incessant heat, the lousy food and the long hot, endless marching didn't do me in because I was driven by ego, vanity and optimism. God, what optimists we were. After the war, knowing what I had endured gave me confidence to weather all kinds of situations, even in dealing with rascals like this fellow," pointing to Blitzen.

"There are aggravations that mere perseverance will see you through," he said, "You cannot endure without perseverance but that is only one quality you have to have to survive something momentous like a shipwreck or a hard, close battle or some crippling disease. The folks who rise up from that kind of adversity need to be hardy and have prudence and foresight. To endure you must respond to the aggravation, actively respond: not passively. Look at Job in comparison with Noah. Job merely persevered. He simply put up with God's various tests, whereas Noah showed resourcefulness. The Bible attributes Job's perseverance to faith. I don't dispute that but for me the story of Noah is more impressive because it's not just about perseverance. Noah took action. In a contest between Noah and Job, I'm sure Noah would be the winner."

"The idea that the meek will inherit the Earth is nonsense. It's just silly, wishful thinking because there are so many meek among us. Yes, those who persevere will inherit the Earth: Indeed that is already the case. The worst of the incompetents, those most easily distracted or those most softened by the pursuit of creature comforts, have long since perished…and good riddance.

"Although the meek survive, they seek protection from the people who are able to lead and to endure.

Show me an army that has just won a major victory and you'll find a leader who taught those men and provided those soldiers with what they needed to know so they could endure the battle and win.

"It is evident to me that God wants the human race to endure. Just look at the tools he has given us so we can achieve it, but in his wisdom he has put a limit on how much he is willing to contribute to our survival. He disdains the stupid, the incompetent and the deviant, and in a system of elimination the race is improved and holds for all creatures, including this troublesome friend of mine." He gave Blitzen a good-natured slap on the rump.

Pointing derisively to the three receding wagons, he said, "Any river worthy of its name between here and where they're bound will do them in. In any contest where nature is the enemy," he said, "you need to be single-minded but notice that those people weren't even trying to fend for themselves. Even with all the wild fruit and berries that are available here, they still mooched their next meal from you. They are not using their wits to protect themselves. Anything will kill them, a little tainted meat, which anyone with a good nose would reject, or maybe even a small summer tornado. It's a good bet that none of them will see their fortieth birthday. Our graveyards are full of their ilk."

"Colonel, you are a most interesting man," said Adda. "You seem to have given a lot more thought to philosophy than anybody I've met, except perhaps our father. On occasion he was rather philosophical. Your stimulating speech on endurance raises an interesting question. Since you speak of endurance in almost heroic terms, what in your opinion fuels endurance?"

Out on the open prairie in the mid afternoon sun the back of Mr. Rackliffe's wagon provided our only shade. Tired-out from wrestling with the stubborn ox again Mr. Rackcliffe was now lying down with most of his legs under his wagon in the shade provided by the angle of the last big hoop holding up the canvas cover. The Colonel was leaning against the back of the wagon in the shade. Adda was also leaning there facing the Colonel. I had taken a box down from the wagon and was sitting on it, taking notes as fast as I could write, often asking the Colonel to repeat some idea new to me, all the while flicking off prairie insects that seem to find something of interest about me.

"Conceit, pure and simple." The Colonel paused a bit to organize his response, and then explained what he meant. In my case I went into the military out of patriotism and out of a desire for adventure, but I put myself in a situation where I put my life at risk. Those of us who signed-up for the war were so full of ourselves and the righteousness of our cause. Conceit always springs from a perception of being right. Self-righteousness and conceit go hand in hand.

"America, come what may of the North and the South's current difference of opinion about slavery, will endure and will continue to thrive as a democracy, because we are an aggregate of so many conceited, self-satisfied individuals. You Northerners are just as certain about your beliefs as those of us who live down south. Most of the abolitionists I've met, are so full of themselves, they're nuisances. But the abolitionist cause will prevail, I'm afraid, not so much because you Northerners are right, but because sooner or later we Southerners must put an end to slavery, or the Union will disintegrate.

But we Southerners have such a huge economic interest in preserving slavery that it's now becoming a mater of pride to assert our independence. For the past ten years we have been toying with the idea of secession, even though we know that creating a separate and independent nation could destroy our way of life, including our land-owning aristocracy." He added that he himself didn't belong to that class but that every Southerner was brought up to admire slavery and the plantation system. "It's in our blood and if a war between the North and the South does come to pass, the crux of the conflict will be pride—ours versus yours. I'm afraid that we are indeed headed for secession and war. And maybe it wouldn't be the end of the world if we had two countries…After all, we seem to get along with Canada."

This was quite an unexpected homily, delivered by a well-educated gentleman, who was open and proud of his being proslavery. How will we ever reconcile the incongruity of his philosophy with ours?

Well, the three scruffy eastbound wagons had disappeared quite a while ago and we were still wrestling with the old ox. We were just about to give up when Pete Gillespie appeared with a team and wagon, heading west. Other than hauling a full load of shelled corn in hundred-pound sacks, what Pete was doing on the trail or who he was freighting the corn for, I didn't ask, but he was most cordial.

After our greetings he, too, joined in pushing and shoving the troublesome ox, in an effort to yoke Blitzen. He and the men spent half an hour at it with no more success than they'd had before.

Mr. Rackcliffe, who had hired this pair of oxen and the owner, announced he was ready to give up and wanted to pay-up the Colonel and dismiss the ox team. He added he would take his chances with the hills from here on out. Pete Gillespie said, "Since I'm going back to Eldorado too, why don't you join me?" He suggested that Adda, Mr. Rogers and I throw our trunks up on his wagon and complete the trip with him since his wagon was sturdy and would take the hills better than Mr. Rackliffe's wagon.

By the time Mr. Rackcliffe had hitched up his horse to his wagon and we left, it was close to four o'clock.

We said good-bye to the Colonel, wished him luck with his troublemaking ox and told him that we hoped our paths would cross again.

Pete had two strong horses. He suggested that Mr. Rackliffe proceed ahead of us, so that if he needed help with any of the hills between here and the Chelsea cutoff, Pete and his horses would be available. We traveled in this fashion without trouble to Emporia where Mr. Rogers jumped off and thanked Pete for the ride. When we got to the Chelsea turnoff, we parted company with

Mr. Rackliffe and headed toward Chelsea, and the Hayworths' mill to get Pete's corn ground but whether we were up on the buckboard riding with Pete, or walking along the wagon, all Adda and I could talk about was how stimulating the Colonel was. His entire life seemed shaped by his experiences in the Mexican War. We had met other proslavery individuals but they were all far less complex than this Missouri philosopher, who had such provocative ideas, like his belief that the outcome, namely, of the Mexican War that Texas was now a slave state—resulted from President Polk's clever use of proslavery Democratic volunteers, guided only in a limited way by the Army "regulars."

Just as we began to discuss the points the Colonel had made about endurance, we pulled up at the Hayworths mill.

There was an elegantly painted wagon about the size of our Studebaker in the yard ahead of us fully loaded. The mill had already shut down for the day. The driver, who seemed rather well dressed for the work he was doing (striped blue shirt; fancy shirt-sleeve garters, holding up the shirt's rather puffy sleeves and a fancy flat straw hat, sporting a wide red, white and blue ribbon band), hailed Pete as an old friend.

Just then Jerry Jordan came over. He and Pete quickly decided that if Pete wanted to wait, he could have his corn ground by noon tomorrow.

We will stay overnight here in Chelsea and return with Pete after he gets his supply of corn milled.

I asked Jerry who the prosperous owner of the red wagon was and Jerry said, "That's the mill's wagon. The driver is our salesman. He's just back from his route, which covers all the little burgs within fifty miles of here. He picks up the farmer's grain and we mill it for them. He's got about a hundred sacks of grain, mostly wheat. It's all Kansas wheat, but there are two kinds of it. Every time he comes back with a load of grain, our goal is to get all that grist ground and back to the owners within a week. Yes, sir, we'll be putting out flour in our own white cloth bags soon, just like the big boys in Cincinnati and Chicago." I was glad to see Jerry so enthusiastic.

The Hayworths put us up for the night and I was quite impressed with what they've accomplished with their mill, since they had set it up at about the same time we started our sawmill. I was a little embarrassed by our progress compared to theirs.

Mrs. Hayworth said they'd recently put in a new mill with a secret process, that allows them to mill hard wheat. "The Germans out here prefer hard wheat," she said. "They like it even though the wheat isn't really German. It's actually of Ukrainian origin."

"This new hard-kernelled wheat produces finer flour and makes better bread," she said. "I'll send you home with a fifty-pound bag, so you can try it. In exchange, you can give me your opinion of it.

"When you bake with this wheat, it might be a good idea for you to add a tablespoon of sugar or honey to the dough for each load." She added, "This wheat requires a finer grinding process than our standard stone mill can provide." Her husband proudly let me know that the new mill does not use a conventional millstone. "That," she chimed in," is the 'secret.'"

I asked Mr. Hayworth how they get paid, telling him that we had trouble collecting cash for the jobs we did at the sawmill.

"Well, I'll tell you another secret," he said. "We haven't totally solved the cash problem either, but we've developed a method that has helped us get paid faster. Our driver collects the cash when he makes his rounds," and he said, "I suspect our tickets are much smaller than yours at the sawmill. Our problem is, though we are growing, we could mill three times what we are milling; there's not enough people"

He told us that their red wagon goes out on a route that takes six days and travels to towns that are mostly east of here, since we are on the frontier. On the way out, the driver delivers the flour or corn meal the mill has ground from the farmer's grain, and on his way back to the mill, he picks up the new sacks of grain to be milled.

"We don't wait for the farmers to bring their grain to us. We hope they will, but we don't wait for it to come. No! The farmers simply drop off their grain at their nearest grocers in hundred pound sacks for our driver to pick up for milling by us. Then five or six days later our driver returns with flour or cornmeal and collects a cash payment from the grocer. The transaction works like this. Our driver returns to each grocer a hundred-pounds of flour, which we have put in two fifty-pound bags. The grocer keeps one fifty-pound bag for resale and pays us fifty cents cash on delivery. Therefore we are milling wheat for half a penny a pound or 50 cents per hundredweight. So, the grocer is paying a penny a pound for what he must sell at a profit. The farmer for his 100 pounds of raw wheat gets the other fifty-pounds of flour cash free. The grocer may put the milled flour into smaller bags, but sells it for two or three cents a pound, depending on package size. I'd guess he grosses between a dollar and a dollar-fifty for acting as our agent. The farmer has gotten fifty-pounds of flour milled at a cost to him of 100 pounds of grain with no cash exchanged between himself and the store. The grocer gets his flour at wholesale prices and sells it at least twice what he pays for it. And because it's local, our free delivery eliminates freight costs. The farmer gets flour for his home use without having to layout cash for it, and of course, the amount of wheat the farmer wants milled for his home use is a "drop in the bucket" compared to the volume of his harvested crop.

"Wheat sells for about twice as much as corn, but we use the same transaction system for both the wheat and the corn, yielding the farmer's fifty pounds of cornmeal in exchange for a hundred pounds of his raw corn. The grocer acts as an agent for us and provides a service to the farmer, which provides a profit to him, allowing him to stay in business."

Most farmers are glad not to have to pay cash.

"If they come directly to us in order to get a better deal than they are getting from the grocer, they seldom ask us to do the milling on credit. We don't like credit and the farmers don't like it either.

"The farmer's real problem is not with this small local transaction but with the markets they sell their grain harvest to. There is also a suspicion that the Eastern markets rig grain prices. And the farmer's other problem is getting their grain to the nearest market, which for us is Kansas City."

Before supper, I had time for a chat with Jerry Jordan out by the mill. As I've noted before, Jerry is now the Hayworths' mill master. He said he was getting along, but would rather be with us in Eldorado. It was flattering but also embarrassing to hear him say that he thought of us as "family." He removed his hat to mop his brow, which was pale white because his forehead was rarely exposed to the sun. "Augusta, I'm busy up here but I'm so lonely."

I wanted to ask him what happened to his budding romance with Glennis Bemis, which seemed to me last August to be so promising, but something as personal as that is hardly any of my business, even though Jerry and I are old friends. I told him Adda and I had decided to sell our claims in Eldorado. I paused to get his reaction. He didn't express an opinion, but I sensed that he was both surprised and disappointed by the news.

I told him about my visit with Judge Lambden, adding that I'd decided to give him (Jerry) a share in the sawmill and intended to offer the remaining shares to Mr. Martin, who had expressed interest in buying them. As I explained these arrangements to Jerry, I felt he was a little put off by me. He didn't seem pleased that he would now be an owner in the mill, even though he hadn't been one of the investors. I suspected that he was disgruntled because I had turned down the second offer of marriage he'd made. Sometime after Chase died he had proposed marriage again via another very sweet letter, which I received before my last trip to Lawrence. I'd procrastinated but finally responded, declining his offer. I'm just not ready to remarry. Chase had only been dead ten months and I realized more and more how much we loved each other, I'm not sure I'll ever marry again.

Jerry Jordan is a fine man, was a good friend of Father's and is a sober, hardworking gentleman…all desirable traits for a husband, but I'm still in love with Chase. Knowing that, how could I be an honest wife just now to anybody? (But, of course, I can't explain any of those reasons to Jerry.)

The next morning, as promised, Jerry ground Pete's corn and had the sacks of cornmeal ready by noon.

Loading the corn grist back up on Pete's wagon was hot work in the noonday sun. It was impressive to see how busy this mill is. Wagons with grain seem to be coming in from some distances. And, this mill is not nearly as complicated as our sawmill.

When I had the opportunity, I told Jerry there was a considerable inventory of lumber, mostly pine, stacked-up at the mill. He interrupted and said, "Yes, yes. You seem to forget Chase and I sawed that wood together."

Ignoring his tone, I replied, "That lumber is yours. Use it to finish building your house or sell it, as you see fit." Though I thought he would be pleased with this offer, that didn't seem to be his reaction.

By the time all of Pete's bags of grist were loaded up, it was already mid afternoon. Adda and I climbed up on Pete's wagon and the three of us left for Eldorado.

52

ADDA AND I SELL OUR ELDORADO CLAIMS
July 8 to July 19, 1860

It was a stiflingly hot July 8th before Adda and I got back to Eldorado and there were lots of changes here. None of them seem to me to be for the better. The friends who are still here remain our friends, but with some of the newcomers and some of those we didn't know well, I have noticed a strange but perceptible pettiness.

Adda and I hardly had a fire going in the stove and we had visitors. Mrs. Rackliffe came by with little Ermie, who's now about seven months old, a real little doll. In a flash I recalled little Ermie arriving as a late present on Christmas Day! Mary and her husband are *so* lucky. It pleased me in a strange way to see that little Ermie was still nursing. It was really none of my business, but vicariously, I was pleased.

Mary said she's been collecting the eggs and milking our cow, but the garden has been a fizzle: no rain.

Elizabeth Cordis and Mary Rackliffe dropped in together. They feigned surprise that Pete Gilespie wasn't with us. Someone had spread a rumor that Pete and I had secretly gotten married. Well, I soon laid that one to rest, though I must say the idea contains some humor.

After supper, during the long twilight that brought no relief from the heat, Mrs. McCabe came by with Mrs. Frances and Mrs. Peterson. So we had a house full. It was like old times …sort of. In the old days our life here was based on Father's position and I was Mrs. Chase, a woman with a husband and the beginnings of a business, which we thought would keep the sawmill busy… all that's changed.

Mrs. Peterson asked Adda, "Just what is it, dear, that you two you *do* in Lawrence?" implying, I suppose, that what we did there, didn't have the social distinction of what we had been doing here. Now, this is the same Mrs. Peterson who has two children, good children and good scholars in my school, but who has never sent me a penny for their education, never mind their noon meals.

And it wasn't lost on me when Mrs. Peterson posed her impolite question, that Mrs. Frances' face seemed to express a mean-spirited curiosity. How was it that this lady could possibly be joining Mrs. Peterson in bearing us any ill will? I recalled more vividly that last September, when the Frances' friend, Mr. Trask, came by to pay-up some money he owed Father for surveying but more importantly to ask me to go with him to help with laying out their little baby, who had died the day before. Though I wasn't well myself, I rode up there with him on Pete Gillespie's wagon. The Trask Family was living with the Franceses and the baby died in their house. She certainly must be recalling now that it was I who came up and helped prepare the little baby's body for burial.

Of course all this is vivid in my memory. Chase died exactly ten days later.

Adda, who seemed less enthused to be home than me, sensing a little maliciousness in Mrs. Peterson's question, got up and pretending to swat a spider said, "We are very busy in Lawrence, Mrs. Peterson," several of the teamsters we've met out here are headquartered up in Leavenworth. When they come through, Augusta, and I occasionally entertain some of these gentlemen at the Whitney House, and we sometimes take in their laundry, particularly if they spend the night at the hotel with us. We have it ready for them when they return from their freighting jobs. We make our own soap, using Buffalo tallow we buy from the Indians. I work part-time cleaning up at O'Neill's Livery Stables and we've tried to get a little business going selling eggs door-to-door. I'm trying to get Augusta to take in sewing." Mrs. Peterson became very quiet, probably trying to decide if any of that was true or whether my imaginative sister had dismissed her idle curiosity with a bit of off-color jesting.

The next day I went out to the well for some water. I was relieved that nobody had walked off with our elegant bucket. When I lowered the bucket into it, it took several more cranks longer than usual to hit the water.

The water had a brownish-red tint to it, tasted of iron, smelled of sulfur and was not fit to drink. I had been of the opinion that the purity and availability of well water always remained the same, independent of the level of rainfall. So much for that opinion. I think this well is almost dry.

So, in the afternoon I took my little two tone crock over to the faithful spring that runs out of that small cave in the limestone cliff onto a ledge above the river, the same spring we carried our water from until we got our own well dug. That spring always ran, even in winter, and when the weather got severe a huge set of icicles of pure water built up and we would pick up a rock and knock off big chunks of them. The ice always seemed to me to be heavier than the same amount of water.

When I got to the spring, it was dry. My first reaction was that I'd come to the wrong place; it had been so long since I'd been there. So I walked up and down the limestone ledge, looking to see if it could be anywhere else, but I was correct the first time. The odor of "fish" was everywhere. Below me, the muddy water of the Walnut was flowing sluggishly.

Near the grassy, muddy shore a big old yellow-scaled carp was floundering. For some reason the old fellow kept thrashing and pushing his head in deeper through the thick, syrupy mud toward the grass. I picked up a stick and gently nudged him out into the stream where he disappeared. I wondered if that old carp knew how well off he was when the river was running normal. The water being low and so muddy must have disoriented him. Walking back to the cabin I saw a similarity between the carp and me. I hadn't realized how well off I was when the men folk were alive and were all together as a big family. In hindsight I even remember with pleasure all the boarders coming and going.

When I returned from the spring empty-handed, a small freight outfit was tending their mules down by the saw. Adda was talking to the boss. I recognize him from a previous stopover. He said they had delivered some freight at Fort Riley and were on their way back empty to Fort Leavenworth but asked if they could board with us tonight and stay here as well. With some humor he asked if our rates had gone up since last time. I glanced at one of his wagons, noting the usual water barrel strapped to it.

I said, "My well is too dry for drinking or cooking water, so I'll trade you board and room for ten or fifteen gallons of water, if you can spare it. I suggested he assign one of his men to walk the mules to the river for their water and said, "You'll find that the only green grass around here is along the shore, which the mules will like."

At breakfast the next morning, I asked if these fellows could arrange for one of their westbound outfits to pick up Kate and our Studebaker at the Gates' place and bring them out and, if there is a charge for this, I'll be happy to take care of it. It turned out that one of the mule tenders is a soldier from Fort Riley. He replaced a teamster who was too sick to make the return trip. He said that driving our wagon back out would "beat walking," and he said he'd be happy to oblige.

Before I went to the spring, I prepared some bread dough from the flour Mrs. Hayworth gave us. I was anxious to see what kind of bread that hard, extra-refined wheat flour would make. I made up enough dough for four loaves, added the sugar, as suggested, and let it rise. Adda and I baked it before supper. I've never had such good bread. Mrs. Hayworth's flour gave the bread a chewy golden crust, and the bread was pure white inside, absolutely white. No more coarse brown or black bread for me!

The next Sunday in the afternoon, Adda and I were bustling around the house, still cleaning up after our long absence. Some big fat spiders had taken over one corner of our house and there were daddy long legs all over the place, and bugs, bugs in everything, everywhere. One big old spider had made a web in the stairwell. It must have been a foot in diameter. What an engineer he was. I watched him hover over a green fly that his web had snared. The afternoon light hit his web in the same plane in which the spider had woven it and the sunlight made the strands of the web shine green. As I raised my feather duster to sweep the corner clean, I stopped and wondered, "Who am to destroy his workmanship? It was "Passover" for the spider.

Adda and I examined the spaces between logs for snakes, assuming that if they'd been there, they would have been undisturbed all the weeks we'd been gone.

Since I didn't relish killing a rattler, I was glad we found none.

I'd brought a small bag of fresh yellow corn meal with me from the Hayworths' mill and cooked it last night. I spread it out in a shallow pan to cool overnight. This morning I fried-up two or three pieces for our breakfast, the way Chase liked it with some bacon from the Hayworths. It was delicious.

Some months ago, after Chase died, I found a little black tin box that Father kept his papers in. Actually, I hadn't really found it, because it was never lost. I simply hadn't been able to bring myself to examine the papers. It was too emotional and personal.

What I did do, though, since I'm away from the house so much, was to put the box in my traveling trunk. I had it with me in Lawrence. A few evenings ago I suggested to Adda we sort through the contents together. It was really quite revealing. I won't go into all that now, because my journals seem to be like the afternoon newspaper to some of my curious visitors.

While doing an inventory, I discovered that Father had organized the sawmill ownership around nine shares. In among Father's personal effects, letters, surveying notes, etc. was a brown envelope containing a printed certificate signed by himself and Judge Wakefield. (I recall Father telling me that the Judge was in Eldorado in 1857 when the town was founded. Indeed, on the Fourth of July he gave a speech to commemorate the day. The certificate designates six shares that Samuel Charles Stewart owns in a sawmill located on the Walnut River on the east half of the northeast quarter of Section 15 and the west half of the northwest quarter of section 14.) In the same envelope were two receipts, also witnessed by Judge Wakefield, showing that Henry Martin and Mr. Eastwood had each invested and received a certificate for one share in the mill. According to the papers in Father's box, there were nine shares sold in the mill, but we don't know who owns the ninth share, nor do we know what Mr. Martin paid. This morning, while Adda and I were waiting for Judge Lambden to appear, Mr. Rackliffe and Le Roy Rogers Mrs. Fisk's cousin came by. Mr. Rackliffe wanted to know if they could have the two coils of rope in the shed. They were each 100 feet long. Father and Chase had used the rope to make rough surveying measurements. Father would then take several lengths of an iron chain, which he could snap together in fifty-foot lengths, to make his final surveying measurements.

Apparently Mr. Rackliffe and Mr. Rogers are going to use the rope to make a rough corral each night for Mr. Rackliffe's cattle, as they drive them up towards Topeka.

Mr. Rackliffe found the rope and went home. Mr. Rogers stayed behind and we chatted a while. Mr. Rogers said that when he was finished with herding Mr. Rackliffe's cattle, he'd be returning to Lawrence.

I told Mr. Rogers I'd remembered his politeness in giving Mrs. Fisk his seat in the westbound stage a few weeks ago, and inquired as to her health.

The Rogerses and the Fisks are related clans from Northern Missouri, the section of the state north of the generally east-west flowing Missouri River.

Mr. Rogers is a very interesting fellow. He told us a little about the area where he came from.

"The people there," he said, "are about fifty-fifty abolitionist and proslavery with a lot of latent animosity between the two groups. It's not that there are few slaves or slave owners in northern Missouri. It's just that those who are proslavery feel very strong about it, as a right they may aspire to."

The next day a gentleman named William Little, came by. He looked to be about Mr. Martin's age, but not as old as Father. He told us he was a cattle grower from Chelsea and knew the neighborhood, because Mr. Rackliffe was one of the locals who had been buying calves from him. He said that he'd walked our claims in the past few months and wanted to know considering our current family situation if we would consider selling. "Your location is more or less what I'm looking for, he said. "Prairie farmland with a supply of water from the river, which I'll be able to use for my animals whether we have dry spells or not and that beats pumping well water twice a day even when the weather is nice." Mr. Little raises calves and sells them at six months (or so) to others, like Mr. Rackliffe, who in turn fatten them for market usually with grain and fodder raised by themselves.

Mr. Little grows his own supply of corn, which he uses as cattle feed. He chuckled. "I get a better deal by feeding the corn to my cattle than if I harvest it for sale. When my corn walks off my place on four legs, it's worth a lot more than grain leaving by the sack when I try to sell it for gain. By converting corn to meat, I'm not at the mercy of the Easterners who fix the price of grain to suit their purposes. They are continually rigging both the price of corn and wheat. In the past few years I've seen fall wheat bought at the Kansas City markets as low as forty cents and as high as eighty cents a bushel * and we pay the freight charges to those markets. Sending one hundred bushels of wheat from here to Lawrence costs as much as the wheat is worth. I could raise grain corn for sale but corn is so cheap, I can't afford to freight it. That's why so many of us raise corn as grain and fodder to fatten cattle and walk it to the closest market. That's what your friend Mr. Rackliffe is fixin' to do. He has fattened his calves off his own land. Sometimes he sells yearlings as veal. Out here they call it baby beef."

He paused and chuckled again. "I'm beating those rascals at their own game."

While walking your property, I noticed that there are some falls on the river. I like that, he said with a pleasant smile.

"Should we make a deal, I plan to deepen the ditch at the river above the falls on your place…my place. Putting a weir in the ditch near the river will let me keep a pond or two full of running water without depleting the river. Then I'll let the water drain into your crick. That will keep it always running and wet. I notice that crick runs across all three claims. Your crick then drains back into the river below the falls on one of your claims. Cows like to roam down along a crick, walk in the water and drink out of it. That's probably a more natural way for them to drink than getting their water out of a trough. Breed stock, especially the cows, when they are nursing, need lots of water. I don't have that where I am."

Adda, looking at me, gave me a little wink.

He said his family breed calves in Illinois and he'd continued the family tradition when he came out here. "I need more

---

*A bushel of wheat weighs about sixty pounds, so one hundred pounds at sixty cents per bushel is worth $1.00.

space for my breed stock than I have now up in Chelsea, but land values around Chelsea are up to where, it's now too expensive to expand and you've got a much better source of water down here."

Adda caught that implication. "Mr. Little, she said, "What's your farmland worth?"

Well, if I'm a buyer, about a dollar and fifty cents an acre. If I'm a seller, about two dollars an acre."

Adda went over and poked him playfully on the shoulder, treating Mr. Little as familiarly as if he were one of the teamsters taking a night's lodging with us and said, "Mr. Little, I think you're teasing us a little. We've turned down an offer for over two dollars an acre for all three claims."

I thought to myself, "Well, that's news to me, but I suppose my little sister is just engaging in a little horse trading. Nevertheless I thought Mr. Little might take offense. The price he was telling us was about fifty cents an acre less than we expected, so maybe he was trying to give us a low price, thinking we would take less for our claims. But even so, Adda's behavior was still a little forward. "Adda," I hurried to say, "she means raw, undeveloped land without a house and without available river water."

"Mr. Little," said Adda, "we have three claims, each of 160 acres. My claim and my sister's are on either side of father's parcel, and all three claims come together over there in a 90-degree angle near where the river bends. Our land is well staked out. Father was a surveyor and did all the surveying for our property for the Land office."

Mr. Little said he wasn't sure he could manage three, quarter sections just now. Then he laughed and said, "But I suppose if I don't take all three claims now, I'll envy what I didn't purchase 'til I die."

Adda said, "Yes, and you might not like the neighbor, who ends up buying the third claim, if you don't take all three claims. The owner of the third claim could make your plans for the water and crick difficult."

Mr. Little was quiet. I could see he was probably thinking, "In my vanity to impress these girls, I've revealed too much about the advantage their property has."

Adda asked him if he was planning to sell his place in Chelsea if he bought our claims.

"Yes, I need a better and more reliable source of water for my livestock than what I have up in Chelsea. I'm ready to move. I'm not sure how far west I want to be, but I'm ready."

Adda was quick to understand his last remark. She said, "Our well is so close to being dry that the water ain't fit to drink. Chelsea, where you are, hasn't been getting any more rain than we have. So, I suppose what you are saying is your Chelsea well is as dry as ours is." Then looking at me, she added, "So, that ought to make our river-sided claims worth at least 50¢ an acre more, because no matter how dry it gets, there is always some water running in the river.

Adda told him that Father's claim includes the house, the sheds and the land that goes down to the Walnut. "His parcel is the nicest of the three claims. You could use Augusta's claim to raise your cattle feed. That one is the flattest. How many acres do you need for grain and fodder?" But Mr. Little seemed lost in other thoughts and didn't answer.

"This is the best house in Eldorado," she added, "though the Wattses' building is bigger.

The crick on my claim, is the same one that runs across all three, and my sister's claim also goes along the river. It's her claim that's above the falls."

"Well, yes, but that lower crick is dry now," said Mr. Little. "Has it always been dry?"

"Well, of course not. It's the first time in years, and anyway, if the crick at the river on Augusta's claim was a little deeper, mine wouldn't be dry. Those cricks are a nuisance to us since we have to plow around them," she responded.

He talked about the importance of getting clear title, free of any Indian claims. I told him that I'd discussed our intentions with Judge Lambdin and that we expected him in a day or so. Before Mr. Little left, we made arrangements to send word to him when the judge got here, which we hoped would be this Thursday, July 12th. The Judge will handle the sale of our three claims we told him.

On July 11th, while we were waiting for Judge Lambdin to arrive, Adda and I decided to visit the Martins to discuss their interest in the sawmill.

On the way over there, Adda asked me if we owed Jerry Jordon any back pay for running the sawmill. I said, "No I don't think so. But while we were at the Hayworths, I offered to give him some ownership in the mill. I didn't think you would object if he got one share, the share I received from Mr. Eastridge for the syrup mill." Adda said that was fine with her.

The Martins were, as usual, most cordial and asked us to stay for supper and the night. After supper I explained to them that Adda wanted to live in Lawrence, and that with Chase gone and the short supply of cash customers for lumber, or for the use of the saw, I didn't think I could make a living off the sawmill. I said that I really enjoyed teaching my scholars, though the parents didn't see fit or maybe, they simply couldn't afford to pay.

I told him that I didn't think I wanted to be a widow farmer. "I wasn't all that happy as a young widow in Lawrence either," I added, "but I think I may find work there that I would be more suited for than farming. I enjoy farming but I realize how inexperienced at it I am."

Plowing all that land was a man's job," said Mrs. Martin. "And even for a man, it's not easy, not even when he has a team of horses or oxen."

"Yes, I certainly agree with that." I said.

Mr. Martin knew that this was all small talk leading to the best mutual terms we could arrive at in disposing of the sawmill. After I'd exhausted my reasons for removing from Eldorado, Mr.

Martin pushed himself back from the table, folded his hands on his chest and said, "Well, Mrs. Chase, let's talk about the sawmill."

I told him about discovering the documents for the original investors in the mill, which verified that there were nine shares, but failed to reveal the name of the owner of the ninth share. "Adda and I intend to give Jerry Jordan the share we got from Mr. Eastwood for the syrup mill. Besides your share and that of the missing owner, that leaves six shares. I have a single certificate in Father's name for those six shares, which Judge Lambdin assumes, as Father's heirs, we own and have the right to sell."

"Actually," said Mr. Martin, "I now have two shares—the ninth share now belongs to me too. A year or so ago I bought it from the owner, who went off to the gold fields."

I gave some thought to inquiring who the seller was but thought knowing it, was none of my business and it wouldn't make any difference anyway. Mr. Martin either owned two shares or he didn't. The important thing is we have six shares to sell and that's that.

The next day about noon, Judge Lambdin arrived in his fancy one-horse, two-wheel shay. We got right down to business. The Judge had located Father's original filing of our three claims, but said there was some question as to this particular land purchase. "We'll simply make the estate of your father the selling person for all three claims."

Adda asked him to explain this.

"I don't think it's necessary to go into all the details, some of the aspects might offend you ladies and it's not at all clear whether the original seller for the land your father bought was the Territory or the Federal Government."

"Wait a minute," said Adda, "Can't you find who Father made the payments to…and if our deal with Mr. Little falls through, Augusta and I will have to hang on until we find another buyer. So, we should know who the seller was that we owe money to."

"Your father made payments to the local land office, a Federal officer, but that really doesn't tell us who the seller is."

He added, "These two governing bodies have subtle differences in the rules pertaining to the purchase of new Territorial land and it's my job to find the rule that best fits your case." He smiled and said, "I think I'm pretty good at that."

"What are the rules that affect us?" asked Adda.

"Well, Miss Stewart, I'm not sure that you, or your sister for that matter were legal owners of your claims but we don't have to blab that about."

"Of course, we're the legal owners. Our father paid for our two claims and named Augusta and me as the claims' owner. He went out of his way to show us the forms he filed on our behalf."

"Now don't take offense. I'm not sure you were then of legal age when your father filed the claim on your behalf with the Land Office but I can get around that. The more interesting and perhaps offensive question is whether married or unmarried women are entitled to file claims and own new Territorial land in the first place. The law is not silent on this but it is ambiguous. Kansas Territory is so new there's no case law on this question but there is in states that were territories east of us and it doesn't favor you two clearly enough for me to hang my hat on.

"Wait a minute," said Adda. "Do you mean that women can't file for or own claims on land out here that had never had previous owners? I don't believe it."

The Judge responded, "Well, I said in the beginning that some aspect of this transaction might offend you."

"Augusta is a widow," said Adda. "Her husband had a claim nearby. Will the ownership uncertainty in Territorial law keep Augusta from claiming her husband's land?"

"Well, we'll get to that question later. Let's get on with these three parcels. I'll solve all this by establishing that your deceased father, that is, his estate, is the legal seller of all three claims, since he was your legal guardian until you reached, what we call 'your majority," and since you are his heirs, you'll get the proceedings of any sale of those claims. In that way I'll dispose of the fine points of how you two came by the claims. I'm comfortable with that approach.

"How will you dispose of it?" asked Adda.

"In the practice of law, we simply avoid items that we hope to disposes of and in this case naming your father's estate as the seller avoids the question of ownership. For reasons I've recited, your father's estate has clear title to each of your three claims." The Judge added that if ownership or possession were ever to come under dispute, he would show that he, and the two of us for that matter, had clearly established residency out here. He explained that Father had fulfilled the terms of the 1854 Act of Preemption, a Federal act that applied to the purchase of land in the Territory, so long as we can show that it has not been claimed by or set aside for the Indians. "I've made several careful searches of the records at the Land Office," he said, "and can find no evidence that there are any specific Indian claims on your land. As a surveyor, your father was also very well aware of this act.

"Each claim is limited to 160 acres at a dollar twenty-five per acre. That's two hundred dollars. No payment was required during the first year of residency, but within one year following the filing date the settler is required to make a minimum payment of five percent to hold the land. According to the fling records, your father paid thirty dollars in early November 1857 to cover the minimum 5% requirement for all three of your claims.

"By the way, your father was very careful about the filing. He knew the filing documents might be tampered with in Lecompton, so he filed a duplicate in Leavenworth. The Land Office there had a suspicious fire, but it didn't damage the claims book that contains your father's records. I did some research to make sure of that. You can count on it. If there ever is a question about the ownership of these claims, after you sell them, you won't have to worry about it because the records at the Land Office will prove that your father met all the purchase requirements, including publishing notices in six newspapers of the date, location, etc. of this filing," he laughed, "that particular requirement is just a bit of legal bunkum to keep newspapers in business.

He said that the three claims together cost $600. After the payment of thirty dollars your father made in 1857, the balance due was $570. "The Act of Preemption," he added, "allows a claim to be paid off in three years after the initial minimum payment, although a two year extension is available. My notes show that two years ago, in April '58, your father made a payment of $200, leaving a balance owed of $370.

I looked at Adda. "That was just about the time he was attending the Lawrence Convention. He must have made that payment while he was there."

"Do you know if your father borrowed money to build this house?"

"No," I said, "the first floor, as you can tell, was made from logs. My husband and my Father added the upstairs. We used lumber sawed by our own mill."

"What do you think the house is worth?" he asked me.

"Well, I guess about $500. I am assuming this because while I was in Lawrence, I heard that some newly built houses there, which aren't nearly as large as this, sell for about that much. Those houses are nailed together from parts made in Chicago and brought down by boat. Anyway, you can get one of those frame houses for $500. But that doesn't include the cost of the Lawrence lot. Do you think putting that value of $500 for our house is too much?"

"Well, the two of you must decide that, but it seems reasonable to me," he responded. "Now ladies this brings me to an interesting dilemma, which we must settle amongst ourselves before I meet the prospective buyer. The balance due of $370 is a sizable sum."

Adda interrupted him, "I don't see a dilemma there. If that's what we owe, we'll figure a way to pay it. We're not paupers."

I thought to myself, I wonder if Adda has saved that amount from the whiskey trade she and Aggie Rourke has carried on. While I worked at the Whitney House, I thought it best to not get involved in their activities. Adda had explained their arrangement, so I just assumed they were still carrying on. I certainly didn't intend to ask in front of the Judge. "No, that's not the dilemma," he told Adda. "I was referring to a possible loophole. Congress is considering legislation called the Homestead Act, which allows the settler to earn ownership by merely staying on and improving the land. It's my understanding that a "Homesteading" precedent has already been established in Iowa and parts of the Northwest Territory, such as Ohio, Wisconsin and Michigan. The local governments in those places have used this practice to convey thousands of acres of land to new settlers. But I don't feel adequately comfortable arguing that this doctrine applies to your land out here because the Homestead Act for territories or government-owned land in the new states is still pending.

We've been waiting for Congress to pass the new Federal Homestead Act and the Senate did pass it, only to have President Buchanan (recently) veto it. When the Senate attempted to pass it over the President's veto, they lacked the votes to over ride. The opposing vote was entirely Southern. So, you see why I call the situation ambiguous until a new administration comes in."

What's the risk if we assume that we will ultimately get these homesteading rights?" I asked.

"That's a very astute question. The risk is that the new owner or two of you might have a lien for $370 placed on that house you are going to buy in Lawrence, if we fail to get those rights out here. Sometime in the future a Federal land agent who is auditing the books of the previous land sales here in the Territory might see that under the pending law there is a balance owed of $370 and serve the new owner or you two a notice to pay up."

"What happens if in a year or two the Homestead Act does become law? Will we or the new owner be able to cite the law and get the balance eliminated?" asked Adda.

"Good question. It all depends on how that law gets written or with this recent veto, rewritten. Sometimes a new tax law will include a moratorium on past taxes, meaning that they are forgiven, although that applies specifically to taxes. If Congress ultimately passes the Homestead Act, and the new president signs it, the Government could in effect nullify the $370, if it hasn't been paid, similar to a moratorium. I think it's prudent to wait and see."

"Why not simply tell Mr. Little about this money we owe but suggest to him that it might not be a problem if the Homestead Act is ultimately passed for this territory," she added. "With a two year extension, $370 won't be due until sometime in 1863. By then the act could eliminate the $370. We can give him the facts and let him make the decision."

"Yes," said the Judge. "I could explain it to him as a mortgage owed to the original owner, which in this case, would be either the Territory or the Federal Government."

"Augusta and I think this land, since it fronts on the river, so the buyer will always have access to water is worth two dollars and fifty cents per acre, maybe more, but we'll settle for that. That's $1,200 for all three claims. Minus the $370 we owe, that's $830. Deduct from that your fee of $130 for handling the sale and all the searching you did, and we should clear $700 on the land. If we can get $500 for the house, that's $1,200 for everything. When Augusta and I get back to Lawrence, we want to buy a little house that we had our eyes on, as well as the lot it's on…$1,000 to $1,100 ought to more than cover those costs, but we'll need some additional money for work that needs to be done inside the house. We're hoping to clear something on the sawmill. Can you write all of this in a contract?"

"Miss Stewart, writing contracts is what I do for a living. It's my stock-in-trade. You ladies will actually need two contracts:

one for the property and a simpler one to convey the shares in the sawmill to Mr. Martin.

The Judge asked us if we had reached an agreement with Mr. Little on price and terms for our land.

"Not exactly," I replied, "but I don't think we're very far apart. He likes the idea that he will be able to divert some of the river water to fill up a couple of ponds and keep the crick on Adda's claim running, so that he can always have a source of water for his cattle.

He pumps well water for them now, which, he let us know was a nuisance." I explained to the Judge Mr. Little's rather unusual sort of husbandry. The Judge had a chuckle at my expense and explained that it was not unusual at all. "People have been raising calves from prize breed stock for others to graze or fatten in this fashion for centuries," he said.

Mid afternoon, Mr. Little came by in response to a note I'd sent earlier. In an hour or two we had settled our differences with the help of Judge Lambdin, who incidentally got along very nicely with Mr. Little and handled the $370 item in a way that Mr. Little sees the money as a possible windfall. Mr. Little will write a check payable to us. The Judge will hold it until a deed he drafts is conveyed to Mr. Little.

At around 5 PM Mr. Little said he thought he'd be going. As he rose to get up from the table, he made a little ceremony of rapping our wooden table with his knuckles. He smiled. "I want you two ladies to knock on wood with me," he said. "That's an absolute and ancient guarantee that this transaction will be mutually beneficial to us all." We both smiled at this custom new to us and knocked on wood.

So now our claims are sold. Our deal appears to be favorable to both parties. We'll have our cash as soon as Judge Lambdin delivers the deed and clear title, which will give Mr. Little possession. We'll stay here until all that's done. The Judge is including in the agreement an obligation that Mr. Little will assume the balance of $370, if required, although he thinks he will get his windfall if the Homestead Act goes through and forgives that $370. Judge Lambdin reminded him that if that happens, it would be equivalent to a rebate worth seventy-seven cents an acre. The clincher was by our agreeing not to make a claim on that $370, if it was allowed, he had agreed to $2.50 per acre.

After he left, we invited the Judge to stay for the night; I told him I'd sent word up to Mr. Martin saying we'd like to visit him in the morning to discuss the sale of the sawmill.

The judge agreed to stay over. The supper could have been better. Between the weeds, which didn't get hoed while I was in Lawrence, the lack of spring rain, and the grasshoppers, our vegetable garden hadn't produced much worth eating. The onions and carrots were runts and it took four cabbages the size of my fist to make decent coleslaw. I did boil, and then bake with bacon, some nice white sweet potatoes, but none of them were much bigger than a sore thumb.

After supper the judge got rather philosophical. "I observed Mr. Little this afternoon. He certainly knows what he's up to." He said, "He seems to be in such control of his destiny. Now I certainly don't mean to be offensive, but it seems to me that in contrast to him you and Adda have had your plans and your expectations snatched from you. Tell me, Mrs. Chase, do you think we are able to control our destiny?"

The gravity of his question, coupled with his remarks, caused me to pause. "Well, I said, "maybe sometimes it's not always possible. Our father certainly wasn't able to control his destiny."

"Yes, but didn't he exert some control by choosing to go after the horse thieves, taking a risk for which he lacked sufficient skill and help? Is there a horse in the world worth getting killed for?"

"I think he took the risk of going after them to defend a principal—the principal is that a man has a right to defend his property, especially if there's not a law enforcement agency available to do it for him. I had to control myself to keep from seeming indignant.

"My father did get to control his destiny to some extent, since he was able to come out here to pursue the abolitionist cause and was elected to represent the District.

"My husband, on the other hand, wasn't able to control his destiny, in the way I think you mean the question. He was a fine, hard-working honest man, still less than ten months after our marriage, he was dead…but I don't want to go into that."

"Well," said Judge Lambdin, "I'm old enough to be your father and from what I've experienced, I don't believe we have the ability to control our destiny."

He recited the Shakespeare verse I myself had pondered some time ago:

'There's a Divinity that shapes our ends, rough hew them how we will.'"

"Well, yes," I said, "but there is a difference between a Divinity intervening in our lives and the extent to which we can exert personal control over our ends."

"Well, I was impressed by your friend, Mr. Little," said the judge. "There's someone who is bound and determined to control his destiny. Here we are out on the prairie so new to the white man that most of the land between our two great rivers and the Rocky Mountains has never been explored, never been scratched. And this fellow Little, certainly not a paragon of wisdom, maybe not even a paragon of virtue, has already figured out a how to prosper by refusing to farm conventionally, growing crops he won't get a fair price for. He's relying solely on his skills to be a success, raising cattle and getting a steady supply of water for them so he won't have to depend on Nature's whimsical allotment of rain."

The Judge said that Mr. Little's plan to use a controlled flow of river water to irrigate both land and cattle reminded him of the Romans, who had built aqueducts and other systems to provide water, adding it was one of the best things the Romans did for the provinces they conquered, which helped to bring several hundred years of peace and prosperity to the empire.

Near bedtime I fixed a pot of tea. The Judge didn't seem to want to retire. "How soon do you suppose war will come?" he asked me, bringing up a new topic for discussion. "I think that war could break out any day and if that happens, this Territory will be in trouble because of our location. We'll get the proslavery raiders coming in from Missouri, and we'll get some coming up from the southwest, now that Texas is a proslavery state and has a large militia. It's reasonable to assume that if war comes, Texas will secede and join the Confederates. And I'm afraid that the Indians in the Cherokee Nation might just join the south, although I think the Cherokee Nation itself will remain officially neutral." He said that the Indians had already sided against us, pointing out that during the War for Independence they joined the British to fight against the Colonists."

I found the Judge's comments rather disturbing and gave a few seconds of thought to simply going back to Michigan. But then I shook off that idea, thinking to myself, "No by god! I'm here and I'm going to stay in the Territory and make the best of it. I'm not going to go back to the states like the owners of those three shabby wagons we saw when we were struggling with Blitzen."

Early the next morning just as we were ready to leave for the Martins', the Fort Riley soldier came across the crick driving our wagon. Adda ran over and yelled, "Did you drive all night?" He said something about the noonday heat bothering Kate, so he stayed on the trail as late as he could and got going before sunup. I told him there was some warm coffee on the stove and that he could rustle up a breakfast and rest here as long as he liked.

Adda asked him how he was going to get to Fort Riley from here. He laughed, slapped his thigh and said, "Hey, I marched all the way to Santa Fe, when I was your age."

Adda said, "You're not that old."

I explained that we were on our way to visit some friends and that he could stay as long as he liked.

We left for the Martins' house at 7 AM but it was already hot. Even the early morning breeze was hot and dry. What little prairie grass, not yet eaten by the grasshoppers, had already taken on its tan color of winter dormancy. We seemed to be traveling over a carpet of skittish grasshoppers. Old Kate scares them up off the trail by the dozens and they light everywhere. The grasshoppers have eaten the tops off my carrots right down to the furrow, the same with the onions.

When we arrived, the Martins seemed distressed over the news that two of the families, who came out with them in July of '57, are returning to the States, citing failed crops. Their claims were next to each other. Both their wells went dry. The settlers had both put in about a hundred acres of corn and between the lack of rain and the grasshoppers they'll have no crop this year. Last year they lost two cows due to Spanish Fever. They said one of their reasons for going back is to see if they can get some relief from any abolitionist committees that might have been set up to help our drought-stricken farmers out here in western Kansas.

The sale of our shares to Mr. Martin went quite smoothly. He produced a receipt for the money he invested for his initial share and proposed he pay us six times that amount for our six shares. Mr. Martin must be doing very well. He said he'd been able to get a fair crop of winter wheat each of the three years that they've been here and had a good corn crop every year but this one, which he also turned into beef and sold profitably, but he added this year's crop had been sacrificed to the 'grasshopper god.' He seemed rather unperturbed about losing it.

I hadn't realized it until he said so, that he too uses his corn entirely as cattle feed. Like Mr. Little he too "walks" his crops to market; in fact, he also buys calves from Mr. Little. This whole clever idea, so new to me, yet it is so well established, that it has made my ignorance of it rather embarrassing.

Mr. Martin asked us if he could settle accounts by paying us half in cash and by giving us a promissory note due in two or three years for the balance. We agreed.

"I'll draft two notes," said Judge Lambdin, "one payable to Augusta, the other to Adda, if that will be satisfactory."

We told the Martins about the sale to Mr. Little, without going into details. Mr. Martin said he'd spoken to Mr. Little about the mill, "I think we'll be able to work out an arrangement to leave the mill where it is for the time being," he said. "I might move it later and put a flourmill nearby, adding that he knew Father had bought a boiler big enough to run both the sawmill and a flour mill."

Adda laughed and said, "That's probably why it takes ten days and a cord of wood to get up steam," she said, "that's if the weather is nice."

Mrs. Martin fixed us a nice noontime meal and served lemonade. I appreciated the lemons since they masked the sulfur and iron taste in their water, and wondered where she got them.

She asked us to be seated at her elegantly laid out table. She had used the same decorated white Limoges china that she used for our pre wedding party. I took the same seat I chose during that festive supper a year and a half ago. As I sat down, I noticed I could see myself in the same way in the mirror on their chiffonier on the opposite wall as I had on that night and it was as though all this was taking place then when Chase was alive, as though nothing had changed. I looked to my right in the mirror and saw my beloved husband. The sunlight hitting the mirror obscured his image but it was Chase. No doubt about it. I was still studying my face in their mirror and trying to focus on my husband's face, when off in the distance I thought I heard Mrs. Martin in her delightful English accent ask the judge if he would care to say Grace.

The judge said he'd be honored. He asked the Almighty to bless this food, this home; he asked for guidance and help in farming. He asked for Divine intervention in the drought. As he went on and on, my attention drifted in and out. I heard the sounds of the Judge's words but failed to comprehend a good many of them. I slipped into a little reverie. I was certain for a second or two that Chase was sitting next to me and I waited for him to reach under the table and pull my leg over toward his as he did that January night when I whispered to him that my knees were cold. Just when the judge finished his prayer, I don't know. I had my head bowed and my eyes closed. In the silence that followed I suppose they thought I was still in prayer…and perhaps I was…in my fashion.

Before we left, I asked Mr. Martin if he had a spare pony that we could buy or trade. He said he thought we could work something out.

By midafternoon we were home and the Judge made preparations to leave, saying he thought he'd stop by the Hayworths. I asked him to tell Mr. Hayworth that their new flour made the best bread I've ever had, even with our old oven."

"Their milling business is quite brisk now, said Adda, "and they are doing some C.O.D. milling. I'll bet a lot of farmers in this area owe them money."

"Wouldn't be surprised," said the Judge.

During the next few days, we continued packing.

Today Mr. and Mrs. Little came down from their place in Chelsea where they breed their cattle and sell their calves all over this area.

We've used up two or three more days arranging our return to Lawrence. Mr. Rackliffe came by to ask a favor. He will leave a week from today. His departure from Eldorado will be more complicated than ours. He's looking for help in driving his cattle but he didn't say where they were driving them. I can't get over how prosperous the Rackliffes and Martins have become since moving here, but I'm not at all envious. And Mr. Little's purchase of our place will double his land ownership. It's dawned on me that their gains have come entirely off the land. Poor Tom Cordis wasn't so lucky. Though he farmed a little, his living was dependent on his blacksmith shop. We are simply too far west for sustained commerce. And in hindsight, I suppose that's also why Howland moved his store, likewise the McWhorter Brothers, who, even by selling whiskey by the glass and promoting sporting events (just old-fashioned fist fights under the name of English Boxing), couldn't make a go of it. Well, another couple of days has gone by and we're still here. I hadn't realized just how much time would be consumed getting ready to leave. We're mostly packed-up.

I've taken our half dozen or so laying hens to Mrs. Martin. I traded them along with the cook stove, and Father's surveying equipment for the pony we spoke about three or four days ago, which we will put in harness next to Kate when we leave for Lawrence.

The milk cow stays for Mrs. Little. I'll leave Father's big steel breaking plow for Mr. Little, with my compliments.

We'll leave most of the furniture for the Little's but we've packed our personal effects, including my books, letters and boxes of articles I've been working on. We are taking most of the kitchen "stuff," though I've never replaced all the forks, spoons and knives the Indians took last summer. I think I'll leave the parlor stove. The iron bed has pretty good springs but I haven't decided about it. I guess we are going to need a bed up there, so maybe we should take it too. And I've already packed that long straight-backed bench, where I keep my journals and books. I've also kept the oak rocking chair that Father liked, that we brought from Michigan.

Le Roy Rogers came by to say he'd agreed to help the Rackliffes drive their cattle. They plan on leaving Thursday, July 19th, give or take a day. That's when Adda and I will leave—and, oh yes, Old Dick, the cat; we'll take him back to Lawrence with us. Adda told Dick this morning that his "tomcatting prospects" would improve immensely in Lawrence. The place, she said, is just overrun with lonely female cats…all abolitionists.

Thanks to the Fort Riley soldier who returned with the Studebaker and Kate, Adda and I have it to move our household stuff to Lawrence and we agreed we'd try to get away the morning of July 18th. With painful regret I have given our tools, including Chase's tools, to Pete Gilespie, but we both thought Kate could use a little more rest before starting the trip, so we won't leave until tomorrow.

It was simply too hot to cook a warm meal. As we left the Martins, the Missus gave us a small piece of cold roast. I still had some of that nice white bread from Hayworth's new milling process and some preserved apple butter. As Adda and I sat there eating our cold meal with cold tea, I asked Adda, "Do you remember the day after we left Knoxville, Iowa four years ago this summer, where Father had the steel rim on our wagon tightened-up by that Dutch blacksmith?"

"Well, what I remember about Knoxville was the two of us met General Jim Lane the first time and all three of us listened to a fiery speech of his the evening before. Why?"

"Well, when we got on the road, the next morning the three of us had a big discussion about regrets. It became rather philosophical. You asked Father if he wasn't worried or concerned about having regrets about selling the sawmill and the Gibraltar store. Father got very philosophical about how regrets rise up, manufactured from our fear of failure. We work so hard to prepare ourselves to avoid failure, that when we leave one opportunity as we did in Michigan we hope to find better opportunity out here. As usual I made some notes of that discussion and later put it in my journal as an entry. I'm hoping we don't regret the move we've agreed to, so I looked up what I wrote about that discussion. You want to hear what I wrote?"

"Sure"

I dug out volume I of my journal.

It was our habit to start the day with the three of us riding on the wagon's buckboard. Adda asked Father if now that we'd been gone two weeks or so from the orderliness and security that we had in Michigan, if he was having any regrets.

Father, "Regrets? Regrets about what?"

Adda, "Well, we had a perfectly good sawmill in Gibraltar. It seemed to be running day in and day out, so business must have been pretty good…good enough to keep Augusta and me in nice clothes and in a fancy private boarding school and you had a store in Gibraltar. It seems to me you traded all that for a pretty risky situation in the new territory."

Father, "Well, Adda, regret is certainly one of man's constant worries or concerns. Did we do the right thing? My opportunity in Gibraltar was a "given." But after hearing Jim Lane and Governor Reeder speak in Detroit, I saw several opportunities in the Kansas Territory. As a citizen, concerned with this slavery issue, by going to the new territory I'll have the opportunity to add my vote to the other Free Soilers and abolitionists already there plus the thousands more on their way In that way at least we can put a stop to slavery in that new territory and maybe all the new territories that will become states…and there's all sorts of latent opportunity in all that, almost free land and for the three of us an adventure that we're not apt to get, staying in Gibraltar.

On the other hand, the consequences of going west, as young as we all are, need not be the "end of the world". If things turn bad, if war comes, who knows, maybe we'll go back to Michigan. If war comes, the North will need ships and ships need lumber. If I can't buy back the Gibraltar mill, we might move to some town on the New England Coast, where they build ships, Ill build another sawmill and we'll be a supplier of lumber.

"Will you build a sawmill in the Kansas territory, Father?"

"You betcha! Maybe mill grain and press sorghum, to boot."

Father was quiet for a while, and then he spoke up. "Regrets are for yesterday. Hope and opportunity are for today and particularly tomorrow. The problem with regrets, Adda, is that you can't go back and worry about what could 'a been. That will serve no earthly purpose.

Opportunity, girls, is like beauty. It's in the eyes of the beholders. But I can tell you this, opportunity always looks better to the optimist and I am that, an optimist. The pessimist will usually see too much risk associated with opportunity and will pass it up.

I was busy writing as much of this as I could for an entry into my journal.

"Are you finished reading?"

"Yes."

Adda asked, "Why are you bringing all that up now?"

"Because, I hope later, when we discover the grass isn't much greener in Lawrence than it is out here, that I won't have regrets about our giving up on Eldorado."

"Well, let's just look at our marvelous opportunity out here. We are literally out of water; the well's dry and river water is so muddy you couldn't strain it. This place hasn't seen a good rain for weeks…maybe months, so the garden we counted on is so far gone we couldn't serve a real supper for friends even if we wanted to. Yes! We have a sawmill. We also have an inventory of logs. I told you before, I'm not going to stay, but if you stay, Augusta, at the first snow you can't just curl up and hibernate, you'll need to eat more than wild game.

On the other hand, with two horses and enough grain to get us to Lawrence, we have the opportunity to leave here and use the wits God gave us to live up there. As to your regrets, I won't have any regrets about leaving…none.

We had talked until it was dark. I had lit the lamp before I began reading from my journal. A slight warm, dry breeze had come up, but thank goodness it's been so dry that there's no place for the musquitoes to breed, so we're free of those pests.

July 19, 1860 It dawned hot; the warm dry breeze added to the sense that it would soon be stifling. By 7 AM, it was eighty degrees Fahrenheit. I don't think it had dropped much below that temperature during the night. Yesterday it was over a hundred degrees by noon and it's been like that through all of June and July. The area hadn't had rain since a little sprinkling in early April.

We were packed and ready to go. I had fixed a hasty breakfast and had packed some food to lunch on but I was concerned that some of it might spoil in this heat.

Adda was standing in the doorway, looking south. I went over not so much to partake of the view but to share the sentiments that I knew were in her heart. How different were our circumstances now compared to the expectations we'd had when Father founded Eldorado.

We could see the waves of heat on the prairie, dancing with such wispiness that they made it impossible to tell just where the horizon was.

Without saying anything, Adda slipped an arm around my waste; I did the same with her. Without needing to express it out loud, we both knew this was a complicated farewell to our "place," our father's prize; so it was a farewell to his ambition for our life out here, to be the founder of Eldorado…but, of course, history cannot deny him that…and in addition to bidding adieu to Eldorado' Adda and I were also saying farewell to our own very best intentions, a distillation of our very best hopes, which this community represented for us. Would we ever have another opportunity like Eldorado? I hope that Adda and I will not become prey to disillusion. Morale is a delicate flower that needs to be sustained with success. I also know that it is important that Adda and I stay together, at least until we get over this.

We were ready to leave. We had finished loading up the reliable "Studebaker" yesterday afternoon, parking it so close to the door we could put things on the wagon almost from the doorstep. We gave both horses a good drink of water. Adda had fed them some grain earlier in the morning and had thrown a half-full gunnysack of it on the wagon, knowing that due to the drought it would be hard to find grass for grazing during the next four or five days it would take us to get to Lawrence. As I closed the door and began to climb up on the wagon, Adda asked me what I had in my hand. As I began to give her an answer, I suddenly became very emotional. I used the time and exertion of getting up on the wagon seat to get myself under control.

"Well?" said Adda.

I explained that I was bringing with me two little sacks of seeds: one set was this generation's seeds from those cantaloupes we got on our way through Iowa in the summer of '56 and which I have planted every summer saving the seeds from each crop since then. The other sack contained seed corn from our first crop of Kansas corn, which did so well last year. "I intend to replant the cantaloupe," I said, "and save the seeds and hand them down like an old piece of jewelry that has been in the family for years."

Adda laughed, "I understand that sentiment. I'm keeping Mr. Diggle's watch for the same purpose." Adda hadn't yet climbed up on the wagon. She seemed to be fussing around with the two horses and their harness.

It was already a bright sunny day, not a cloud in the sky, and it promised to be another hot one.

I asked Adda what was the delay.

"As much as I'd enjoy another conversation with the owner of Donder und Blitzen," she said, "I'm counting on these two horses to get us over those hills this side of Clinton so we won't have to call on the service of his two rascals again. But I'm not sure whether the new pony should be on Kate's right side or left."

For a minute or so Adda stood between the two horses, rubbing their manes and talking softly to both of them. Suddenly she swung her body up on the buckboard, gave me an affectionate slap on the left leg, snapped the reins and yelled, "Gaddyap there, Kate."

Neither of us looked back.

Thursday, July 19, 1860

On the way from Eldorado to Lawrence, Kansas Territory.

In less than a month I'll be 21.
Adda is nineteen years old.

INDEX

A

Abbe Prevost 207
Abolitionists
    32nd degree abolitionists, 252, 254
Abolitionist in Oberlin, 223,
Act of 1854
Act of Preemption, 292
Alsace, 81
Apostle Paul, 182
American slavery, 93
Apostle Paul, 182
Archer, Nebraska, 196,
Army Camp at Frederick, Maryland, 166
Arms, Deputy Marshal, 248

B

Baltimore's, 34, 35
Baltimore's Catholic Community, 34
Barrett, Mrs., 128
Bathsheba, 193
Beecher, Reverend Henry Ward, 168
    Beecher's Bibles (the sharp rifle) 168
Beerop, Mr. mules, 74
Belfast to Boston, 73
Bemis Family, 30
Bemis, Glennis, 86, 95, 115
    Sings Bach's "Ave Maria", 115
Benton family
    the pot luck dinner, 88
Blasting powder, 91,
Book of Job, 182
Booze Bros. Whiskey, 34
Boston, 34

Boston Atlas, 164
Boston Traveler, 139, 148
Bowie Knives, gift from John Brown to girls, 161
Bowles Brothers. 148
Bowles, John (Daguerrian's Studio)
    served under Col. Harvey, 149
Bowles, William served under Colonel Harvey, 148
Breckinridge, John from Kentucky, 69
Brooklyn, NY, 22
Brooks, Mrs., 60
Brown, John, v, viii, 101,
   Old John Brown", 102, 138
   John Brown and Harpers Ferry, 163
   John Brown in the 1850s, 160
   John Brown sentenced to be hung In Virginia – Federal Troops,- 164
    John Brown's activity in Lawrence, 165
Buchanan, Mr. & Mrs. 240
Buffalo tallow, 281
Burns, Bobby, 47
Butler/Hunter County, x

C

Cabbageworm problem, 81, 118
Caesar Augustus, 175, 246
Cain and Abel, 193
California, 67
Calvinists, 35
Camp Creek, 130,
Capt. Cook, 18
Capt. Henry, U.S. Army, 196
Captain John Wesley Stewart, 163
Carver, Mr., 128
Cary, (Mr. and Mrs.) 216, 248
    healthy baby boy, 216
Cato, Judge, 183,

Charity, 177
Charleston, 68
"Charley", the horse, 13
Chase, Jacob Eastman, xi , 111, 125 (photo)
    Chase's guitar, 195
Chelsea, K.T., 3, 74
   On the Walnut River in, 86
Cherokee Nation, 64
Chicago, 44
    Chicago papers, 68,
Christ, 175
Christian era, 176
Christian literature, 178
Christmas Day, 200
Cincinnati House, 40, 133
Civil War, xii
Close Order Drill, 245
Comanches, 72, 75
Confederacy   6
Confederates, 299
Congregationalists from Ohio, 189
Connelly, Jason, 136
Conner, Jerry (J. D.), 6, 14
    as Sheriff, 73
Conner's Store, 45
Cook, John E., 212
    executed December 16th, 1859, 212
Cooke, St. George, Colonel
Cooper, James Fennimore   27
Corcoran and Riggs Bank, 1, 38
Cordis, Thomas, 13, 14, 23
    Eldorado's blacksmith
   Quotes "John the Disciple
  Wife, Elizabeth , 18, 21, 72. 107, 122, 279,
Corinthians, 175
    Paul, 175
      First Corinthians chapter 113, 178

County Clare, 90
Court of St. James, 92
Crabtree, Dr., 63
Cracklin, Capt. Mount Oread Rifles, 147
Crocker, Mrs., 241
Curl, Mr.,(First Funeral in Eldorado 88
Cuter, Amos, 241

D

Dagarian's Gallery 144
 Daguerreotype, 144
Daughters of Laban, Leah and Rachel, 193
Davenport, Iowa, 198
Davenport (nickname), 198
Davenport stage The, 84
Davies County, Missouri, 145
Deep South, 167
Defoe, Daniel, *Moll Flanders*, 190
Dempsey, from Galway , 86, 92
Denver, CO, xi , 136
Detroit , viii, 21
Dickens, Charles, serial stories, 211
Diggle, Mr. Randolph H., 1, 143
        the bank embezzler, 151
            heavy gold watch chain, 154, 308
            indicted proslavery embezzler, 157
            Diggle bank fraud case, 183
District 17 in Territorial Legislature, 4
Donder and Blitzen, 261
Doniphan, Kentucky born lawyer, 262
        and the Mexican War
Donkey's breakfast, 222
Double truss, Roof, 11
Douglas, Stephen A., Senator from Illinois, 69
        North Star newspaper, 236
Dred Scott Decision, 68, 173

Duck Creek, 224
 Clinton to Duck Creek, 261

E

Eastridge, Mr. & Mrs., 41, 42, 48
Eastwood, Mr., 6
Eclipse of moon – full- February 6th 1860, 210, 214
Economic Balloon in 1857, xi
Egypt, 176
Eldorado xi
 First accidental death, 37
 First couple in Eldorado to marry, 29
 Abandoned to the Indians, 71
 Augusta - First School "Marm", 187
 First Sunday School, 239
Eldorado, K. T. cofounders, x
Eldorado Ladies Undertakers Guild, 201
Eldorado leaderless, xi
Eldorado Education Committee, 194
Eldridge, Colonel Shalor's Free State Hotel, 103
Elephant, "Going to see", 49
Eli Whitney, 2
Elks, Benevolent and Protective Order of the, 156
Emerson, Ralph W. in Boston, 168
Emporia, K.T. , 3, 86, 131, 238
English colony, 34
English companies in Canada, 34
English detectives in Wales, 90
English Sheriff, 89
English-Style house framing, 11
Enos, Mr., 220
Eureka, 129
European whisky, 145

F

Fall River, 128,
Fanny (Mrs. Gates daughter), 140
Federal Homestead Act, 294,
"feminine" health, (Aggie Rourke), 135
Fifield, Donnali v,
Fisk, Mrs., 257
Fort Gibson, 44
Fort Leavenworth, 22
Fort Riley, xi, 72, 75
Fontanel and Origano, 84
Fourth Ward N.Y.C., 92
Mrs. Frame, 79
Frances, Nelson, 105
Francis & Loutrel (frontice page)
Free Soilers, viii, ix
Free State Constitution, 224, 242
Free Stators in Plymouth, 138
Fremont, Mr. John, 229,
     a good Whig, 265

G

Garrison, William Lloyd, 213,
Gates, Mrs., 40, 84
Gibraltar on Lake Erie, Michigan , viii
Gillespie, Pete, 75, 79, 99
Glacial ice field, 225
Gold Strike –Rocky Mountains-1857, xi
     goldfields Kansas Territory, 44, 290
Gordon, Mr. Andrew, 31
Graton, John, 248
Gunn's Book of Medicine, 107

H

Harney, Gen. William S., 22
Harper's Ferry, 166
Harrison, Mr., (also called Albert Hazlett), 212
Hayworth's gristmill, 86, 96,
Hazlett, Albert (also called William H Harrison, 212)
Henry, Captain, U. S. Army, 196
Hildebrand, Mr. William , 85
Hinton, Richard (English reporter), 101, 102
History of Oppression, 173
Homestead Act, 294
"Hop" at the Eldridge House, 198
Howland, Erastus, 33, 94
    First grocer in Eldorado 30
Hudson River Valley orchards, 81

I

Indian Creek, 130, 221, 237
Indians
    Dead Indians, 83
    Cheyenne, Kaw (Kansa), Apache, Kiowa,
      Arapaho, Shawnee, Otoe, Comanche, 72
Indians in the Cherokee Nation, 299
Independent Democrat of New Hampshire, 199
Irish
    Exiles, 91
    Irish Democrats, 92
    Irish politics in New York, 92,
    Irish Whigs, 92
    Irish whiskey made in Missouri, 145
    Irish generals- Mexican War, 265
    Newspaper clippings, 92
Ireland, 88
    free Ireland, 91
Isinglass window, 201
Israel at time of Christ, 175

J

Jacob, 193
    Love for Rachel, 193
January 23, 1860, First anniversary Augusta and Jacob Chase, 208
Jones, Sheriff (proslavery) from Missouri, 148
Jordan, Jeremiah, 13, 23, 39, 51
    flotation logs, 55
    Hayworth's mill foreman, 76
Joseph, in Egypt, 193

K

Kagi, John, Associate of John Brown, 103, 140, 166
Kansas as "Bloody Kansans", 8
Kansas City, 71
Kansas Historical Quarterly vol. 21-29
Kansas-Nebraska Act of 1854
Kansas State Historical Society, v, 29
Kansas Territory. 22, 193

Kearney, General Stephen, 262
King David, 193
Kingdom of Heaven, 178
Kinner, Calvin, 33
Knowles, Mary, from Massachusetts, 106
Knoxville, Iowa, 304

L

Lake Erie , viii
Lamb, the Brooklyn doctor, 140
Lambden Judge, 237, 260,
    Father's original filing of three claims, 290
Lane, General Jim , viii, ix
    General Lane's Army, 158

Lawrence, Kansas , xi, 22, 49
Leavenworth *Evening Transcript*, 84
Leavenworth *Territorial Register*, 210
Leavenworth, 84, 158
    Abraham Lincoln debating in, 210
LeCompte, Judge, the Chief Justice of the Territory, 144, 152,
Lecompton road, 131
Ledger-new cloth bound ordered from Brooklyn, 211
Legal presumption of innocence, 152
Leslie magazines, 211
Leviticus, 175
Lewis, Doctor, 140
"Likeness" of Laura Augusta Stewart at 20 years, 150
"Likeness" of Laura August Stewart Chase…20 years old and a widow, 159
Limerick and Clonmel, Ireland, 89
Lincoln, Abraham, President from Illinois, 68
Little, William, 285
London, 14
Louis XVI's France, vii
Louisiana Purchase "Great American Desert" 3
Lund, James L., v

M

Martin, Henry (Mr. and Mrs. From England), 12, 14
Mason County, 266
Massachusetts, 124
McCabe, Mrs., 280
McKinney, Mrs., 189
McWhorters, Grocers 6, 33
Medary, Samuel Territorial Governor, (1858 to 1860), 131, 184
Methodists, 141
Mexican War, ix , 22, 139, 167, 245
Minneola Constitution, 189
Minneola Convention, 242
Missouri , viii , 39

John Brown led raiding party, 149
Missouri Volunteer Regiment of Foot Soldiers, 262
Missourians, 140
Montague, D.H. from Plymouth, 243, 253
Monterey, Mexico, 266
Mormons, 177, 266
Morphine, prescribed to relieve intense pain, 141
    (an overdose killed Chase?) 142
Moses, 176
Mortise & Tenon, 12
Mount Oread Company, 135

N

Napoleon, 246
National Anti-Slavery Society, 213
Navy beans, 55
Nebraska City (in Nebraska Territory), 167
Negroes, 165,
New England, 35
    New England Coast, 305
New Hampshire, 71, 78, 200
New Hampshire Street, 151
New Testament, 182
    Paul's metaphors, 182
New York, 92
New York Harbor, 92
New York Times, 22
New York Tribune, 140
Noah, 269
Northern Democrats, 69
Northern Missouri, 285,

O

Ohio, 51
Olathe, 208

Old Country, 87
Old Testament religion, 86
O'Neill's Livery Stables, 281
Onondaga County, NY, 64, 81
Osages, 71
Osage Trail, 224

P

"Pains-Childbirth", 204
Parker House of Boston, 100
Parsons, Reverend, 139
Pate, Colonel, 140
Pennsylvania mines, 35
Pennsylvania smoke less coal oil (Kerosene, 33
Perkins, Reverend, 17, 21, 27, 171
Perseverance, endurance and leadership, 269
Peterson, Mrs., 280
Philadelphia, 11
Phillips, William A., 101, 140, 165
    claim at Duck Creek, 224
    from a speaker's agency out of Chicago 241
Pierce, Alfred, 138
Pierce, President Franklin pardoned all, 148, 183
Pike's Peak, 87, 136
Platte River Route, 268
Plains Indians, 77
Plumb, Preston B., (founder of Emporia, K.T.), 128, 131
  (Leader of 1856 supply train)
Polk, President's Army (Mexican War), 92
Pony Creek Army Camp, 196,
Popular Sovereignty, 68, 175
Post, Miss Minnie, 238
Potato famine - Irish, 73
Potomac River, 166
Powder monkey, 91
P.O.W. camp ix, x

Powers, Ramon, v
Prevost, Abbe, *Minon Lescaut*, 190
Prisoners, 88 were charged, 148

Q

Quaker Households, 131

R

Rackliffes, Sumner and Mary, 13, 21, 80, 117, 119, 200, 279
Red Sea, 176
Redpath, James, 101, 103
Reeder, Governor Andrew H., 148, 248
Rhode Island Street, xii
Rice, Mr. George, 43, 51, 61,
Riggs Bank, 1, 143
    Bank's note, 4
Ritchie, John, 238
Riverboat crews,

Robinson, Dr., 131
Robinson, Frank O., 22, 33, 101
Robinson, Governor Charles
   Wife Sara, v, 245,
Robinson, Mrs. Alfred (Sister-in-law)
    Governor Robinson's brother's family, 245
Rocky Mountains, 298
Rocky Mountain gold miner, 136,
Rogers, Mr. Leroy (Mrs. Fisk's cousin), 264,
Roman Centurions, 175
Roman Law, 175
Roman rule, 175
Rome, 35
Rourke, Aggie, 3, 65
    Cincinnati House Cook, 125
    sells whiskey, 145

Russell, Majors and Waddell Freight outfit, 197

S

Samson and Delilah, 193
Santa Fe Trail, 65, 105
Sawmill, 48
Scarecrows, 45
Schaefer, Mrs., 107
Schoolbooks, 192
Schweitzer, Dr. of Philadelphia, 116
Scotch Boiler, 47
    Steam up the boiler for inspection, 46
Scott, Winfield, - a Whig, 265
Scottish Presbyterians, 47
Scriptures for guidance, 176
Sculley's livery, 84
Searle, A. D., 248
Sermon on the Mount, 177
Shakespeare verse, 298
Shareholders of the sawmill, 121
Sharps rifles, ix, 54
    Sharps carbine, 78
    called Beecher's Bibles, 168
Sidney, Iowa, 45
Sir Chester Drawers, 78
Slave State, x
Smith, Mr. (widower), 75, 101
Smith, Gen. Persifer, 22, 266
Snakes, 190
Soley, Mr. A. C., 22
Sorghum Mill , 4
South Hampton, England, 92
Southern Proslavery Democrats, 68, 247
Southern Missouri, 103
Spanish Fever, 106,
Sparrows, (called spatzie), 81

Spitting tobacco juice, 141
Stagliano, Kim, v
Stein, Mr., 247,
Stendhal *"The Charter House of Parma"*
   The Scarlet and the Black, 189,
Stevens, Aaron, as Ed Whipple, 167
Stewart
    Adelaide (Adda) Henrietta Stewart , 109 (photo)
        signature: bank loan, 38
        Addie Stewart Graton, 63, 80
            Alice Graton, Kincaid, 63
    Charles Samuel Stewart, 231
        Building and Running Sawmills
        Horse, Sam's Black Canadian called "Puss"
        Voting District #17, x
        President of Eldorado, 2
        Bank loan, 37
    Grandma Hannah Gates Stewart, 231
    Ransom Stewart (uncle) in Trent, 77
    John Wesley Stewart, 63, 64
        Grandfather from Massachusetts 64, 65
    Stewart Clan Magazine, 63
St. Louis . 39, 71, 165
    St Louis via New Orleans, 265
Stone Nathan, 218
Storrs' place, 238
Stowe, Harriet Beecher, 94
Summary Judgment to dismiss, 152
Supreme Court, 173
Swift, Francis, Kansas Territory militia, 40
Syrup mill, 1

T

Tabor, 149
Tappan, Sam, 138
Taylor, Dick, 26, 33

Taylor, Pres. Zackary, 92, 265
    Buena Vista, 265
Teacher pay rates in Western Iowa, 192,
Teetotalers, 46
Tempus and Fugit, 233
Tenth Commandment, 134, 102
Ten Commandments, 192
Territorial Capital Building, 183
Territorial Commissioners for Indian Affairs, 72
Terryalt, 87
    (secret societies back in Ireland)
Texas as a Slave State ix, xi, 22
    Home of Capt John Wesley Stewart, 64
Tongues of Angels, 178,
Topeka, 284,
Toronto, 47
Trask, Mr. , 106
Trunnels, 12
Turner's Hall, 198,

U

Ukrainian wheat origin, 274
Underground Railroad, 103, 149, 196,
Unemployment in 1857, 44
United Brethren Church, 17
University of Kansas Libraries, Lawrence, KS, 63
Upham, David, 95
U. S. Army: viii
U. S. Army scrip in lieu of cash, 6
U. S. Senate, x
Utah Expedition, 22

V

Van Buren, Arkansas, 64
    court room re: Sam's killer, 64

W

Wakefield, John A. (ex territorial judge, cofounder Eldorado) 284
Wales, 89, 90
Walnut River, K.T., x , 75
    in Chelsea, 86
    on the Walnut River in 86
Washington, Pres. George, 246
Watt, Mr. James (Scotch inventor, 47
Weibly, Dr. Marcus 13, 14, 18, 33
    Madeira, 18
Weibly, Mrs., 14
Weinbury, Mr. 195
West Point graduates, 246
    in Mexican War, 265
Wexford, Ireland, 90
Whig Party, 105
Whipple, Capt. Ed, (under Gen. Lane) as Aaron Stevens 167
White House, x
White Water, 219
Whittier, Mr. 32
Whitney House, Lawrence, K. T., 27, 100, 133
W.O.P., 92
    Without Papers, 92
Woodruff, Mr. William, 195
    Mrs., 238
Woodward, Mr. Philip, 218
Worldy, Sam Stewart's killer, 64

Y

Young, Mr. James, 41

Breinigsville, PA USA
24 November 2009
228107BV00002B/12/P